S0-AGB-675

FRONTIER GOVERNOR
Samuel J. Crawford of Kansas

FRONTIER GOVERNOR

★ SAMUEL J. CRAWFORD OF KANSAS ★

by
Mark A. Plummer

THE UNIVERSITY PRESS OF KANSAS
Lawrence / Manhattan / Wichita

© Copyright 1971 by the University Press
of Kansas

Standard Book Number 7006-0080-9

Library of Congress Catalog Card Number 72-161656

Printed in the United States of America

Designed by Fritz Reiber

F
686
C 9
P55

for

Betty
Robert
&
Lisa

177063

CONTENTS

ILLUSTRATIONS ix

FOREWORD xi

1 YOUNG CRAWFORD MIGRATES TO KANSAS
(1835-1861) 1

2 COLONEL CRAWFORD IN THE CIVIL WAR
(1861-1864) 9

3 THE WAR AND THE ELECTION OF 1864 25

4 THE YOUNG GOVERNOR 43

5 RECONSTRUCTION AND THE ELECTION OF 1866 65

6 RAILROADS AND SPECULATORS 83

7 A "LAME DUCK" TERM AND A BID
FOR CONGRESS 101

8 CRAWFORD AND THE INDIAN PROBLEM 113

9 A DECADE OF DEFEAT 135

10 A NEW CAREER 157

NOTES 175

BIBLIOGRAPHY 199

INDEX 205

ILLUSTRATIONS

Facing Page

Samuel Johnson Crawford, Governor of Kansas, 1865-1868   50

James Henry Lane, United States Senator, 1861-1866   51

Edmund Gibson Ross, United States Senator, 1866-1871   51

Thomas Carney, Governor of Kansas, 1863-1865   51

Samuel Clarke Pomeroy, United States Senator, 1861-1873   51

Sterling Price, Major General, Confederate States Army   66

Samuel Ryan Curtis, Major General, United States Army   66

James Gillpatrick Blunt, Major General, United States Army   66

George Armstrong Custer, Brevet Major General,
    United States Army   66

Sterling Price's army moving south along the Kansas-Missouri
    state line after Westport   67

Home of Governor Crawford at 435 Harrison, Topeka,
    in the 1880s   67

MAPS

Civil War on the Frontier, 1861-1865   12

Cherokee and Osage Indian Land Controversies, 1866-1868   84

Kansas and Indian Territory, 1868-1869   127

FOREWORD

The Kansas frontier brought rapid success to Samuel J. Crawford. At age twenty-nine, he was Kansas's youngest governor. He was elected as an authentic Civil War hero who had displayed bravery in numerous battles in the Western theater and who had commanded a regiment of black soldiers. As governor, he was involved in reconstruction politics, the 1867 peace treaty with the southern plains Indians at Medicine Lodge, the building of the Kansas Pacific railroad, and the rapid settlement of the state. He resigned his position as the state's chief executive to lead the Nineteenth Kansas Cavalry in an expedition against the Indians in the winter of 1868–1869. His campaigning against the Indians brought him into contact with Generals William T. Sherman, Phil Sheridan, and George Custer. Crawford's early political success was followed by frustration. He repeatedly attempted to obtain a U. S. House or Senate seat, but he was thwarted by the corrupt election practices of the "gilded age." He joined the Liberal Republican and the Greenback parties but he later opposed the Populists. He found monetary success, however, by prosecuting claims against the national government on behalf of the state, numerous Indian tribes, and individual claimants. He died in 1913 at the age of seventy-eight.

I have tried to use the story of Crawford's political career as a means to throw some light on the "dark ages" of Kansas history, that is, the period between the much publicized "Bleeding Kansas" territorial years and the Populist era. If I have had any success in this venture, it has been because I have received generous aid from many unselfish persons. It was Dudley Cornish, author of the pioneering study of black soldiers, *The Sable Arm,* who first suggested Crawford to me as a worthwhile study. Robert Johannsen, now of the University of Illinois, helped me initiate the study. George L. Anderson, of the University of Kansas, contributed more to the study and to the author than I can ever repay. John G. Clark, also of the University of Kansas, offered timely encouragement.

The entire staff of the Kansas State Historical Society in Topeka made research in the society headquarters most pleasant. I find this opinion shared by researchers from across the country who have worked there. Nyle Miller, Robert Richmond, Joseph Snell, Forrest R. Blackburn, Lela Barnes, Elsie Beine, Portia Allbert, and Shirley Borgulund are names of staff members who come to mind as being exceptionally helpful. The Society also granted me permission to quote from an article I had written which was published in the *Kansas Historical Quarterly.* All of the illustrations are made possible by courtesy of the Society. I am indebted to Illinois State University for granting me a sabbatical leave which was used, in part, to rewrite the book manuscript. The Research Committee of the Graduate School provided some financial assistance for typing which was expertly done by Alberta Carr. Marty Turbett also did some of the typing. Jim Schneiderman made the most out of the information available and drew the maps. My wife, Betty, contributed greatly to the literacy of the book. She has been involved in every step of the process from the first typing and editing to the final draft.

M. A. P.

1

YOUNG CRAWFORD MIGRATES TO KANSAS (1835-1861)

In the early spring of 1859 a tall, slender young man from Indiana crossed an imaginary line near Kansas City which separated the slave state of Missouri from the disputed territory of Kansas. He was Samuel Johnson Crawford, and he had come to Kansas in search of opportunity. He would not be disillusioned for he would be elected to the state legislature in a few months; become a colonel in a Kansas regiment in a few years; and be elected governor, the youngest in the history of the state, before he reached his thirtieth birthday. After being twice elected governor, Crawford would become famous as an Indian fighter, be a prominent political figure in Kansas politics for half a century, and become a millionaire as a claims agent. He would live through some of the most exciting and important events of

American history. He would witness the breakup of the Union, participate in the war that followed, and have some influence on the reconstruction of the state and nation.

There was nothing extraordinary about young Crawford's coming to Kansas. Since the opening of the territory in 1854, thousands of young men had come to Kansas. Most of them came from the Ohio River valley states. Nearly ten thousand people born in Indiana were settled in Kansas by 1860.[1] Crawford was repeating the action taken by his father in moving to the frontier. His parents, William and Jane Morrow Crawford, were born in North Carolina. They moved to territorial Indiana in 1815, five years after their marriage. According to Samuel Crawford's "court" biographies they moved because of ". . . an unconquerable prejudice to the institution of slavery."[2] Samuel Johnson Crawford was born on April 10, 1835, twenty-five years after his parents' marriage, on a farm near Bedford, Lawrence County, Indiana. The boy attended the public schools and also an academy at Bedford. At age twenty-one, he became a student-at-law in the law office of S. W. Short of Bedford and was soon admitted to the bar. In the fall of 1857, he became a student at the Law School of Cincinnati College, from which he was graduated in 1858.

Crawford reached his twenty-first birthday in time to vote for John C. Fremont and the new Republican party in 1856. By 1859, a Free-State party was in control of the Kansas Territorial Legislature and the formation of a Republican party was imminent. Perhaps an enterprising young Republican lawyer could build himself a great future on the frontier. Crawford was a bachelor and there was little to hold him in Indiana. As Crawford put it some years later: "I bade adieu to friends and the scenes of childhood, and turned my face toward Kansas, a new planet then rising in the West, and struggling to throw off the barnacle of human slavery. . . ."[3]

It was not a difficult trip from Crawford's home to territorial Kansas. It took him only eight hours by rail to reach St. Louis. From there he took a Missouri River steamer to Kansas City. On

March 1, 1859, he left Kansas City and journeyed to the village of Garnett in Anderson County, some seventy-five miles to the southwest. Young Sam Crawford was attracted to that town because of its beautiful natural setting and its friendly people. The fact that it was the county seat must have added to its attractiveness to a young lawyer in search of a place to practice. He took quarters in the new Quality Hill Hotel and sent for his law library.[4]

By the time of Crawford's arrival it was evident that Kansas would eventually be admitted to the Union as a free state. On November 19, 1858, President James Buchanan had appointed Samuel Medary, an Ohio Democrat, as governor of the territory. Medary was determined to allow the people of the territory to express themselves, and he ordered an election held to determine whether or not the people wanted a new constitutional convention. The election was held March 28, 1859, and the vote was 5,306 for the calling of a constitutional convention and 1,425 against.

Before such a convention could be held, the free-state sentiment of the state was further crystallized by the formation of the Republican party in Kansas.[5] There was some opposition by the conservative wing of the Free-State party to such a movement. They feared it was a scheme of James H. Lane to win a seat for himself in the United States Senate.[6] Nevertheless, a convention call was made for May 18 at Osawatomie. There was a great deal of excitement attendant to the meeting, not only because it meant the formation of a new party in Kansas but because it was to be attended by Horace Greeley, the Republican editor of the New York *Tribune*. The diversity of opinion was greater than might be supposed at a Republican organizational meeting. There were many radical abolitionists there who favored Negro suffrage, but there were also many there who were "black-law men," that is, they wanted to forbid slavery but they also wanted to exclude the Negro from Kansas. The conservative element seemed to have the upper hand. Horace Greeley was not invited to address the convention, but the meeting did recess to hear him. The convention went on record as favoring the Declaration of Independence, but it refused to condone anything as radical as Negro suffrage.[7] Three of the sixty-two delegates were from Anderson County. Crawford was not one of the voting delegates, but he may have attended as an observer.[8]

On June 7, 1859, the delegates to the constitutional convention were selected by popular election. The Republicans cast only 7,374 votes to 6,155 for the Democrats, but the Republicans gained thirty-five delegates while the Democrats captured only seventeen.[9] The delegates met at Wyandotte on July 5 to begin work on the constitution which was to become the basic political document for the future state of Kansas. They labored over the constitution until July 29, at which time thirty-four Republicans signed the document. The Democrats refused to sign. The Constitution was antislavery; but in keeping with the views of most Kansans, it excluded the Negro from voting. Article V, Section 1 read: "Every white male person . . . shall be deemed a qualified elector. . . ."[10] A proposal to exclude the Negro from the public schools was narrowly defeated. James G. Blunt, who represented Crawford's home county, was one of the leaders who fought against such an exclusion.[11]

The Wyandotte Constitution was submitted to the people of the territory on October 4, 1859, and it was adopted by a margin of nearly two to one. The Republican party then held a nominating convention in Topeka in November in preparation for the election of state officials which was scheduled for December. Samuel J. Crawford, twenty-four years old, a resident of Kansas less than nine months, was nominated by the Republican party for the House of Representatives from Anderson County. He was elected on December 6, 1859. No official figures are available as to his margin of victory. Governor Charles Robinson was elected by more than a seven to five margin and the Republican state senators from Crawford's district were elected by a two to one margin. Crawford's margin was unofficially reported to be about the same as that of the state senators. The Republicans elected a twenty-two to three majority in the Senate and a sixty-four to eleven majority in the House.[12]

But the newly elected legislature could not serve until statehood was achieved and statehood was now dependent on events over which Kansans had little control. John Brown's raid on Harper's Ferry in the fall of 1859 foreshadowed the difficulties which would lead to the breakup of the Union, but in 1860 there was still hope that such a split could be averted. In April 1860 the House voted to admit Kansas, but the proposal met with defeat in the Senate. The Senate continued to delay Kansas statehood until many of the Southern senators withdrew.

In the meantime, Kansas continued to be ruled by a territorial legislature which by this time had a large majority of free-staters. The appointed governor and the legislature wrangled over where to meet. The governor called upon the legislature to convene at Lecompton on January 2, 1860. They met and voted to move to Lawrence. The governor vetoed such a move, but the legislature overrode his veto. Kansas Republicans sent delegates to the national nominating convention in Chicago in May. These delegates preferred Seward, but Lincoln was an acceptable candidate.[13]

In 1860, Kansans had their minds upon concerns other than their admission to the Union. It was the year of the great drought. The difficulties of Kansans were publicized throughout the free states and money and supplies came pouring in from the East. Samuel C. Pomeroy, who was to become one of the first United States senators from Kansas, became the relief administrator. This position and his election were not completely separated; he was accused of using the relief money to support his political ambitions as well as drawing on it for personal use.[14] This charge, which was probably true, was to set the tone of the senatorial elections for at least the first two decades of Kansas statehood. According to Crawford, the drought of 1860, although severe, caused "no real suffering for food." Anderson County even refused to accept the aid which was offered. "The whole scheme was a fraud, and it gave Kansas a set-back from which the territory and the state did not recover for many years." Crawford believed that the aid solicitors were working for themselves rather than for humanity.[15]

The Republican victory in November 1860 gave new hope to Kansas and her dreams of statehood. On January 21, 1861, soon after the withdrawal of many Southern senators, the Senate passed a bill to admit Kansas by a margin of thirty-six to sixteen. A week later, the House gave the plan an even larger majority. On January 29, President Buchanan signed the bill which would make Kansas the thirty-fourth state of the Union. There were celebrations all around the state; Kansans had at last achieved the political privileges which accompany statehood, and they knew how to use such privileges. There was a great exodus from Kansas toward Washington and the March 4 inauguration of Abraham Lincoln.[16]

The new state officials had waited from the time of their election in December 1859 until statehood was proclaimed in 1861 to occupy their official positions. Governor Charles Robinson was sworn in as governor on February 9, and he in turn called for a meeting of the legislature on March 26, at Topeka. The activity in Topeka had been feverish for several weeks. The town's hotels were filled with senatorial candidates who promised jobs and provided for the immediate needs of the new legislators.[17] Into this beehive of activity came Samuel Crawford, not yet twenty-six years old. The House and Senate were organized, committees were duly chosen, and the governor's message was heard. With these formalities out of the way the legislature could get down to the business of electing two new United States senators.

The leading candidates were described in a letter from John J. Ingalls to his father, dated Atchison, March 21, 1861:

> . . . There are several candidates in the field, but only four of any prominence—Parrott, Pomeroy, Lane and Stanton; the two first north of the Kansas River and the others south. Mr. Parrott is the late delegate for two terms from

the territory, and will probably succeed. With Pomeroy you are familiar. . . . If abdomen was a test, he would be sure to triumph; but as brains enter into the contest somewhat, his chances are small. General Lane is another notorious character in early Kansas history and one of the most remarkable men I ever knew; a perfect demagogue, charlatan, knave— everything that is infamous and detestable in private life, and yet possessed of a certain indefatigable energy, magnetism and nerve, which conquers adversity and achieves success. The chances are immensely in his favor. . . .[18]

The struggle was largely confined to the first three mentioned: Marcus J. Parrott, Samuel C. Pomeroy, and James Henry Lane. All were veterans of the territorial wars and all were determined to achieve success. Parrott had an arrangement with C. W. Babcock and D. W. Wilder whereby they were to support him in return for control of the patronage of Kansas.[19] Pomeroy had used the relief work of 1860–61 to good advantage and he was accused of offering cash in exchange for votes.[20] Lane helped finance a newspaper for John Speer in Lawrence which he believed to be necessary to the success of his venture.[21] He also promised federal jobs to anyone who could be of service to him, not always remembering which jobs he had already promised.[22]

Lane and Parrott reached an understanding some weeks before the voting began by which they agreed to support each other's candidacy. This conspiracy crumbled, however, when the State Senate, on All Fools' Day, passed a motion to elect one candidate south of the Kansas River and another from north of the river. Parrott and Lane were both nominated for the south side and their supporters were thrown into confusion. After considerable maneuvering, a Pomeroy-Lane combination was effected whereby the election should be held at a joint session of the legislature. The alliance had thirteen of the twenty-five Senate votes committed to such a scheme. The date set for the joint session was April 4.[23]

The roll was called about 2:30 P.M. at the joint session. It was agreed that each legislator would have two votes but that the House and Senate votes should be counted by their respective clerks. After that, bedlam reigned. There was only one ballot taken but it took more than two hours to complete because there was a great amount of vote changing. According to Wilder, the vote for Lane fluctuated between 45 and 64; for Pomeroy it was between 49 and 57; and for Parrott it was between 47 and 60.[24] The tally sheet of John J. Ingalls, secretary of the joint convention, shows that more than half the legislators changed their votes at least once. Crawford was one of that minority group which made no changes at all. He voted for James H. Lane and M. J. Parrott.[25] After two hours of confusion the vote was tallied. It read: Lane, 55 votes; Pomeroy, 52; Parrott, 49; Stanton, 21; and a scattering among five other candidates. Finally, it was announced that James Henry Lane and Samuel C. Pomeroy were elected as the first United States senators from the new state of Kansas.[26]

The legislature could now settle down to the work at hand. Crawford was appointed chairman of the Committee on Counties and County Lines. He also served on the military committee. Crawford's service as a member of the state legislature was to last less than six weeks. When news came of the firing on Fort Sumter and the President's April 15 call for seventy-five thousand volunteers, the legislature as Crawford put it, "had no charms for me." Governor Charles Robinson soon tendered him a commission to recruit a company from Anderson and Franklin Counties and he readily accepted. He was granted leave of absence from his seat in the House on the tenth of May.[27]

2

COLONEL CRAWFORD IN THE CIVIL WAR (1861-1864)

The war fever ran high in Kansas in May and it was not difficult to organize a company of men. Crawford managed to recruit a full company in less than a week after leaving the House of Representatives. He appointed a recruiting officer in neighboring Franklin County and announced a great public meeting for Saturday, May 14, 1861, at Garnett. The meeting was a success and the Garnett contingent marched off to war later the same day. They received a noisy send-off from their fellow townspeople before proceeding to Ohio City, in Franklin County, where other recruits joined the company. An election of company officers was held and Crawford was named captain and John G. Lindsey and A. R. Morton were named lieutenants. In Ohio City, the company not only received a noisy welcome but was treated to a speech by State Senator P. P. Elder, who presented Crawford with his grandfather's sword, which he said had been used in the Revolutionary War. It took the company two days to reach Lawrence, where they were again welcomed and honored in a parade, complete with drum and fife music. Other companies soon gathered in Lawrence and a regiment was formed. The next month was spent in drill and waiting in Lawrence.[1]

Among those who had accompanied Crawford's company to Lawrence was James G. Blunt, who was to become the state's only major general. Blunt was dissatisfied with the delay in getting into the war. He believed the delay was caused by the political maneuverings of Governor Charles Robinson. Blunt therefore left the Second Regiment, which had not yet been mustered into service, and joined the forces being recruited by Senator James H. Lane, Robinson's political rival in Kansas.[2]

The Second Regiment was ordered to report to Kansas City to be mustered into the army on June 20, 1861, for three months' service. The official designation given to the unit was the Second Kansas Volunteer Infantry. The regiment was immediately ordered to proceed to southern Missouri to join the forces of General Nathaniel Lyon. Camp was made near Springfield, Missouri, and there was more drilling and waiting. The Second Kansas first came under fire in a minor engagement at Forsyth, Missouri, on July 22, followed by another minor skirmish at a place called Dug Springs.[3] The latter battle was fought without authorization in order to obtain drinking water on a hot August day.[4]

Crawford and the Second Kansas Infantry received their first real taste of war in the battle of Wilson's Creek, near Springfield, on August 10. This was one of the bloodiest battles fought in the West during the entire war. At stake was southern Missouri, perhaps even all of Missouri. The Union forces were under the command of General Lyon, who had only about six thousand troops at his command. He was opposed by the forces of Confederate Generals Ben McCullouch and Sterling Price, said to have more than fifteen thousand troops.[5] The Second Kansas Infantry, under the command of Colonel Robert Mitchell, was held in reserve during much of the early morning fighting at Wilson's Creek. The Confederates attempted a flanking movement on the Union left. Lt. Col. Charles W. Blair approached General Lyon and asked if he should order the Second forward to strengthen the Union left. The General assented and he and Colonel Mitchell led the advance toward the crest of a hill which appeared to afford a stronger defensive position. Suddenly there was a volley of gunfire from an ambush and General Lyon fell mortally wounded. Colonel Mitchell was also wounded. The Union line hesitated and then charged the enemy, forcing them back beyond the crest of the hill. The battle continued but orders were soon received to retire as soon as it could be done in good order. The regiment suffered casualties numbering 70, while their sister regiment, the First Kansas Infantry, lost 284 men. The Union casualties totaled 1,235. The Confederates suffered a similar loss of men.[6]

Although the Union troops had been forced to retire, the battle forestalled the capture of Missouri because the Confederates were exhausted. The battle-weary Union forces moved up the military road until they reached Rolla on August 18. Crawford was ordered to accompany the wounded to St. Louis by rail. He returned to his regiment the next day. During the next month, the Second Kansas was involved in many minor skirmishes against irregular troops in Missouri. The regiment reached Leavenworth on September 7, but it was soon ordered to reinforce the Union troops at Lexington, Missouri, who were under attack by a Confederate force under the command of Sterling Price. Before the regiment could reach the battlefield, Price broke off the engagement and retreated south. The Second Kansas camped at Wyandotte a few days before returning to Fort Leavenworth to be mustered out on October 31, 1861.[7]

Captain Crawford and Major W. F. Cloud were among those retained in service to help in organizing a new regiment for a longer term of service. The work was not completed until the

spring of 1862, when the new recruits, plus a number of transferred companies, were organized as the Second Kansas Cavalry.
The new regiment was mustered in at Shawnee Town, April 15,
1862. The muster roll listed the following information concerning

Civil War on the Frontier, 1861-1865,
with Crawford's Principal Engagements (x)

Captain Crawford: age, 26; height, 6'1"; brown hair; hazel colored eyes; fair complexion; single.[8]

The next six months saw Crawford and the Second Kansas Cavalry ordered to Fort Riley and then on to New Mexico via the Santa Fe trail. There were no military battles of any consequence fought during this tour, but there were some political battles. Colonel Mitchell was promoted to general in April, thus leaving the new Second Kansas without a regimental commander. Lieutenant Colonel Owen A. Bassett of Lawrence was the second-ranking officer and he expected to be promoted to colonel and made commander. He received a commission as colonel from Governor Robinson in May, but General James G. Blunt, the new commander of the Department of Kansas, refused to allow his muster.[9]

Senator Lane had been fencing with the political forces of Governor Robinson over the control of the regiments recruited in Kansas since the beginning of the war. The Second Infantry and the Second Cavalry had been commissioned and largely controlled by Robinson but Lane was able to gain authority to recruit and officer some additional regiments. After an abortive attempt at being general and senator simultaneously, Lane had finally persuaded Lincoln and the War Department that a new Department of Kansas should be established. Lane's friend Blunt was promoted to general in April 1862 and in May he was given command of the Department of Kansas, which included not only Kansas, but also the Nebraska, Colorado, and the Indian Territory. The officers and men of the Second apparently backed Bassett, but Blunt continued to refuse the promotion. Bassett never did receive the promotion although he did serve as regimental commander during most of the unit's history.[10]

Crawford arrived at Fort Scott on September 20, 1862, after a two-thousand-mile expedition which had taken him to Texas, New Mexico, Colorado, and western Kansas. The Kansas political wars had continued during his absence. In August, Lane had wrangled an appointment as "recruiting commissioner" and had set about to form several additional regiments. One of these regiments, the Twelfth Kansas Infantry, was commanded by Colonel Charles W. Adams, Lane's son-in-law. Crawford was offered a lieutenant colonelcy in this unit but he declined because, according to his memoirs, he preferred cavalry to infantry. This explanation seems inadequate because he later accepted the command of a black infantry regiment. Crawford always professed great disdain toward what he called "political soldiers." Perhaps he did not want to become closely associated with the Lane political group. He may have had reason to believe that he would be promoted in his own unit because, on September 30, he was made acting-major and put in command of a battalion of the Second Kansas Cavalry.[11]

Late in 1862, rumors began to be heard about a great Confederate army being recruited in Arkansas in preparation for another invasion of Missouri. The skirmishes in southwest Missouri and northwest Arkansas became more determined. In early October a Confederate force gathered near Newtonia, Missouri, but it was forced to retreat into Arkansas after a short battle. The Confederate forces then split, with one force going south to Huntsville, Arkansas, and the other force under Confederate General Douglas H. Cooper and Stand Watie, the Cherokee Indian leader, moving toward Indian Territory. Cooper and Watie had a force estimated at five thousand to seven thousand men, mostly Indians. They made camp near Maysville, which was located near the intersection of the Missouri, Arkansas, and Indian Territory boundaries. General Blunt, in command of a force of about six thousand men, including the Second Kansas, was ordered from Fort Scott to reinforce the Union troops in southwest Missouri. After the Confederate withdrawal from Missouri, Blunt was allowed to pursue Cooper and Watie toward Indian Territory.[12]

Blunt proposed to surprise Cooper and destroy his army; but as he neared Maysville, the enemy pickets fell back and warned the Confederate army of Blunt's approach. The forces of Cooper and Watie formed a defensive line near Old Fort Wayne on the morning of October 22. To their immediate front was about one-half mile of open field. Blunt ordered the Second Kansas Cavalry to dismount and advance to a fence which was only about two hundred yards from the Confederate lines. A Confederate battery then opened fire making their position untenable. Crawford was in command of five companies which were in the direct line of fire. He was forced to retreat to a position of cover or charge the battery. Without orders, he acted upon the axiom which was to become his battlefield credo: "When in trouble, charge!" Crawford led his men over the intervening fence, across an open field, and captured the battery. According to one eyewitness, he was the first to reach one of the guns, which he struck with his Revolutionary War sword, and exclaimed, "You are ours, damn you!" Crawford ordered Captain Henry Hopkins to turn the guns on the Confederates, but Hopkins's men lacked the necessary firing caps and Crawford then ordered Lieutenant Horace Moore to move the guns back to the Union lines. This was done, and before the Confederates could counterattack, additional units of Blunt's force came up to join the fighting. The Confederate army was then forced to withdraw in disorder, leaving all of its artillery and most of its supplies behind. Blunt later reported to his superior that the enemy had fled across the Arkansas River at Fort Gibson, seventy miles away. According to Cooper's report, this loss of artillery deterred his army from joining the Confederate force which was planning the invasion of Missouri.[13]

Crawford was commended in the official reports sent to headquarters by both Lieutenant Colonel Bassett and General Blunt, something of an accomplishment since these two men represented the two warring factions in Kansas politics. Blunt credited Crawford with making a "gallant charge, driving in their center, capturing their artillery, and bringing it in triumph from the field," for which "great credit is due for his gallantry...."[14]

Crawford and Blunt had much in common. Both came from Anderson County, Kansas, both were young and dashing, both

were fearless, perhaps to the extent of being foolhardy. Blunt
liked to ride far in the lead of his troops, sometimes wearing
civilian clothes and asking questions of civilians in enemy territory. Crawford in his autobiography related that he and General
Blunt rode out with only three men on the day before the battle
at Old Fort Wayne to ". . . have some fun with [the enemy's]
next picket post." They escaped a patrol of sixty Confederates
only because of their fleet horses.[15] Blunt came to rely upon
Crawford more and more from the time of the battle of Old Fort
Wayne; yet there is nothing to indicate that Crawford had joined
the Lane-Blunt political forces. Captain Crawford performed the
duties usually assigned to a major or a colonel during his tour
with the Second Kansas Cavalry, and yet he was not promoted.

Blunt relied on Crawford to get things done, in and out of
battle. After the battle at Old Fort Wayne, his command was
short of rations and a wagon train was overdue from Fort Scott.
He ordered Crawford to take one hundred men and investigate the
delay. Crawford found the train near Carthage, Missouri, under
the command of Captain Morton, a quartermaster. There were
bushwhackers and other diversions in abundance in that area and
the train had been moving with caution. Crawford ordered the
train to leave at daylight the next morning, but several hours after
sunrise the train was still motionless and the officer's tent had not
yet been struck. Lieutenant Edwin Manning reported to Crawford that the quartermaster was enjoying a leisurely breakfast in
the company of three or four women. Crawford, according to
Manning's story, approached Morton, who said he was in command and would move when he got ready, to which Crawford
replied, "You damned scoundrel, this train will move at once, and
if you and your harem get ready in time you can march in the
rear with the guard." Crawford further threatened to tie Morton
to a wagon until they reached camp and then have him shot
before breakfast.[16]

The Confederate threat to Missouri was not removed either
by Blunt's victory at Old Fort Wayne or by the coming of winter.

Confederate General Thomas Hindman recruited an army from his base at Little Rock and soon began to build up the strength of the Confederate army in northern Arkansas. General Schofield retired to St. Louis for the winter, leaving Blunt and about five thousand troops to guard the mountain passes in northwest Arkansas. Another force remained at Springfield under the command of General Francis Herron. Hindman collected a force of about 11,500 men, with which he was determined to attack Blunt before obeying an order to send all available men to Vicksburg. Blunt learned of Hindman's intentions and decided to attack the Confederate forces before they reached full strength. The Confederates were at Cane Hill, about forty miles north of Van Buren, Arkansas. He made a forced march of thirty-five miles on November 27, and arrived at Cane Hill on November 28. A bitter battle followed, but Blunt was successful in gaining Cane Hill, a good defensive position. Crawford was mentioned prominently in the official reports of the battle. Crawford and A. P. Russell were credited with leading the dismounted charge which spelled success.[17]

The losses at Cane Hill were not great on either side and General Hindman planned to attack Blunt before reinforcements could arrive from Springfield. Meanwhile, Hindman learned that Herron was already near Fayetteville with a force of six thousand men. He decided to make a feint toward Blunt at Cane Hill and attack Herron before he could consolidate his forces with those of Blunt. The result was a major battle at Prairie Grove, December 7, 1862. Hindman approached Herron and successfully masked his intentions until Blunt heard the gunfire which opened the battle. Blunt immediately ordered his division to the relief of Herron. Blunt arrived in time to help ward off Hindman's attack but he missed a great deal of the fighting and the bulk of casualties were suffered by Herron's men. Nightfall finally stopped the fighting. Each army had suffered about thirteen hundred casualties. The next morning General Hindman requested an armistice to bury his dead. Blunt assented and Hindman used this time to organize his army and retreat south to the Arkansas River.[18]

Crawford received more laurels from his superiors for his part in the battle of Prairie Grove. Blunt commended Crawford for his command of a battalion which displayed great gallantry. Colonel W. F. Cloud's official report describes a Confederate flanking movement which was defeated because of the "nerve and courage that Captain Crawford was able to infuse into his men, by his brilliant example and courageous bearing. . . ."[19]

According to Blunt's account, his army was ordered back to Springfield for the winter by General Schofield. Blunt disregarded the order and followed Hindman's army to the Arkansas River at Van Buren. A battle was fought with the Confederate rear guard at Dripping Springs and four steamboats were captured and burned. This ended the attempted invasion of Missouri and Blunt's forces retired to southwest Missouri for the winter.[20]

At the close of the campaign in northern Arkansas in 1862, the line officers of the Second Kansas Cavalry petitioned Governor Robinson requesting that Crawford be promoted to colonel and given command of the regiment. Lieutenant Colonel Owen A. Bassett, the commander of the regiment, was unpopular with his officers and they apparently hoped that Crawford's promotion would displace him as their commander. Perhaps Robinson had noted the close connection between Crawford and Blunt, and remembering that Blunt had refused to sanction many of the governor's appointments, he refused to promote Crawford.[21]

Failing to gain Crawford's promotion, thirteen of the officers of the Second Kansas Cavalry decided to take a more direct line of action in an attempt to replace their commander. In a letter to Bassett, dated January 4, 1863, they wrote:

> We the undersigned officers of the 2nd Regiment Kansas Volunteers do most respectfully ask you to resign your position as Lieutenant Colonel of this Regiment. In making the request, we are not influenced by any *personal* feelings

whatever; but we feel it due the Regiment, as well as our-
selves, that a change be made, and some one appointed to
fill the position who can command the fullest respect and
confidence of the men and officers. From the very com-
mencement of this campaign, we have watched you closely,
and with the deepest interest, hoping that in each engagement you would acquit yourself with credit to the Regiment, and redeem the reputation you *have* once been associated with. But we find that instead, each time has but
tended to confirm the oft expressed opinion of a large majority, and to day (we are pained to admit) we are satisfied
that all confidence in you as a fit officer to command us in
action is entirely gone.

We desire an officer who will not falter amid danger,
when *duty* calls him; one who does not consider the place
where his men are ordered "too hot" for him; one who will
lead us into battle instead of *ordering;* one who will help us
to sustain the present reputation we now enjoy; in short, a
man whom we can respect as a brave and efficient commander.

We do not deem it necessary to particularize. You understand our feelings and must know that where there is
a total lack of confidence there can be no efficiency. We
therefore respectfully *but earnestly* request you to hand in
your resignation as early as possible.[22]

The letter was signed by thirteen officers, representing eight of the
ten companies in the regiment. Crawford's name appears at the
top of the list of signatures, perhaps because he was commander
of Company "A."

On March 14, Bassett sent the letter to Colonel William F.
Cloud, the District of Southwest Missouri commander, asking
that it be sent on to Departmental Headquarters with the recommendation that a court of inquiry be called to investigate the
charges against him. On March 29, General Samuel Curtis

ordered a general court martial. The court martial was set for June 10, but a continuance was granted and the trial opened on July 10. The formal charges included: "Misbehaving himself before the enemy." "Conduct unbecoming an officer and gentleman." The specifications charged that Bassett had abandoned his men during the battles of Coon Creek, Old Fort Wayne, and Prairie Grove; that he had stated that the regiment could do just as well without him in battle; and that he had retained some money stolen from an Arkansas citizen. The court heard three days of testimony, but the judge advocate asked the court for a delay in order to obtain certain important witnesses. The court adjourned for thirty days, but there is no record of its ever reconvening. General John McNeil ordered the records forwarded to his headquarters; and on August 6, Bassett was cleared on grounds that there was insufficient evidence presented to sustain a charge.[23]

While Bassett was involved in the court martial episode, Captain Crawford was given the temporary command of the regiment during the summer of 1863. The officers of the Second Kansas were thus successful in replacing Bassett, but they did not succeed in obtaining for Crawford the rank of colonel, the prescribed rank for a regimental commander. The official records and the memoirs of the men involved provide no clue as to the political implications, if any, of the court martial. Bassett was one of Governor Robinson's appointees, but so was Crawford, although he had become more closely associated with Blunt in the northwest Arkansas campaign.

There was little military activity in the Kansas-Missouri area in the summer of 1863, but there was no decrease in the political maneuvering. Lane had been successful in discrediting the Robinson administration; and Thomas Carney, a Lane supporter, was elected governor in November 1862. Carney, however, also came into conflict with Lane over the control of the Kansas regiments and the political wars waxed as hot as before. Blunt was promoted to major general in May; but in June 1863 Major General John

Schofield ordered the district of Kansas subdivided into two divisions. Blunt lost most of his command in Kansas and was confined to Indian Territory and some small areas in southern Kansas and Arkansas. As Blunt said: "My command was reduced in proportion as my rank was increased." This was a serious blow to Lane, who had also lost his almost exclusive right to officer the Kansas regiments.[24]

General Blunt refused to remain inactive in spite of the decreased size of his command. After being stripped of the northern part of his former command he briefly contented himself with recruiting two new regiments at Fort Scott. Reports of Confederate activity near Fort Gibson soon gave him an excuse to lead an expedition into Indian Territory. Leaving the recruiting of the two new regiments to Major T. J. Anderson, who would later become Crawford's adjutant general, Blunt set off toward Fort Gibson with a small command. Blunt learned that a Union force of fifteen hundred men, nominally under the control of another department, was operating either in or near his diminished district. He ordered them to join his command. Included in this command was the Second Kansas Cavalry with Crawford as acting regimental commander. Blunt called in his widely scattered troops until he had an aggregate of about forty-five hundred men, then he set out toward the Canadian River in search of the enemy. Crawford was ordered to take the Second Kansas and parts of the Third Wisconsin Cavalry and Fourteenth Kansas Cavalry and swing around to the west by way of North Fork Town and then come in on the enemy flank at Perryville. Crawford burned the quartermaster stores at North Fork Town and captured a Confederate paymaster who was in possession of $40,000 in Confederate money. The disposition of this money became a campaign issue when Crawford ran for governor in 1864. Crawford then rejoined Blunt at Perryville on August 25. The Confederate forces had formed on the crest of a hill, but a flanking movement forced them to retreat to the Red River. Blunt then ordered the pursuit of the forces of General William Cabell, who had taken his men toward Fort Smith before the engagement at Perryville. Colonel Cloud was in command, as Blunt had become very ill; Crawford was in command of the Second Kansas. Cabell's Confederate army was forced to fall back beyond Fort Smith to Backbone Mountain. There, on September 1, after two hours of bitter fighting, Cabell retreated, leaving Fort Smith to be occupied by the Union army.[25]

Blunt was soon strong enough to return to Fort Scott to continue the work of organizing the Fourteenth Kansas and the Second Kansas Colored Infantry. Before leaving, he offered to appoint Crawford commander of the Second Colored, a position which would carry the rank of colonel. Captain Crawford had serious objections to commanding colored infantry, but he also had serious objections to remaining a captain throughout the war. There seemed to be no hope of gaining a promotion in his own unit; all the promotions seemed to be coming to men in the Lane-backed regiments. He finally resolved to accept the promotion and the new black regiment.[26]

Crawford returned to Fort Scott to assist in the organization of the Second Kansas Colored Infantry (also known as the Eighty-third U. S. Colored Infantry). In late October, Blunt put Crawford in charge of a supply train consisting of more than six hundred government wagons. The train started for Fort Smith with units of Crawford's own Second Colored, parts of the Third Wisconsin and the Fourteenth Kansas Cavalry as an escort. The train was harassed by bushwhackers during most of the journey to Fort Smith, but it arrived without serious loss.[27]

Crawford picked a camp site for the Second Colored Infantry near Fort Smith. For the nine hundred officers and enlisted men he set up a rigid training schedule which included drill each day and a dress parade once a week. According to Crawford's account, many of the politically appointed white officers soon began to hand in their resignations. Crawford then accepted officer applications from the white troops stationed nearby. He was thus able to choose his officers from more than sixty qualified candidates. He also subjected the enlisted men to a rigid physical examination, which led to the discharge of two hundred men. After four months of strict discipline and rigorous training, Crawford believed he had a battleworthy regiment.[28]

In the spring of 1864, the War Department ordered a coordinated attack upon Shreveport, Louisiana. The plan was for General N. P. Banks to approach up the Red River from the south while General Frederick Steele and General John Thayer would join forces and approach from the north. Colonel Crawford's untried Second Colored Infantry formed a part of General Steele's army. This army pushed into southwest Arkansas with twelve thousand men. Steele reached Camden, Arkansas, but he was cut off from his source of supply by Confederate cavalry units shadowing his forces, so he ordered a retreat toward Little Rock. Before starting the retreat, Steele had made repeated attempts to procure supplies. Most of these efforts met with failure. One of the more noteworthy attempts resulted in the notorious battle of Poison Springs, April 18. In this engagement, 117 men of the First Kansas Colored Infantry were killed, many after they had surrendered or had been wounded. This "black flag" policy of the South toward the Negro troops was a serious threat to the morale of the black regiments. To counter this threat, Crawford called a council of his officers at which it was decided to take no Confederate prisoners in any future engagements. "Remember Poison Springs" was to become the battle cry of the Second Kansas Colored Infantry.[29]

On April 26, General Steele started back toward Little Rock. He was constantly harassed by the forces of Generals Sterling Price and Kirby Smith. On April 29, during a rainstorm, Steele's forces reached the Saline River at Jenkins' Ferry, where they laid a pontoon bridge. Several regiments, under the command of General Samuel Rice, were assigned to guard the approach to the bridge. The next morning at about 8:00 A.M., Crawford, who was camped near the bridge, heard gunfire to his front. He rode up to General Rice and asked for orders. Rice asked the name of his

unit, and upon being told, responded, "They won't fight." Crawford told him "in language more emphatic than Christian," that
they would fight as well as any other regiment.[30] Rice then
ordered Crawford to relieve the Fifteenth Indiana at the front.
There was heavy fighting for about two hours and then the enemy
brought three guns to a position about 250 yards in front of
Crawford's regiment. Crawford asked for and received permission to "fix bayonets and charge." The regiment advanced amid
cheering and shouts of "remember Poison Springs," until the
battery was captured. The regiment suffered seventy casualties
and Crawford had his horse shot out from under him. Crawford
was commended in General Rice's official report for his "most
marked gallantry" in the battle of Jenkins' Ferry.[31]

The unsuccessful expedition returned to Little Rock and
General Thayer took his men back to Fort Smith. Crawford's
regiment spent the summer in and around Fort Smith, making an
occasional short expedition into Indian Territory. Crawford spent
very little time with his regiment after his June appointment as
president of a general court martial. An inspection and grand
review was held at Fort Smith on the Fourth of July. General
Thayer, the division commander, complimented Crawford upon
the appearance of his regiment. He also asked Crawford to lead
a proposed cavalry expedition to the Red River. Crawford was
recommended for promotion to brigadier general; but before he
was appointed, news came from Topeka which was to change the
course of his career.[32]

3

THE WAR
AND
THE ELECTION
OF
1864

In September 1864 Colonel Crawford was nominated, not for brigadier-general as he had hoped, but for governor of Kansas. The story of that nomination is a complicated and disputed one which hinged on a political situation peculiar to Kansas. The dominant figure was Senator Lane. His political fortunes had risen and fallen many times, but he had always managed to be on top at election time. In the summer of 1864, his political prospects reached a new low. Former Governor Charles Robinson and Governor Thomas Carney were against him. He had lost the support of many of the influential newspapers of the state. The opposition resolved to elect a ticket which would depose Lane when his term expired in 1865. Lane, however, still controlled most of the federal patronage in Kansas; and he had powerful friends in the army. The result was that the Republicans in Kansas nominated, not one, but two tickets in September 1864. The Republican State Convention met in Topeka on September 8, and the Republican Union State Convention (the anti-Lane Republicans) met in the same city on the thirteenth. Both conventions claimed to represent the regular Republican party.[1]

The excitement in Topeka was great on the eve of the Republican State Convention. Senator Lane had stumped the state during August, but he chose not to attend the convention. In his absence, no one seemed to know just what the convention would do or whom it would choose. A reporter for the Leavenworth *Conservative* listed Thomas A. Osborn, Samuel J. Crawford, and George Crawford as the leading candidates for governor.[2] George Crawford, who was no relation to Samuel, was a perennial candidate for governor who was purported to have Lane's support. Samuel Crawford's strength was said to be based on the soldier delegates who were in town. Thomas A. Osborn, from Doniphan County, represented the northern counties of the state.[3] W. W. H. Lawrence, from the city of Lawrence, was another leading candidate.

The convention was called to order by Jacob Stotler, the secretary of the State Central Committee. Convention officers were elected and the appropriate committees were appointed. The first floor fight came when the Committee on Credentials reported in favor of accepting one delegate from each Kansas regiment which had sent representatives. The adoption of this report would have allowed the admittance of only about four soldier delegates. A minority report was presented which would entitle each white regiment to three delegates and each colored regiment to one delegate. D. R. Anthony, a Lane supporter, spoke for the minority report. The minority report was amended to exclude the delegates from the colored regiments. The amended minority report was accepted. This gave the soldier delegation about twelve, rather than four, representatives.[4] Among those, other than Anthony, who urged the admission of the additional army delegates were

E. C. Manning and D. E. Ballard. Both of these men had fought in the battle of Old Fort Wayne with Crawford. Manning made the motion to accept the minority report, and Ballard served on the Committee on Credentials. Henry Hopkins and J. B. McAfee, who had also been very closely associated with Crawford in the campaigns in Arkansas, were among those chosen to represent the army. McAfee was the chaplain of the Second Kansas Colored Infantry.[5] Before adjourning the first session of the convention, an informal ballot was taken for governor. The results were: George A. Crawford, 23; W. W. H. Lawrence, 21; Samuel J. Crawford, 16; T. A. Osborn, 12; S. D. Houston, 3; J. C. Burnett, 3; J. W. Scott, 3; and R. Riddle, 1; for a grand total of 82 votes. The meeting then adjourned until the evening session.[6]

The evening session was called to order at seven, and a motion was passed to proceed to the formal balloting for governor. The result of the first ballot was very similar to the afternoon informal ballot. George Crawford was leading with 25; W. W. H. Lawrence polled 19; Samuel Crawford was third with 18; Thomas A. Osborn, 10; and three other candidates shared 10 votes. The convention then voted to eliminate the two candidates with the fewest votes. This left only five candidates in the race. The next ballot eliminated two more candidates and left George Crawford with 29; Samuel Crawford, 33; and W. W. H. Lawrence, 21. On the fourth ballot, George Crawford maintained his 29 votes while Colonel Crawford's total jumped to 41 at the expense of Lawrence. The convention then restricted the choice to the two top candidates, George and Samuel Crawford. On the fifth and final ballot, Samuel J. Crawford was nominated by a vote of 51 to 31.[7]

How could a twenty-nine-year-old youth, who was a virtual newcomer to Kansas politics, be nominated to the state's chief executive position? A number of explanations have been offered by the participants in that convention. The question revolves largely around the part played by Senator Jim Lane in the nomination. Crawford's friends generally expressed the belief that Samuel Crawford was not Lane's choice for the nomination, while Crawford's political enemies generally expressed the view that he was Lane's lackey.

According to Josiah McAfee, who became Crawford's private secretary in 1865, Crawford's army friends approached Senator Lane at the Planter's House in Leavenworth a few days before the convention. They asked him to support the colonel for governor. Lane professed his friendship for Crawford but declined to support him, saying, "Gentlemen, you are too late. I have made other arrangements. Colonel Crawford's friends should have brought him out at an earlier date."[8]

E. C. Manning, a lifelong friend, who was a participant in the convention, maintained that Crawford's nomination was the result of adept management by D. E. Ballard and himself at the convention. Their first victory was gained when they persuaded D. R. Anthony of Leavenworth to support the admittance of the army delegates. Their second victory came when they persuaded the representatives of the northern tier of counties, who were chafing over the neglect of their interests on the part of the politicians from Lawrence, Leavenworth, and Atchison, to unite behind Colonel Crawford. They reasoned that since Crawford's hometown was Garnett he would not be controlled by the "big city" politicians. They thereby persuaded Osborn, representing the northern tier, to withdraw in favor of Crawford. The clincher, according to Manning, was a compact with the delegates from Lawrence whereby Crawford's supporters would back Sidney Clarke for Congress in return for the votes previously cast for W. W. H. Lawrence for governor. The bargain was carried out and Samuel J. Crawford was nominated on the next ballot. Clarke was subsequently nominated on the first ballot.[9] Crawford's campaign managers may also have promised support for some of W. W. H. Lawrence's business enterprises. Crawford had been in the governor's chair only a few days when he wrote to Senator Lane asking for assistance for W. W. H. Lawrence in the matter of a freight contract from Fort Leavenworth. Crawford wrote Lane that he would count any assistance to Lawrence as "a personal and special favor."[10]

The testimony of D. R. Anthony generally confirms that of McAfee and Manning. Anthony believed that Lane had agreed to support George Crawford but that he may also have promised help to W. W. H. Lawrence. He reasons that the Lane men did not generally support Samuel Crawford in the early ballots. In addition, he cites the fact that the Lane papers withheld their support for the nominee of the convention for several days. This was certainly true of the Leavenworth *Conservative,* usually considered the Lane organ.[11]

Crawford's political enemies did not share his friends' view that Lane did not control the convention. T. B. Murdock, later the editor of the Eldorado *Republican,* was one of those who believed that Lane controlled the convention from the start. According to him, Lane called several of his associates, including John Speer, Sidney Clarke, and Jacob Stotler, together for a meeting. The alleged meeting took place in a St. Louis hotel shortly before the convention. Lane, after ordering drinks for all present said: "Gentlemen, we have an important duty to perform . . . we must have a military candidate for governor of Kansas and that man should be Samuel Crawford."[12] Marsh Murdock, writing in his Wichita *Eagle* in 1886, described a buggy ride he took with Lane shortly before the convention. Lane told Murdock that Crawford should be nominated at all costs. Murdock replied that "Georgie" was a splendid man and would make a popular race. Lane, according to Murdock, turned sharply and said, "Great God, man, I mean Colonel Sam of the second nigger."[13]

Jacob Stotler, who was chairman of the Republican State Central Committee during the convention, remembered Samuel Crawford as Lane's choice from the start of the campaign. Lane believed that the military record of Crawford would be an asset to the ticket. According to Stotler, Crawford could not have been nominated without Lane's support. Lawrence, Osborn, and Houston were Lane men and they transferred their votes to

Samuel Crawford. Stotler remembered Lane as being highly pleased with Crawford's nomination.[14]

The Murdocks were brothers and Jacob Stotler was their brother-in-law. Marsh Murdock asked Governor Crawford for several favors during his administration. Apparently none of these was forthcoming. Jacob Stotler seems to have supported Crawford's political ambitions until 1872, when Crawford bolted the Republican party to support the Liberal Republican party. Stotler described Crawford as an "ungrateful wretch" who had been nominated for governor by Jim Lane in 1864. Crawford replied in kind, accusing Stotler and his brothers-in-law of soliciting bribes from him. Milton Reynolds, who reopened the controversy with his "Made Governor by Lane" article in the January 24, 1886, Kansas City *Times,* had also been rebuked by Crawford. The governor had sent letters and telegrams to important congressmen opposing Reynolds's nomination for United States assessor for Kansas, labeling him a notorious "copperhead."[15]

The fact that Sidney Clarke was nominated on the first ballot for congressman would seem to prove that Lane was not in control of the convention, provided it can be shown that Clarke had broken with Lane by convention time. Unfortunately, the precise time of their estrangement is not entirely clear. According to Jacob Stotler, who wrote that Lane controlled the nomination of Crawford, Lane did not control the congressional nomination. Stotler claimed to have been an eyewitness to a bitter quarrel between Lane and Clarke which took place in the Landis House in Leavenworth a few weeks before the 1864 general election. Lane wanted A. C. Wilder to be returned to Congress, and he was keenly disappointed at Clarke's nomination. Lane told Clarke, according to Stotler, that he never dreamed that he had any chance for the congressional nomination. Had he foreseen such a possibility he would have walked to Topeka from St. Louis, if necessary, in order to defeat Clarke. John Speer, Lane's confidant and biographer, also wrote that Lane opposed the nomination of Clarke. Clarke, however, had served as Lane's private secretary;

and at the time of the convention, he was the state's provost marshal, a position he could not have held for long without Lane's approval. Web Wilder, the brother of incumbent A. C. Wilder and a long-time Lane associate, broke with Lane soon after his brother's defeat, blaming the defeat on Lane. On September 6, two days before the convention, there was a published report in an anti-Lane newspaper that Clarke was slated for the nomination by the Lane forces. This seems to rule out Clarke as a surprise candidate.[16]

There is no evidence that Lane and Crawford ever met before the nominating convention. Lane was in Washington a great deal while Crawford's tour of duty kept him out of Kansas through most of the war. Lane exercised a great influence in the matter of promotions in the army, especially in the Negro outfits which he helped organize, but Crawford's promotions were not out of line with his record. In fact, they were somewhat tardy. Crawford's brigade commander in the battle of Jenkins' Ferry had been Colonel C. W. Adams, who was Lane's son-in-law and political associate.[17] T. J. Anderson, a Lane man and later Governor Crawford's adjutant general, was running the civil government in northwest Arkansas when Crawford returned to Fort Smith from the Camden campaign.[18] Crawford was also in almost constant contact with General Blunt during the war. Blunt, of course, was Lane's *alter ego* in the army. The soldier delegation representing the Kansas regiments stationed around Fort Smith probably could not have attended the convention if Lane had objected. On the other hand, the leaders of the army delegation were men who had served with Crawford in the Second Kansas Cavalry, a regiment organized by Governor Robinson. At any rate, the delegates from the Kansas regiments represented only about one-eighth of the total number of convention delegates.

It seems apparent that Lane did exercise some control over the convention. He was not, however, in a strong enough position to dictate the convention's every move. It seems more likely that he had several acceptable candidates; perhaps he had even encouraged the candidacy of several persons. He may have encouraged the sending of a delegation from the army knowing that the delegation would not be hostile to his interests. He then left the convention free to choose from among those persons who were favorable to his senatorial candidacy. Samuel Crawford had been out of the state for four years and he had not been identified as being closely connected with any particular faction within the party. He had had little opportunity to make enemies within the party. He did not represent any of the geographic blocs within the state and was therefore acceptable to them all as a second choice. When the northern tier counties found that they did not have enough strength to carry Osborn, their candidate, they fell in with the Crawford army delegation. This gave Ballard and Manning, as Crawford's managers, enough strength to exchange votes with the Clarke supporters. Crawford's managers were thus able to parlay their sixteen votes on the informal ballot into fifty-one votes on the fifth and final ballot. This was neither the first nor the last time in the history of American politics that a dark-horse candidate would be a successful compromise nominee.

Colonel Crawford received word of his nomination at Fort Smith. According to his own account, he was reluctant to accept because he was expecting a promotion to brigadier general and an important assignment and because he had a low opinion of politicians.[19] He quickly accepted the nomination, however, and wrote a lengthy formal letter of acceptance dated September 30. Two years later, when Crawford was making a bid for reelection, it was charged that Crawford's original letter was vain and impolitic and had to be rewritten for publication during the 1864 campaign.[20]

Crawford left his unit in Fort Smith on October 12, but he was not able to campaign in Kansas until October 27, a scant ten days before the election. The Price raid across Missouri was to interrupt his campaign but at the same time secure his election. Upon reaching Fort Scott on October 17, Crawford received an order to report to General Blunt at Hickman Mills, Missouri.[21]

In September 1864 Confederate General Sterling Price had begun a diversionary raid into Missouri. He demonstrated before St. Louis then turned toward Jefferson City. His force was not strong enough to make a determined move in eastern Missouri so he started moving west below the Missouri River toward Kansas City. Reports as to his whereabouts in mid-October varied from south of the Arkansas River to northwest Missouri. General Samuel Curtis of the Department of Kansas ordered the massing of his U. S. troops on the border and asked Governor Carney to call out the Kansas state militia. On October 8, Carney issued the appropriate orders and General George W. Deitzler was put in charge of the militia. On October 10, General Curtis proclaimed martial law in Kansas and ordered General Blunt's forces to the Kansas City area. Price's force reached Lexington on October 20, and was met by Blunt, thus positively establishing the whereabouts of Price. General Alfred Pleasonton had been ordered by General William S. Rosecrans, of the Department of Missouri, to follow Price from the east, but he was not yet in contact with Price's rear guard and his exact position was unknown to the Curtis command.[22] This was the situation when Crawford reached the Kansas City area on October 20. He was unable to report to Blunt as directed because Blunt was at Lexington. General Curtis suggested that Crawford aid Governor Carney and General Deitzler in bringing the Kansas militia to the front, but "for political reasons [Crawford's] services were respectively declined." The Kansas militia, under the control of Carney, was staffed by anti-Lane Union Republicans, while General Curtis and the U. S. forces were assisted by "volunteer aides" including Senators Lane and Pomeroy and candidate Crawford.[23] Curtis was aware that the governor suspected the calling of the militia to be a Lane scheme to get the voters out of the state on election day. It was a very difficult situation for Curtis because he could not be sure that the militia would leave the state if needed. He was convinced that they would not go many miles from Kansas soil. As late as October 19, many anti-Lane newspapers were "denouncing the whole thing as a fraud . . . and expressing a belief that Price had left the country."[24]

General Blunt fell back to the Little Blue River on October 21, where he had prepared a strong position. He fought a brief engagement there but was ordered by General Curtis to fall back to the Big Blue River, where the likelihood of receiving the aid of the Kansas militia was greater. But the Big Blue, or the army behind it, was not strong enough to prevent the crossing of Price's troops on October 22. Fortunately for Curtis, Pleasonton's force had caught up with Price from the east and attacked his rear guard in the afternoon of the twenty-second. Curtis received word of Pleasonton's arrival about six o'clock in the evening. The news was circulated and the morale of the army greatly strengthened.[25]

The stage was set for the battle of Westport, October 23, 1864. Exactly what happened on the evening before that battle has become a controversy. In Crawford's version, published forty-seven years later, Curtis had decided, after his reverses in the battle of Big Blue, to abandon Kansas City and retreat toward Leavenworth. Crawford claimed that he met with Curtis, Blunt, and Lane at the Gillis House in Kansas City. All of Curtis's aides insisted on standing at Westport. The situation became so serious, according to Crawford, that some of the officers took General Blunt aside and insisted that the only thing to do was to put General Curtis under arrest and allow Blunt to assume command. General Blunt replied, "That is a serious thing to do." Crawford and the other officers answered, "Not so serious as for this army to run away like cowards and let Price sack Kansas City and devastate southern Kansas." Blunt then returned to Curtis and inquired "in no uncertain tones" what he proposed to do. Curtis, seeing the determination depicted on his face, answered, "If you say fight, then fight it is." Blunt said fight.[26] Neither Curtis nor Lane in their official reports made mention of such a meeting, although it is not likely that they would report such an incident.[27] During the period of extended crisis the defenses of Kansas City had been greatly improved. In dispatches as late as 10:15 A.M.,

October 21, Curtis spoke of his purpose to defend the Big Blue and Kansas City, which were his strong points.[28] General Blunt, writing in April 1866, made no mention of any staff meeting with Curtis during the night of October 22. He did write that he had learned that Curtis had commanded his troops to fall back to Kansas City, an order which Blunt countermanded, for Blunt meant to attack the enemy at Westport.[29] Crawford, writing more than forty years later, may not have remembered the detailed happenings and conversations of the night of October 22, 1864. Curtis was a cautious individual, while candidate Crawford had many reasons to want the army to make a strong stand in defense of the Kansas border. It is probable that Curtis wanted to defend Kansas City with the aid of the Kansas militia rather than extend himself to Westport or beyond. He may therefore have ordered his troops back to Kansas City only to have Blunt countermand the orders of a part of his army. With Pleasonton known to be in position to attack the rear of Price's army and the Kansas militia's increased strength and willingness to fight in Missouri, Curtis may have given in to Blunt. It is extremely doubtful, however, that Curtis ever ordered a retreat to Leavenworth.

With General Pleasonton's army on the east, the Missouri River on the north, and Curtis's reinforced army on the west, Price's army was in a precarious position. The fight started early on the morning of the twenty-third. Crawford rode with Blunt. On one occasion, Crawford ordered two company commanders to "sound the advance and charge," a solution which worked quite as well as it had worked for Crawford's own units at Old Fort Wayne and Jenkins' Ferry. Other sections of Blunt's command effected similar charges at the same time.[30] At 11:00 A.M., General Curtis led the final charge himself. By 11:30 A.M., Curtis could telegraph his superior that "victory was ours." By 2:00 P.M., the enemy had been driven south and Curtis had linked his army with that of Pleasonton.[31] Thus ended one of the major battles of the West. Nearly thirty thousand troops had been assembled, less than ten thousand of them Confederates. The majority of the Union forces, however, was made up of untrained militia.

The Kansas militiamen residing in northern Kansas were released at the suggestion of General Deitzler and Governor Carney. The reduced Union force then began its pursuit of Price down the Kansas-Missouri line toward Fort Scott. The border was the dividing line between the jurisdiction of Generals Pleasonton and Curtis, a situation which caused some delay in following Price. There was a great deal of movement with only minor skirmishes during the next two days.[32] It was the kind of running battle in which a general is unable to exert complete control over his army. The role of the junior officer thus becomes much more important. Colonel Crawford insisted on pressing the enemy and when General Curtis did not move fast enough to please him, he rode on ahead looking for a fight. Before dawn on October 25, General Curtis's forces came upon Price's army near the Marais des Cygnes River. There were few casualties, as Price was only fighting a rear guard action. Later the same day, however, an important battle was fought at Mine Creek.[33]

Crawford played a prominent role in the battle of Mine Creek. When he came upon the Confederates, who had formed a rear guard at Mine Creek, he believed an immediate charge to be in order. He ordered the skirmish line to advance and sent word back to General Blunt asking for assistance. Blunt, according to Crawford, was still chafing over jurisdictional disputes and he declined to take part in the battle, "in terms which could not be found in the New Testament."[34] Units of Pleasonton's brigade then came up to within sight of the enemy. Crawford conferred with Colonels John F. Philips and Frederick Benteen, explaining the enemy's position and suggesting that they charge at once. He told them he would explain everything to their commanding officer. Philips and Benteen charged into the fray and within thirty minutes the enemy's lines were broken. During the fighting, Crawford rode among the various units urging them forward and coordinating the attack. He personally led at least one of the charges.[35] During the confusion and disorganization of Price's army a Corporal James Dunlavy succeeded in capturing Major-General John Marmaduke. General William Cabell and more than five hundred Confederates were also captured. In addition, Price was forced to abandon most of his train and give up any designs he may have had on Fort Scott. Price turned his retreat to the southeast, away from Fort Scott and the threat to Kansas was ended. Crawford was disappointed that Price's whole army was not destroyed, but he earned commendations from Generals Blunt and Curtis and his role in the battle would be a great asset in his role as candidate for governor.[36]

On the twenty-seventh of October, just eleven days before the election, Crawford was relieved from further duty as volunteer aide-de-camp. Although Crawford's active political campaign in his own behalf had been postponed because of the Price raid, his military actions, coupled with other political developments which hinged on the Price raid, did more to promote his election than he could possibly have accomplished by taking the stump. When he accepted the nomination, the chances of election for Crawford and the Lane Republicans were uncertain. After the Price raid, his election was assured.

On September 9, 1864, Solon O. Thacher who was to be the Union Republican (anti-Lane) candidate for governor wrote: "The Lane ticket is terribly weak . . . we can rid the State of the throes of these fellows."[37] Charles Robinson, former governor and an ardent Lane hater, wrote to his wife on October 1: "Politics look quite favorable for the state ticket. It is generally thought the Thacher ticket will be elected."[38] Sol Miller, editor of the anti-Lane White Cloud *Kansas Chief,* wrote: "Had the Convention raked the State over with a fine tooth comb, it could not have gathered a smaller and weaker set of men to place on their ticket."[39] Even the paper usually considered the Lane organ, the Leavenworth *Daily Conservative,* was slow to come to the support of the ticket. Two days after the Republican convention the *Conservative* said: "In saying that we do not approve of the Topeka nominations we simply repeat the observations of every honest man. The ticket is a poor one, will not be elected, and will have our undivided opposition."[40] The following five days there was no mention of state politics in the *Conservative;* and then on the sixteenth, the entire Republican ticket, with the exception of Clarke, the candidate for Congress, was printed under the masthead. There was a terse announcement: "For reasons which it is unnecessary to state, my editorial connection with the *Conservative* ceases as of this date." It was signed Wm. W. Bloss.[41] The same issue came out in support of "Colonel Samuel J. Crawford . . . one of the most upright and manly citizens of the State," who possessed a "reputation inferior to that of no Kansas soldier." "Crawford, Kansas' own war hero" was to be the Republican paper's theme when it became necessary to mention the gubernatorial candidate at all. For the most part, however, the campaign was fought on other issues. The Republican strategy was to take the offensive by identifying the Union Republicans as the Carney-Fusion-Fraud party. The Union Republicans were accused of being Copperheads because they accepted the support of the Kansas Democratic party, which put up no state slate.[42]

The opposition papers hardly knew how to attack such a man. "Who is S. J. Crawford?" wrote J. W. Roberts in his Oskaloosa *Independent.*[43] The Atchison *Freedom's Champion* wrote: "Of Crawford, nothing is known save that he is a Colonel of a Negro regiment. Probably not ten men in this county were aware of his existence."[44] Sol Miller, dedicated enemy of Lane, could only write in his *Kansas Chief* that: "We have nothing to say against . . . Col. Crawford, except that he does not possess the ability requisite for a Governor of our State."[45] These were mild words for Sol Miller. On October 21, the Leavenworth *Times* published an attack on Crawford, accusing him of having misappropriated some Confederate funds which he was said to have captured in September 1863. According to the story, he had taken several prisoners and forty thousand Confederate dollars in the capture of a wagon train. He was accused of delivering the money to his commanding officer, who kept $30,000 and gave $10,000 to Crawford to divide among his officers.[46] A subsequent exposé was promised, but the battle of Westport was soon to divert attention away from this charge. No more evidence was presented, although the *Times* often spoke of "Ten Thousand Dollar Crawford."[47]

Early in October, the leading figures of both political factions knew that there was some danger of an invasion by the army of Price. General Curtis knew of this danger as early as October 2 and he made it a practice to keep both Governor Carney and Jim Lane, as well as the leading newspapers, informed of the danger to Kansas.[48] Governor Carney doubted that Kansas was in danger, but he called out the militia at the insistence of General Curtis. The Lane faction bet their political future that Price would attempt to invade Kansas. The Leavenworth *Conservative* began its campaign to get the militia to the border. As early as October 8, when the exact location of Price was not yet known, it proclaimed: "The people must arouse. This is no *scare*. You must stop the enemy or suffer your homes to be devastated."[49] On October 11, the *Conservative* read: "Patriots, Rally! . . . every loyal man who is able to carry a musket should leap to the defense of our homes and firesides. . . . Then rally, rally, we say—every man—with a cheer and a will, and our triumph is certain."[50]

When nothing was heard from Price for several days, the Union Republicans became suspicious. A letter written from Shawnee by former Governor Robinson on October 16 shows their frame of mind:

> I am here in camp to defend the border . . . business is stopped and everybody is forced into the service . . . Govr Carney, Thacher, Ingalls, Web. Wilder [are here].
>
> It is beginning to be thought that our being called out is all a sham and trick of Lane and Curtis to make political capital—We cannot have any thing of importance as to the

movements of Price. . . . I have no doubt Price has gone
South. . . . No body thinks we shall have anything to do but
go home in a few days and attend to our business. . . .

Political affairs are prospering finely. . . . Thacher has
been through the Northern Counties and he says there will
not be but three Lane members of the Legislature north of
the River. . . . I think the old devil has gone up. He is on
Genl. Curtis's staff but keeps very quiet and is very blue.[51]

Governor Carney called on General Curtis to express his
apprehensions lest the mobilization be a scheme to "transport the
people beyond the convenient exercise of their elective franchise."[52] By the nineteenth, the Leavenworth *Times* was calling
for the repeal of martial law and sending the militiamen back to
their homes. On October 20, the *Times* said: "We respectfully
request General Curtis and his staff to either find somebody to
fight or else take his miliary clamps from off Kansas and let her
citizens return to their homes."[53] This was the same day that
Blunt and Price met at Lexington and only three days before the
battle of Westport. Meanwhile the *Conservative,* probably acting
on better information furnished by Curtis's aide-de-camp Lane,
bet everything on Price materializing. It was difficult to keep the
men at the border, and the *Conservative* exhorted the boys to
stand firm, "repel all and every party influence and cheerfully
obey the Department Orders."[54] On October 21, the *Conservative*
taunted the *Times* for having suggested the return home of the
militia, saying, "This is the way pro-slavery *Times* strengthens
the military arm of the Government." By the twenty-second, the
Conservative was in a position to make numerous digs at the
Times: "Discovery. The *Times* has discovered that Price was
not South of the Arkansas, as they asserted when they recommended the militia disband." Wm. M. Bloss, former editor of the
Conservative, who had gone over to the *Times,* had gone to the
front to see for himself and had received a minor wound. The
Conservative taunted: "Query? If Price is not in Missouri, who

shot Bloss?" Another short item read: "Let every man go to the front, says Jeff Davis. Let every man go to the rear says the Leavenworth *Times*." On the twenty-third, the day of the battle of Westport, the *Conservative* announced that it would be published irregularly because its staff had gone to the front.[55]

John Speer, in his biography of Lane, wrote: "When the campaign against Price had ended, the election of all the Republican state officers was practically settled."[56] Speer was quite right. The *Conservative* had a field day:

> *Lost*
>
> A liberal reward will be paid for the recovery of that Proclamation of Thomas Carney, prepared by him and read in the camps of the Kansas Militia on Thursday, in which he proposed to order the soldiers home, and in which our recent battles were denounced as "humbugs," Jim Lane Frauds & c.[57]

The *Times* was reduced to desperate name calling with reference to "Ten Thousand Dollar Crawford," the "cotton stealer."[58] On October 30, Robinson, writing to his wife, was trying to convince himself, without much success, that there was still hope:

> The war excitement has blown over and politics rule the house. . . . The political prospects look encouraging. Lane however has the assistance of Lincoln as much as ever. . . . They are unworthy the support of any man. The longer I live the more I am disgusted with Lincoln.[59]

On October 27, Crawford was released from further service to begin his political campaign. He had performed well at Westport and had been a hero at Mine Creek. His bravery was proven and the timing of the battle of Mine Creek was helpful—only two weeks before the election. The Republican papers made much out of his record. With only ten days left before the election, Crawford was unable to campaign very actively. He was scheduled to speak in Fort Scott on October 30, but had to excuse himself as being sick.[60] The *Conservative* published a speaking schedule for Lane and Crawford which would have taken them to fifteen cities in five days. He was not able to speak at all the announced meetings. He made no appearance at the scheduled Leavenworth meeting. He apparently spoke at Lawrence on November 7, the eve of the election. The Lawrence *Tribune* said simply: "His remarks were brief and to the point—worthy of the man and the cause." One opposition journalist characterized his speeches as being vain, unchivalrous, and ". . . fit for the bar-room."[61]

The election was held on Tuesday, November 8, 1864. Crawford was the most popular Republican on the ballot, leading the ticket by more than one thousand votes. He defeated Thacher 13,387 to 8,448. Crawford's vote included 2,181 soldier votes. A legislature favorable to Lane's reelection was chosen.[62]

The Lane-Crawford opponents held many post-mortems. Sol Miller blamed some of the anti-Lane press for taunting Crawford about being with a Negro regiment. He had previously drawn up an elaborate list of fifteen newspapers which were committed to Lane through government printing contracts, government positions, and bribes.[63] Perhaps Lane had followed the advice of one of his correspondents, who said the way to win elections was "to work hard and don't spare the cash."[64] In despair, Robinson wrote to his wife: ". . . the *Sheisters* are in a working majority in this state and I think Lane is a true representative of the majority of the people."[65] The chain of events which led to the election of the Lane-Crawford ticket, however, was beyond the control of the "sheisters," Robinson, or Crawford. Sterling Price's raid was the unwitting instrument which assured Crawford's election.

4

THE
YOUNG
GOVERNOR

On Monday, January 9, 1865, precisely at noon, Samuel J. Crawford was ushered into Representative Hall in Topeka. A large audience watched as State Supreme Court Justice Jacob Safford administered the oath of office and Colonel Crawford became Governor Crawford. Incumbent Governor Thomas Carney tendered the great seal of the state and extended his good wishes to his successor.[1] Crawford, not yet thirty years old, must have been awed by the prospect of becoming the chief executive of a state government with so few apparent resources. Years later he wrote: "As a matter of fact, we had nothing with which to set up housekeeping, except the State Seal, a lease on some leaky buildings, and quite an assortment of bills payable."[2] The war had forced the postponement of the construction of many necessary state buildings. The state had no capitol building, no state colleges, no ample penitentiary, and almost no credit. While the war continued, there was constant anxiety along the state's borders for fear of bushwhackers or Indians. Then there was the prospect of the first draft in Kansas. After the end of the war, there would be new problems connected with reconstruction. Perhaps the most serious of Crawford's problems would be dealing with the audacious politicians who expected to share in the political spoils.

Crawford began his first term with a considerable handicap. He was young and inexperienced, having been in public office only six weeks before entering the army. His administrative experience was largely limited to his command of troops. His absence from the state during most of the four years of Kansas statehood made it difficult for him to be well informed concerning state affairs. On the other side of the ledger, however, Crawford could count a number of important assets. The newspapers of the state gave him almost unanimous support, especially during the first year of his administration,[3] and he enjoyed the admiration of the people of the state because of his war record. He was not closely identified with any of the geographic or special interest factions within the state, and his absence from the active political scene left him largely free from specific commitments to his political followers. In addition, he had made a number of firm friends in the army on whom he could count for support, and these men occupied many of the more responsible positions throughout the state upon their return home. Finally, he had the strong Lane organization behind him.

Crawford's first message to the legislature was characteristic of his first year in office. It was a cautious document which consisted of summaries of reports from the various departments of the state government. It was presented to a combined session of the House and Senate on January 11 by the governor's private secretary, Josiah McAfee. The message included a summary of the condition of the state's educational system, a financial report, a progress report on the penitentiary, and a few encouraging remarks concerning immigration into the state.[4]

The legislators could be excused for being something less than spellbound by the governor's routine message because they were anticipating the upcoming election of a United States senator, always a riotous event in early Kansas history. The House and Senate met in joint session on the afternoon of Thursday, January 12, for the election. Special seats were brought in for the guests who wished to view the spectacle. Governor Crawford was invited to occupy a seat next to the Speaker. John Speer, Lane's faithful friend, surprised no one by nominating Lane. Four other candidates were nominated and the balloting began. In a matter of minutes, Lane's election was assured; he received eighty-two votes while his four opponents received a total of only sixteen. A signal was given from the chamber window whereupon a cannon boomed, a band played "Hail to the Chief," and a cavalry unit wheeled into a marching column. General Blunt had ordered a squadron of United States cavalry, a battery of artillery, and a military band to Topeka for the occasion. The joint convention voted to adjourn, and a crowd assembled in front of the Topeka House to hear speeches by Crawford, General Blunt, Congressman-elect Sidney Clarke, and many others. The next night there was a "senatorial banquet" in honor of Lane. Toasts were made to the president, the senate, the state, the military, the navy, the legislature, the press, the bar, and so on until the five hundred guests lost count. The dinner ended at 1:00 A.M., and General Blunt's band played music for dancing until dawn.[5]

The legislature somehow mustered a quorum on Monday morning, but by Wednesday they had voted to adjourn for a long weekend in order to accept the invitation of John D. Perry, president of the Union Pacific Railroad, Eastern Division, to come to Wyandotte for another banquet and grand ball. The state officials were taken to Lawrence by conveyances which ranged from a stagecoach to a one-horse shay. The party of two hundred congregated at Lawrence, the end of the track, and was taken by rail to Wyandotte.[6] The lawmakers reconvened on Monday, January 23, and adjourned the session on February 20. The legislature authorized some necessary building bonds, unanimously approved the thirteenth amendment to the United States Constitution, and passed some minor bills.[7] In addition, the generous legislators voted to set the governor's annual salary at $2,000 and to allow his private secretary $1,200.[8] With the governor thus provided for, they could adjourn in good conscience and leave the machinery of state in the hands of the administration.

Crawford was besieged with requests for appointments to state office. Actually he had few political plums to distribute. He appointed hundreds of justices of the peace and notaries public, but he apparently made no attempt to exclude his political enemies from these positions.[9] Most of Crawford's major appointments were confined to the state militia, and the majority of these went to Crawford's army associates. This personal consideration seemed to have been more important than the appointment of those officers who were readily identified as "Lane men." Of course, many of the appointees could be simultaneously classified as Crawford's friends and "Lane men." W. F. Cloud was appointed adjutant general, J. K. Rankin was made paymaster general, D. E. Ballard was appointed quartermaster general, and Edmund G. Ross was appointed aide-de-camp. All four of these men had served with Crawford in the Second Kansas Cavalry. Crawford also used his reservoir of army friends for many of his civilian appointments. Josiah McAfee, the former chaplain of the Second Kansas Colored, was appointed the governor's private secretary; John K. Rankin, in addition to being paymaster general, was appointed director of the State Normal School. There were other names, M. R. Dutton, John Ritchie, John A. Martin, and T. J. Anderson, for example, who were considered "Lane men"; but the majority of Crawford's appointments were personal army acquaintances—men known to Crawford long before he became closely connected with Jim Lane.[10]

When Crawford took office on January 9, 1865, he found a draft pending. Thanks to the intense war feeling in Kansas and the exceptional recruiting ability of Jim Lane and his agents, Kansas had escaped the draft throughout the war. Nevertheless, a draft was ordered by Provost Marshal Brigadier General James B. Fry on December 19, 1864. By his accounting, Kansas had fallen short of her quota by more than a thousand men. Crawford, in his January 11 message to the legislature, claimed that Kansas had furnished 16,337 men for Kansas regiments and a substantial number to regiments of other states; but he noted that "from some cause we have not received credit for all the troops furnished by the State."[11] A discrepancy in the figures of the state and federal government is not surprising because there were a number of enlistments which defied classification. For example, the First and Second Kansas Colored Regiments recruited a total of 2,116 men. According to the state adjutant general's report, only six of these men came from states other than Kansas, even though most of the Negroes actually were from Arkansas and Missouri.[12] Another troublesome category was the Indians. The legislature passed a Concurrent Resolution on January 20 calling on the provost marshal to credit the state with the enlistment of three Indian regiments and to revoke the draft.[13]

The War Department informed the provost marshal's office in Leavenworth on January 23 that the revised quota for the draft in Kansas was 1,222 men.[14] Now that a definite call had been made, Crawford became deeply concerned. On February 1, he wrote to Sidney Clarke in Washington to see if something could be done to stop the draft. Crawford told Clarke, who was the congressman-elect and Kansas provost marshal, that "Kansas should not be disgraced by a draft when she is ahead on all calls—having furnished more men in proportion to her population than any other state in the Union." Crawford said he could raise another volunteer regiment if given authority and time, and he asked Clarke to go with Lane to call on the provost marshal general and have the assignment withdrawn.[15] The governor next tried a more direct approach. On February 10, he wrote a letter to Provost Marshal Fry asking that the draft be suspended. It was a lengthy letter which was well organized and persuasive. Crawford argued that Kansas had furnished more soldiers proportionately than any other state reckoned on the basis of congressional districts, election statistics, or the latest census.[16]

The Leavenworth *Times,* which had been the chief opposition paper before the election, but had more recently been more supportive toward Crawford, began to print criticism of the governor for not preventing the draft. In an article headed "The Draft" and addressed to the governor of Kansas, a correspondent asked why this "great injustice had been done to the state?" The paper answered with another question: ". . . is it because you, sir, and our Senators and member of Congress, have been derelict in your duty to your State . . . ?" The correspondent could not resist adding that while Thomas Carney was governor "he was ceaseless in his vigilance in protecting his State from wrong and from the General Government. . . ." Crawford had not yet been in office a month, but the *Times* article asked: "Do you suppose that your constituents will sustain you in sitting timidly by and see that this injustice is done the State without any effort on your part to prevent it?"[17] On February 19, the *Times* announced that orders had been given to start the draft immediately and the Leavenworth draftees would be announced in about ten days.[18]

The legislature adjourned on February 20, leaving the governor free to leave the state capital. Two days later Crawford telegraphed Secretary of War E. M. Stanton from Leavenworth asking that the draft be suspended in Kansas until he could reach Washington the following week. At the same time he advised Lane of his action and told him to see Stanton.[19] Crawford stayed in Leavenworth on the night of February 22, and he explained to the *Conservative* that he was going to Washington to confer with the secretary of war in an attempt to get the draft suspended. He claimed that Kansas had more than filled her quota, but if he failed to convince the secretary of this, then he would ask for time to fill the quota with additional volunteers.[20]

Crawford left Leavenworth for Washington the next day, but Leavenworth set out to effect her own solution to the problem. The Leavenworth papers urged a great drive for volunteers, encouraged by bounties if necessary, in order to avoid the draft. By March 3, the *Times* could announce with pride that 161 recruits had been enlisted in Leavenworth, enough to prevent a draft in that city.[21]

Crawford arrived in Washington and presented a report his adjutant general had prepared which showed that Kansas should have been credited with 19,812 enlistments while they had been credited with only 15,961, a difference of 3,851. Crawford called on Secretary Edwin Stanton, who was reluctant to suspend any draft calls because many other governors were also there appealing for similar considerations and because Grant was now stalemated in Virginia and the need for troops seemed to be great. Stanton referred the matter to a Colonel Vincent, who certified an additional 3,039 men. This put Kansas almost two thousand over its quota, but it also put Stanton in an awkward position. He finally agreed to suspend the draft in Kansas, but he asked Crawford to keep the news quiet. On March 20, Crawford telegraphed from Washington to his private secretary in Topeka, "I have received credit for three thousand thirty nine additional troops—Draft suspended . . . not to be published."[22] Crawford had received credit for the additional numbers ten days earlier, but Stanton apparently had not yet officially ordered the suspension. By March 16, three Leavenworth papers had printed rumors of the suspension. The *Conservative* and *Evening Bulletin* credited Crawford with having been the prime mover and a few days later even the *Times* reprinted a dispatch from Senator S. C. Pomeroy which gave considerable credit to Crawford.[23]

Stanton was not new to handling state politicians. He invited Crawford to join a party which took a revenue cutter down to City Point, Virginia, to observe the Army of the Potomac before

Richmond. The visiting statesmen were treated to an introduction to Grant and allowed to watch a battle from a signal station. When Crawford arrived back in Leavenworth on April 11, he found that some of the draftees had been held. He telegraphed the provost marshal in Washington asking for their release. Four days later an order was received discharging the drafted men. During the interval, however, they had been sent on to St. Louis. Crawford returned to Washington in June and secured an order for the release of these men, who were in General Edward Canby's jurisdiction. This order was delayed and those draftees who had been assigned to the Tenth Kansas Regiment remained in service until the entire regiment was mustered out. Thus Stanton got the needed men and satisfied the Kansas political situation at the same time.[24]

While Crawford was on his return trip to Kansas, Lee surrendered to Grant at Appomattox. Crawford arrived in Leavenworth on April 11 and found the city in a joyous mood. The assassination of Lincoln on April 14 turned joy into sorrow in Kansas. Crawford had been highly impressed with Lincoln when he attended the inauguration.[25] On April 15, 1865, he issued the following proclamation from the executive office in Topeka:

An inscrutable but all-wise Providence has suddenly visited the nation amid its rejoicings and newborn hopes.

President Lincoln has been wickedly assassinated; a loyal people are shedding bitter tears of sorrow; grief, the most poignant, fills the heart of every true patriot in the land; a calamity that seems almost unbearable has visited the nation! Let us submit with Christian resignation to the great affliction—kiss the hand that smites us, remembering that it is our Father's will.

I do recommend that in respect to the memory of the slain hero and patriot, the public and private buildings in the State be draped in mourning, so far as practicable, for the space of ten days; and that on Sunday the 23rd inst.,

Samuel Johnson Crawford
Governor of Kansas
1865-1868

All photos courtesy the Kansas State Historical Society, Topeka

James Henry Lane
United States Senator
1861-1866

Edmund Gibson Ross
United States Senator
1866-1871

Thomas Carney
Governor of Kansas
1863-1865

Samuel Clarke Pomeroy
United States Senator
1861-1873

especial prayers be offered to the Almighty God that He will sanctify this great calamity to the good of our bereaved country.

In witness whereof, I have hereunto caused the great seal of the State to be affixed, at Topeka, this 15th day of April, 1865.

S. J. Crawford, Governor[26]

The end of the war signaled the beginning of a new era in Kansas as well as the other states. The heading of an article in a Kansas paper in August 1865 summed up a new attitude: "Peace-Business," it read.[27] The papers were no longer filled with military and political events; they turned to such matters as railroad promotion and land speculation.[28] The Kansas legislature which met on January 9, 1866, was the first to complete a session in time of peace. Earlier legislatures had authorized the establishment of certain state institutions, but very little money, labor, or material had been available for construction. The 1866 legislature passed bills which provided for the construction of a state capitol, an additional wing on the penitentiary, and some funds for the state university, agricultural college, and a normal school. These funds were certainly needed. Crawford's first message to the legislature, for example, had included a report which stated that of the thirty-two prisoners who had been confined during the previous year, seventeen had been pardoned and seven had escaped. Statistics continued in a similar vein until the completion of the new penitentiary wing. The state university and the agricultural college opened their doors in 1866 and the normal school was soon in operation. The cornerstone for the capitol was laid October 17, 1866.[29]

One of Crawford's routine responsibilities was to sell the state bonds which the legislature authorized for construction of certain buildings. In 1865, he had made a trip to New York City to enlist a fiscal agent. He found the state's credit rating very low. During the war, some state bonds had sold as low as 65 per cent of face value. Crawford again traveled to New York in April 1866 to try to sell $60,000 worth of penitentiary bonds and $70,000 in public improvement bonds. Advisers there told him he would get no more than seventy-five cents on the dollar. He then went to Washington and did not return to New York until late May. This time he managed to sell the bonds at ninety-one cents on the dollar through Fisk, Hatch and Company. On May 26, he wired his secretary from New York: "Bonds received and sold at 91 push forward on the Penitentiary and Capitol Buildings." According to Jacob Stotler's story, Crawford carried the bills home pinned inside his clothes but had to send them back to New York by express because they were too large to change in Kansas.[30]

Another of the routine problems which occupied Governor Crawford's time was the matter of the Price raid claims. In his message to the legislature in 1866, he reported the state held incomplete claims against the federal government for almost $400,000.[31] The state contended that the militia had been ordered into service by federal officers and the state was therefore entitled to compensation for the materials used and the damage sustained. Crawford went to Washington in the spring of 1866 to try to bolster the claim. On April 25, he wrote to McAfee, his secretary: "Our Militia claim to the amount of $259,000 has passed the Senate and will come up in the House tomorrow or the next day—It will pass I think, although nothing is certain in this detestable hole until you get in." The bill was postponed and Crawford returned home. Later in the session Congressman Sidney Clarke telegraphed Crawford: "Price raid claims in danger of defeat I think Anderson or yourself should come here immediately. . . ."[32] Crawford sent Adjutant General T. J. Anderson with a portfolio full of documents and statements which substantiated the state's claims. The bill died in committee, however, because the state had not assumed the responsibility for the debts as other states had done. Anderson came home and wrote a report suggesting that the state assume the debt and then again present its bill.[33] Crawford recommended that the legislature authorize the issuance of scrip for the claims in his 1867 message, but the legislature was unwilling to assume the claims, which by this time had risen to almost $500,000. Consequently, they authorized the appointment of a commission to reexamine the claims. Crawford appointed D. E. Ballard, W. N. Hanby, and W. H. Fitzpatrick to the commission. They threw out $118,654 of the claims as excessive or fraudulent. The state issued the scrip in 1867, but Congress did not reimburse the state until 1873, and then only partially. Crawford, who was appointed state agent for Kansas in 1877, continued to press the claims as late as 1891.[34]

One of the most significant developments which took place during the Crawford administration was the immigration movement. The 1860 United States Census indicated that Kansas had a population of 107,206. A state census dated May 1866 credited Kansas with a total population of 140,179. The United States Census of 1870 showed that Kansas population had jumped to 364,300. From these figures it can be estimated that the population of the state more than doubled during Crawford's two terms.[35] Immigration was a subject included in all four of Crawford's annual messages to the legislature. His proposals were moderate, but he was never able to obtain any substantial appropriation for this purpose.[36]

The 1865 Kansas legislature failed to take any effective action on the subject of immigration. After adjournment, Crawford found that he had the power under an 1864 statute to write a pamphlet for distribution among prospective immigrants which would describe the opportunities in Kansas. Crawford and J. B. McAfee accordingly wrote a twenty-four-page booklet entitled, "The State of Kansas, A Home for Immigrants," which went to press about November 1865. In this pamphlet, Crawford described the boundaries, population, climate, rivers, soil, railroads, schools, and unoccupied lands of Kansas. He minimized the 1860 drought, saying that it was no worse than elsewhere; it was only that greedy men had misrepresented the facts in order to obtain a large sum of money for pretended relief work. Most of the pamphlet was reasonably factual, but Crawford occasionally embellished the attributes of his state: "The winters are short, dry, and pleasant . . . during the summer there is always a cool, refreshing breeze, which makes even the hottest days and nights delightful," and again: "The climate of Kansas is, without exception, the most desirable in the United States." The pamphlet also included a copy of the homestead act and some sample application forms.[37] Crawford's efforts attracted some attention in the Kansas press and the notices were generally favorable. The Leavenworth *Conservative* wrote:

> It is well known that Governor Crawford has been deeply interested in the subject [of immigration] and has done all he could officially or privately to excite an interest in the matter. As there was no appropriation, his labors were necessarily circumscribed. He has a pamphlet now in press that will soon be ready for distribution. It contains much valuable information, and cannot fail to do much towards directing immigrants to our state. . . .[38]

During the legislative sessions of 1866, certain legislators came to Crawford and offered to back the immigration appropriations provided Crawford would agree in advance to appoint a Mr. Dean as the state immigration agent. Dean, a Canadian, had some connection with the Lawrence Land Company, and he had the support of the Lawrence *State Journal*. Crawford refused to appoint an alien and the legislature refused to vote an appropriation. The *State Journal* placed the blame on Crawford, saying that the friends of an immigration bill refused to vote for the bill because they believed Crawford would appoint some incompetent person. The Leavenworth *Times* took a similar position. They accused Crawford of using the fact that Mr. Dean was an alien as a subterfuge for refusing his appointment. The real reason, according to the *Times* Topeka correspondent, was that Crawford "intended to appoint some *seed*" who would waste the public money. Crawford, it was claimed: ". . . rather than not have his will carried out, was willing that no effort towards securing an emigration bill should be made." The Leavenworth *Conservative,* although having no objection to Mr. Dean, took the position that the governor could not very well appoint an agent who was not subject to the laws of the United States. The legislature, the *Conservative* reasoned, should have considered the "measure meritorious in itself" without attempting to usurp the governor's appointive powers. The only criticism of Crawford's position was that he had not named publicly "the men who had the effrontery to trifle with the public welfare to advance their own interests."[39]

The immigration bill came up again in the 1867 legislative session, but it was defeated once again; whereupon, Crawford used the authority of an earlier statute to appoint an Immigration Commission consisting of George A. Crawford, his former rival for the Republican gubernatorial nomination; Judge L. D. Bailey; and himself as commissioners. Under their auspices, thirty thousand circulars and pamphlets were broadcast throughout the country. Crawford believed that Kansas was gaining fifty thousand immigrants a year, but he was sure that figure could be doubled with a liberal appropriation.[40]

It would be misleading to conclude that Crawford, without material aid from the legislature, succeeded in inducing some two hundred thousand immigrants to Kansas during his administration. The chief factors were beyond his control. Probably the most important factor was the influence of free or cheap land in Kansas.[41] The war had temporarily curtailed the westward movement and when peace came it was resumed with greater vigor than before. Another important factor was the building of the railroads into Kansas. The Union Pacific, Eastern Division, for example, was as far west as Junction City by the summer of 1866. By early 1867, more than three hundred miles of track had been laid in Kansas. In another year, there would be more than five hundred miles.[42] Crawford had labored long and hard in the interest of immigration, and he had shown imagination in attempting to induce immigration without legislative support; but his efforts were probably responsible for no more than a small percentage of the increased immigration.

Crawford's handling of the routine matters of state during his first term indicates that he was a reasonably capable administrator. He was able to deal with problems concerning immigration, the state institutions, and the draft without much reference to the political factions. Senator Jim Lane apparently allowed him free rein in dealing with purely state matters; but when reconstruction became an issue in the state, as well as the nation, Crawford was forced to tread lightly.

The reconstruction issue began to have political repercussions in Kansas about February 1866, the month of President Andrew Johnson's veto of the Freedmen's Bureau bill. In January, Lane had come to Leavenworth, where he made a speech endorsing Johnson's reconstruction policy. From there, he wired Crawford in Topeka telling him to make arrangements to obtain "Representative Hall" for a public meeting on January 11. At the meeting, Lane made another strong speech endorsing the president; Crawford, Jake Stotler, the secretary of the state party, and Sol Miller lent their support to Lane. The last two named were soon to become bitter enemies of Lane on the reconstruction issue.[43]

After the president's veto of the Freedmen's Bureau bill, the temper of Kansas began to favor the radicals. The Atchison *Free Press* reported that twenty-five of thirty Kansas newspapers disapproved of the president's veto. This figure may not be completely reliable, but a survey of the newspapers during February and March indicates that a strong majority became dissatisfied with Johnson's reconstruction program after the February veto of the Freedmen's Bureau bill and the subsequent March 18 veto of the civil rights bill.[44] Lane was placed in a very difficult position. He needed Johnson's patronage, but he also needed political support at home.

Lane chose to secure his federal patronage by supporting the president. He used his federal appointments as a device to consolidate his power in Kansas by having some of his old enemies appointed to federal jobs. James L. McDowell, who opposed the Lane ticket in the 1864 election, was made postmaster of Leavenworth, displacing D. R. Anthony; John A. Martin, editor of the Atchison *Daily Champion,* was given a postmastership. An arrangement was made with Thomas Carney, the former governor and Lane's bitter enemy in 1863–64, whereby Lane would support Carney for Pomeroy's Senate seat in 1867.[45] Crawford, if he was being honest with his friend General James G. Blunt, knew little about this combination. In late March, he wrote to Blunt: "Political affairs seem to be moving along without much excitement. . . . As for political combinations that may have been formed, I care but little about them. The time has not come for such a move—early combinations are very apt to be broken up by the people."[46]

Lane voted for the civil rights bill in March, but he voted against overriding the veto. On April 6, he made a speech in the Senate in which he supported the policy of the president but bitterly denied that he was obligated to Johnson. Opposition to Lane in Kansas continued to mount. A public meeting was held in Lawrence strongly condemning Lane's course. A leader in that meeting was Edmund G. Ross. By April, the opposition was condemning not only Lane, but his supporters as well, including Governor Crawford.[47]

Crawford left Topeka for Washington and New York in late March in order to sell some state bonds and to push the Price raid claims. On April 25, he wrote from Washington to his private secretary, J. B. McAfee: "There is not so much political excitement here as you all imagine; true a great many Congressmen are very bitter against the President, and declare he has gone over to the enemy. They may be correct, I hope not. He looks honest and talks very fair. . . ."[48]

The pressure from the radicals continued to build up against Lane, and something had to be done if Lane was to retain control of the Republican party in Kansas. The following letter was written by Ward Burlingame, the newly appointed editor of the Leavenworth *Conservative,* who had been Lane's private secretary during the first part of 1866:

> *(Strictly Private)*   *Leavenworth, May 18, 1866*
> Dear General—[Senator Lane]
>   Your favor of the 11th inst. is at hand.
>   I am very glad to know that your course will be as you say on the Reconstruction plan. All our friends, including Carney, McDowell, Sleeper, Delahay &c are much pleased with your determination. I find that a majority of the people unmistakably sympathise with Congress, and we cannot afford that our enemies shall reap all the advantages of such a state of things. But few of the presses denounce you, under the lead of the *Bulletin,* and the Reconstruction settlement will fix you all right. . . .
>   Crawford should arrange to show his hand at the earliest moment. Some of the papers are criticising him sharply. Clarke is stronger than Pomeroy, and we must lay him out in a regular Republican Convention, if anywhere. Anything like a distinct "Soldier's ticket" would be a farce. We can give the soldiers a splendid show, and strengthen our ticket by so doing. For instance, Crawford for Gov. Jno. A. Martin for Lt. Gov. (he will gladly accept if he can't go to Congress) a soldier in Swallow's place, if necessary, as he cares nothing about re-election, and Barker's place must be supplied in any event.
>   I sent you brief articles from *Conservative.* We must run in the radical groove.
>
> > *Truly yours*
> > *Ward Burlingame*[49]

Lane must have received this letter while Crawford was in New York selling state bonds. On May 25, Thomas Carney wired

Crawford from Washington: "How long will you remain cant you come here is important." This was followed the next day by a telegram signed by both Carney and Lane: "Come over here to-night—cannot go there now. Important."[50]

There was apparently a meeting held the night of May 26 in Washington with Lane, Carney, Crawford, James McDowell, John Speer, and some others in attendance. It was a "grand council" meeting to plan their strategy for the next election. The result of the meeting, according to D. R. Anthony, was that Lane would insist that the president allow him to support the congressional reconstruction in order to gain the approval of the Kansas radicals. Crawford was to run for reelection as governor and Carney was to be given Pomeroy's Senate seat in 1867. All of Lane's supporters would come out for the congressional reconstruction plan. On June 8, Senator Lane voted with the radicals in favor of the fourteenth amendment. Three days later Lane obtained a leave of absence and went home to mend his political fences. He was never to return to Washington.[51]

The period of Crawford's absence from the state coincided with the completion of the break between Congress and the president. Johnson's veto of the civil rights bill came on March 27, the day Crawford left Kansas. Before Crawford returned, the civil rights bill veto was overriden and the rupture was complete. Crawford was able to avoid taking a definite stand on the reconstruction issue because of his absence from the state until his return in June. Had he made a public stand on the issue in April or early May he would have risked losing support of either the strong radical element in Kansas or the support of Jim Lane. When he returned in June, he no longer had to choose.

Crawford grasped at the first opportunity to show his radical beliefs after his return home about the first of June. He did not have to wait long. On June 5, the following letter was addressed to Crawford:

Leavenworth, June 5, 1866
His Excellency, S. J. Crawford,
Governor of Kansas
Dear Sir:

The undersigned, citizens of Leavenworth and supporters of your administration profoundly interested in the grave political questions which now agitate the public mind, and especially solicitous for such an adjustment of existing differences as will tend to establish justice and secure the stability and prosperity of the country, most respectfully invite you to address a public meeting in this city, on the topics of general political interest, at such time as may suit your convenience.

Trusting that we may receive an early and favorable response, we have the honor to be,

Very respectfully your obedient servants

Robert Crozier, Jno. C. Vaughan, C. J. Hanks, Ward Burlingame, M. H. Insley, M. W. Delahay, T. A. Osborn, S. N. Latta and many others.[52]

Crawford wasted no time planting himself squarely in the radical camp. He replied to the letter immediately:

Executive Office
Topeka, June 7th, 1866

Gentlemen:

I have the honor to acknowledge the receipt of your communication of the 5th inst., requesting me to address the citizens of Leavenworth upon the great National measures now agitating the public mind.

It is the imperative duty of the Government to grant the most ample protection to all the loyal peoples of the South, regardless of color, and this I believe, will be secured by the existing Freedmen's Bureau, in connection with the military and civil rights bill—a most just and equitable one in all of its provisions. I regard the President's veto of this bill as wholly wrong, and his objections such as no loyal man should have interposed. . . .

I fully approve the report of the Committee on Reconstruction as amended by the Senate regarding it as the best practical measure that can now be adopted. . . .

As soon as the States lately in rebellion, or in any one of them, should adopt the Constitutional amendment . . . and elect men to Congress who could take the test oath (which should not be made less stringent), those members should be admitted, and thereby all that we have gained in battle be secured by legislation.

S. J. Crawford
Governor[53]

The Kansas radicals under the leadership of the vociferous D. R. Anthony, editor of the Leavenworth *Evening Bulletin,* and the colorful Sol Miller of the White Cloud *Chief* immediately charged that it was all just another of Lane's schemes to control the state. "Come in and See the Baby," Anthony jeered in the *Bulletin,* charging that the Lane political family had decided it was politically expedient to go over to the radical side, and Crawford was to be the first to be christened. Their charges centered around these accusations: the letters were prearranged by Lane and his henchmen; the signers of the Leavenworth letter were all Johnson-Lane men; Crawford had waited much too long to make his position known; the newly adopted radical position of Lane and his friends was insincere.[54]

The pro-Lane papers, on the other hand, endorsed both the motive and the contents of the letter. The *Conservative* quoted the two letters on June 9 and commented that it came as no surprise since Crawford had always been in favor of congressional reconstruction. The Leavenworth *Times,* the Carney paper, called Crawford's letter "sensible." The Lawrence *Kansas Tribune,* edited by John Speer, called the letter "straightforward" and "manly." Speer also took Crawford's opponents to task for accusing Crawford of being pro-Johnson. Speer explained that Crawford had left the state on the very day the news of Johnson's veto of the civil rights bill had reached the state, and his opponents took advantage of this situation to misrepresent his position.[55] It may be well to note that M. H. Insley, owner of the *Conservative,* Thomas Carney, part-owner of the *Times,* and John Speer, editor of the *Kansas Tribune,* were in Washington in May to confer with Lane.[56]

There seems to be some truth in the charges made by the Kansas radicals concerning the letter from the Leavenworth group and Crawford's reply. The letter to Crawford asking his views was prearranged, probably as he passed through Leavenworth on his return from Washington. He later admitted that it was prompted by a friend in Leavenworth. He asserted, however, that he was not aware who was going to sign it; and the sole purpose of the letter was not deception, but "the only object on his part was to get an opportunity to make a public expression of his sentiments, having been importuned to do so."[57]

There was also considerable substance to the charge that the signers of the Leavenworth letter were Johnson and Lane men. Robert Crozier, chief justice of the Kansas Supreme Court, was elected with Lane's support in 1863; John C. Vaughan was editor of the Leavenworth *Times,* the Carney organ which supported Johnson; C. J. Hanks, a brother-in-law to Mark Delahay, had been a U. S. district clerk; Ward Burlingame was editor of the *Conservative* and had been private secretary to Lane; M. H. Insley was the owner of the *Conservative*; M. W. Delahay, a U. S. district judge, had been appointed through the influence of Lane; T. A. Osborn was a U.S. marshal; and S. N. Latta had been an Indian agent.[58] All these men owed a political debt to Lane or Johnson.

The radicals argued that Crawford would have made his position clear much sooner if he had been sincere. Sol Miller wrote that Crawford would have been a radical if he had been left alone, but he was under the influence of a certain "well-known scheming politician." Miller declared that radical friends of Crawford had repeatedly urged him to define his position, but "not a whimper" was heard until Lane realized that Crawford could not be reelected without becoming a radical. Whereupon a group of Lane supporters asked Crawford to make a statement. The result was a declaration of radical principles which his radical friends had not been able to "coax, pump or squeeze out of him."[59]

Governor Crawford's connection with Senator Lane came to an abrupt end in the summer of 1866. Lane had made a trip home from Washington in June in an attempt to strengthen his political position. He met with little success and he started back to Washington on June 22. Three days later, it was reported that he was seriously ill in St. Louis and his doctors advised that he return to Kansas. He was taken to the government farm located on the Fort Leavenworth reservation, where his brother-in-law, J. W. McCall, and some friends kept constant watch on him, fearing that he was insane. On Sunday, July 1, he slipped away from his friends and placed a pistol in his mouth, firing a shot which passed through the roof of his mouth and came out the top of his head. Miraculously, he lived for ten days before dying on July 11. Thus ended an era in Kansas political history.[60] Crawford did not visit Lane during the ten days he lay on the verge of death, in spite of the repeated pleas of Lane's friends. Word of Lane's death reached Crawford at Garnett, his hometown, on July 12. Crawford attended Lane's funeral at Lawrence on Friday the thirteenth.[61]

5

RECONSTRUCTION AND THE ELECTION OF 1866

"Kansas Politics Muddled—Predicament of the Governor," read the heading over a story filed on July 13, 1866, by the Leavenworth correspondent of the Chicago *Tribune*.[1] The heading was succinct. Lane died less than two months before the scheduled Kansas Republican Nominating Convention, leaving the party he had dominated since its inception without a leader. If Crawford were to be renominated, he would have to gather some of the shattered pieces of the Lane organization and combine them with other dissentious factions and form a new organization. The first accessible tool was the interim appointment of a United States senator. It would be a cohesive or a destructive tool depending upon its use. Crawford's delicate position was well defined in the Chicago *Tribune*:

. . . Politicians are in a muddle, and are anxiously awaiting the announcement of the appointment of Lane's successor. There are an innumerable amount of candidates in the field. Every man who has ever been a justice of peace or private in a militia company, is a candidate for the United States Senate. The appointment of any man for the time that intervenes between the present and the meeting of the Legislature would have such an effect as to kill him [the Governor] politically. It would make a political enemy of every one who is an aspirant for that position, and those who expect to be or would accept it if tendered to them. The position in which the Governor is placed by the death of Lane, is one that is unenviable in every respect. Being a candidate for reelection, he must either draw the enmity of every man who desires the place by making an appointment, or he will be charged with sustaining "my policy" by refusing to appoint in case the Freedmen's Bureau Bill is defeated by one vote.[2]

After the Lane funeral, Crawford made a short tour into southern Kansas; perhaps he wanted to escape from his Leavenworth, Topeka, and Lawrence "advisers" and collect his thoughts. He returned to Topeka in a few days and began screening candidates for the Senate seat. The leading candidates were General James G. Blunt, Crawford's old commander; John Speer, Lane's faithful friend; Reverend H. D. Fisher, a pioneer Kansas preacher-politician; and former Governor Thomas Carney. Blunt had an initial advantage because of his friendship with Crawford. He had, in fact, accompanied the governor on his retreat to southern Kansas. Speer had the backing of some remnants of the Lane organization. Fisher had powerful church backing and Carney enjoyed the support of a group of influential businessmen in Leavenworth.[3]

On Tuesday afternoon, July 17, Crawford apparently met with John Speer and C. W. Adams. The latter had been Lane's

Sterling Price
Major General
Confederate States Army

Samuel Ryan Curtis
Major General
United States Army

James Gillpatrick Blunt
Major General
United States Army

George Armstrong Custer
Brevet Major General
United States Army

Sterling Price's army moving south along the Kansas-Missouri state line after Westport.
Taken from S. J. Reader painting.

Home of Governor Crawford at 435 Harrison, Topeka in the 1880s.
Left to right: son George, wife Isabel, father-in-law Enoch Chase, and daughter Florence.

son-in-law and political associate. Crawford may have promised Speer the nomination, as his enemies later alleged, but news came from Washington the same day which may have relieved the pressure for an immediate appointment. Leonard Smith, a Leavenworth speculator, wired Crawford from Washington: "Congress will adjourn next week—make no appointment." Crawford also must have known by then that the second Freedmen's Bureau bill had been passed over the President's veto on the day before, thus relieving much of the anxiety of the Kansas radicals. On Wednesday, Missouri Senator John Henderson wired from Washington, D. C.: "We hope to adjourn by the 23rd inst., but may be delayed until the 25th; we shall certainly leave in a few days." On Thursday, another telegram came from Leonard Smith and M. H. Insley, the owner of the Leavenworth *Conservative,* which read: "All Kansas men and our friends in both houses of Congress recommend you not to appoint a Senator now."[4]

The Henderson telegram brought only a brief respite in the feverish activity in Topeka, because Crawford arrived at a decision the following day. He appointed Edmund G. Ross to the United States Senate. The appointment in the secretary of state's commission book is dated July 19, although the announcement was not made until the next day. The appointment caught Crawford's friends and enemies alike by surprise. On July 20, a day after the actual appointment, but before the announcement, the Leavenworth *Conservative* and the Topeka *Record* predicted that no appointment would be made because of the pending adjournment of Congress.[5] Speer's backers in Lawrence learned of Crawford's intended appointment sometime on the afternoon of the nineteenth. Their telegrams reflected their dismay: "By all means don't appoint E. G. Ross—Speer's appointment would be much more acceptable to the people"; "Give us John Speer or nobody"; ". . . If you appoint Major Ross you will go to Hell in this county"; and from C. W. Adams, "For God's sake don't appoint Major Ross."[6]

Edmund G. Ross was outside the circle of Lane supporters, although he had been John Speer's partner in the Lawrence *Kansas Tribune*. He was a forty-year-old newspaperman with almost no political following or experience. The question then arises: why did Crawford choose such a man who was not even a candidate? One possible answer is that each of the announced candidates was unacceptable to some faction of the party. Speer had been too closely identified with Lane and Johnson; the nomination of Carney would alienate the Pomeroy faction, because Senator Pomeroy's backers believed that Lane and Carney had been plotting to remove Pomeroy from the Senate at the next election; and Fisher was purported to have no strength with the veterans. Ross on the other hand was acceptable to the radicals because he had denounced Johnson's course of action, he was acceptable to the Pomeroy group because he posed no threat to them, he was a popular veteran of the late war, and the fact that he had been John Speer's partner in the *Tribune* might win him the support of some of the Lane element. If this was Crawford's line of thinking, it proved to be correct in all but one particular: Speer was so disappointed because of his unsuccessful bid for the Senate seat that he became one of Crawford's bitterest enemies. Most of the old Lane faction, however, fell in line behind Crawford, largely because they had nowhere else to turn.

There are other plausible reasons why Crawford may have chosen Ross. Even before Lane's death, applicants and "advisers" began to importune the governor concerning the senatorial appointment. Crawford later wrote that "some of the applicants pressed their claims with a tenacity of purpose disgusting in the extreme."[7] Crawford had known Ross since they had served together in the Second Kansas Regiment and he had great respect for him. After the war, Ross had been appointed to a lieutenant colonelcy in the State Militia at Governor Crawford's request.[8]

According to one story, Crawford sent Ross a note asking him to come to Topeka for a conference. Ross approached the governor and began to commend another candidate when Crawford informed him that he had not called him for consultation but rather to tender him the appointment to the United States Senate. "We need a man with backbone in the Senate. I saw what you did at [the battle of] Prairie Grove, and I want *you* for Senator."[9] Crawford later explained the appointment by saying: "I knew him to be an honest, straightforward soldier of sterling worth and unflinching courage; and on that account he was appointed. I had seen him on the field of battle amid shot and shell that tried men's souls, and I knew he could be trusted."[10] Perhaps Crawford became disgusted by the constant harassment by the applicants and decided to choose a man he knew and trusted; a man who had not solicited the position; a man much like himself in many respects. It is doubtful, however, that Crawford lost sight of the fact that the appointment of Ross might be a device through which the party could be reunited and his own renomination secured.

Ross left for Washington on the night of the nineteenth. He was well on his way when the announcement of the appointment was made public the next day.[11] The appointment had the desired effect; some of the newspapers representing each of the various factions approved of the appointment. Crawford was criticized for his vacillation, but most of the Kansas newspapers approved of Ross. He was, after all, a fellow newspaperman. The Leavenworth *Conservative* commented: "His appointment was as unexpected by him as it will be gratifying to thousands of faithful Kansas soldiers." This statement came from a paper whose editor had been urging the appointment of John Speer.[12] The Leavenworth *Times*, the Carney organ, simply reported the appointment and offered no editorial comment. Even the White Cloud *Chief*, perhaps the most radical paper in the state, wrote:

We confess, the Governor has shown remarkable sharpness in this appointment. He has gone outside the scrambling politicians, and committed himself to no factions; he has chosen a man whose record is clean, all through, and he has made an appointment to which it is impossible for any reasonable man to take exception.[13]

The Burlington *Kansas Patriot,* another radical paper, conceded that Ross was outside "the Crawford present supporting ring and that's good."[14]

If Crawford's enemies were temporarily caught off guard, they soon regained their composure. When the attack on Crawford was renewed, it was largely on the basis that Crawford's vacillation in choosing a senator had shown his weakness. Sol Miller, the most humorous writer among the early Kansas newspapermen, wrote that a number of stories had been heard in Topeka concerning the governor's indecision. One story was that Crawford gave the appointment to Reverend H. D. Fisher and then took it back, whereupon he gave it to John Speer, who rented the best rooms in town for a celebration, but Ross came by and Crawford gave him the appointment. Ross left town immediately before the governor could retrieve the appointment again. Another of Miller's stories was to the effect that Crawford lined up W. F. Cloud, Blunt, Speer, and Fisher and played a boy's game called "Spit, Spit, Spot! Tell me who shall be Senator, or I'll smash you on the spot!" but the finger pointed out the window where Ross happened to be passing by and he was made senator.[15] George T. Anthony was even more critical of Crawford's vacillations. In an article under the heading "Too Late," he wrote that John Speer had been given the appointment but the governor had sent an officer with a writ to retrieve the appointment. The officer rode so fast he killed two horses and arrived just two minutes before train time and Speer's scheduled departure. The article advised Ross not to be careless with his commission. Anthony, who never took half measures, wrote that ". . . the ball that went through Lane's head, took from the Governor all his brains."[16] John Speer related that the common expression in Topeka before the appointment was: "Well, who is Senator now?" The answer:

"If you tell me the last man who saw the Governor, I'll name the promised man."[17]

J. P. Greer of the Topeka *Tribune,* himself a candidate for the gubernatorial nomination, wrote a play in honor of the Ross appointment. He called it a "Tragic Comedy." In one of the scenes, Crawford is alone wrestling with the problem of a senatorial appointment; he says to himself: "Hark! I hear in the distance, the rattle of buggy wheels, and the sound of the office hunter's bugle. The pressure is getting too great, I must appoint or the importunities of friends may produce an aberration of my mind. . . ." In scene two, the candidates, including Blunt, Cloud, Fisher, Speer, and Ross, are given an audience with the governor, and each utters some platitude indicative of his character. In the third and final scene, the governor has at last made up his mind. He says to his private secretary: ". . . write quickly my appointment of Mopus [Ross], he will do my bidding—send him forth by the light of the *moon,* tell him to keep sacred our plans for the future canvass, and when he gets to Washington, I command that he appear to Andy 'Moses' [Johnson]. . . ."[18]

The day after the announcement of the appointment, John Speer wrote an article under the heading "Gov. Crawford's Imbecility and Treachery." Speer expected to receive the nomination himself and when he learned that his partner in the *Tribune* had been chosen, he was furious. He fired volleys off in all directions, accusing Crawford of being a weak man who owed his political existence solely to Lane. Speer said he could stand the "imbecility" of Crawford but he could not forgive the greater crime: "ingratitude." He contended that a friend of Lane's should have been chosen in memory of that great man. Speer served notice that he would fight the renomination of Crawford: "We have done with him. Let him rest in the obscurity which mingled imbecility and treachery merit. The name ought not to be breathed in conversation. A few days will develop a [new] standard bearer."[19]

The criticism of J. P. Greer, Sol Miller, George Anthony, and John Speer was countered by several newspapers. The Leavenworth *Conservative* continued to support Crawford as did the Junction City *Union*. George W. Martin of the *Union* noted that Crawford had been charged with indecision and vacillation; he answered: "He has exhibited none of these traits toward us, while those with whom we daily associate, and who knew the man during all his military career, assure us that he possesses no such characteristics."[20] The position of most of the newspapers was to express mild approval of the Ross appointment without commenting on Crawford's alleged "indecisiveness." The editors may have realized that it would not be entirely consistent to criticize the appointment while praising the appointee. They may also have noted that, the jokes about Crawford's indecisiveness notwithstanding, the appointment was made less than a week after Lane's funeral.

As September 5, 1866, the announced date of the Kansas Republican Nominating Convention, neared, Crawford's opposition was reduced to two main sources. The chief source of opposition was from the radicals who believed Crawford "wore Johnson's collar." The other source of opposition was John Speer, who continued to publish anything and everything that might embarrass the governor. The radicals who opposed Crawford charged that the governor's June letter on reconstruction had been insincere and prearranged. They also charged that Crawford had taken "as near a Johnson man as he dared" when he chose Ross for the Senate.[21] To prove that Crawford was a Johnson man, the radicals pointed out that Crawford had spoken at the Johnson endorsement meeting "last winter." The meeting in question was the January Topeka meeting in which Lane endorsed the position of the president. This, of course, was before the open break between Congress and the president. The more serious charge was that Lane, Crawford, and Chester Thomas had approached the president in May on behalf of a Major Chavez, who wanted to obtain an Indian Agency in the New Mexico territory. According to George Anthony, Crawford told Johnson that he and his friends could carry the state for the President in exchange for federal patronage.[22] Crawford's friends answered this accusation by having Chester Thomas write a letter to the president of the Republican Nominating Convention asserting that Crawford had made no such statement. Thomas wrote that he accompanied Lane, Crawford, and Chavez on a visit to the president in May. They urged the appointment of Chavez, but only on the ground that he had been a soldier of Kansas. Whether the candidates favored the president's policy or not ". . . was not alluded to in my presence by any one." Crawford steadfastly maintained that he had opposed the president's position since his veto of the Freedmen's Bureau bill. He contended that the only reason he had not issued a statement before the June letter condemning Johnson was that he had supposed everyone knew his true sentiments.[23]

A week before the scheduled nominating convention, John Speer published a letter calculated to further embarrass the governor. The letter was purported to be a copy of the one Crawford had written in 1864 accepting the gubernatorial nomination. The letter was impolitic and vain; Speer claimed that a new one had to be written for publication by Crawford's friends. The letter which Speer published is quoted in full; sections of the letter which do not appear in the version published in 1864 are in brackets:[24]

Fort Smith, Arkansas
September 30, 1864

Dear Sir:

I am in receipt of a letter from John T. Cox, President of the Republican State Convention assembled at Topeka, Kansas, on the 8th inst., informing me that I was nominated as the candidate, at the next election, for Governor of Kansas; and requested [sic] me, if the action of that body meets my approval, to signify my assent to Jacob Stotler, Secretary of the State Central Committee.

This nomination came to me unexpectedly, while endeavoring to discharge my duties as an officer in the army.

Previous to the assembling of the convention, I was urged by many friends in the army, and citizens of Kansas, to allow my name to be used in connection with that office; but owing to the unparalleled activity of the enemy in our immediate front, and their repeated efforts to cut off our communication, and destroy our transportation, I gave the matter but little attention, knowing that it would be impossible for me to be present at the State Convention.

I am happy to know that the people of Kansas fully appreciate the services of their friends in the army, who have been battling against the tide of rebellion.

While the war continues (and God grant that it may until the last vestige of treason is blotted from our land), and while our State is surrounded by an enemy ready for invasion any time, [I believe with the Convention we should have a Governor of military experience, and who has the ability and courage to discharge the responsibilities of that office without fear, favor or prevarication.]

[It is not at all improbable that the enemy, before the termination of this war, will attempt the execution of more extensive raids and bloodier massacres than heretofore.]

[In that event the citizens of Kansas will realize the importance of having a military man as their chief executive officer.]

[The Governor should thoroughly understand how to organize troops to make them effective, and should know every necessary qualification which a man should possess before he is commissioned as an officer in the army.]

[Upon the officer depends the efficiency, and safety of the army; often have brave soldiers been disgraced or slaughtered on the field of battle, through the blundering stupidity of incompetent or cowardly officers. For these and other reasons.] fully appreciating the responsibility, and duties of the position, I accept the nomination, and if elected shall do everything within my power to advance the interest of the country, the efficiency of the army, and the welfare and prosperity of our own proud State.

Let the loyal men of the country stand together, fight together, re-elect and support the honest President, who has guided our Government thus far safely through this bloody struggle, and our armies will continue to move onward, until every traitor throughout this war-torn land is either bayoneted into the "last ditch," or bows in humble submission to the laws of our country. Then we will have a *Government* firm, free and prosperous, with our own proud banner, the true emblem of American liberty, the pure and spotless ensign of universal freedom, waving in triumph over all opposition.

Movements of the enemy may detain me, but I will be in Kansas at the earliest possible moment.

I am very respectfully,

Your obedient servant
Samuel J. Crawford[25]

It is difficult to judge the authenticity of this letter. Speer, in his comments about the letter, stated that the letter was squelched by Crawford's friends in Kansas, but a copy was published in a Fort Smith, Arkansas, paper. A check of the Fort Smith *New Era,* apparently the only paper published there at that time, failed to turn up any such letter.[26] On the other hand, there were two independent sources who made mention of the letter at widely separated times. Jacob Stotler, to whom the letter was addressed, wrote in 1872 that he had seen the letter in 1864 "and had it been published there would have been a lively time among the 'bolters.'" He contended that Crawford's friends in Leavenworth had written a new letter for publication.[27] It should be noted that Stotler and Crawford had become bitter enemies just before this charge was published. A correspondent of the Atchison *Freedom's Champion* wrote a dispatch, datelined Fort Gibson, November 10, 1864, in which he made much of Crawford's egotism.

He noted that Crawford's acceptance letter told how Kansas needed a military man, a courageous man, and then he modestly accepted.[28] The letter published in 1864 contained no allusion to the state's need for a military and a courageous man, but Speer's version did. John J. Ingalls, who was editor of *Freedom's Champion*, was also the opposition candidate for lieutenant governor in 1864, but the content of the dispatch from Fort Gibson indicates that there was another letter as early as November 1864. Speer's version of the letter is not entirely out of character for Crawford when his age and the circumstances at the time are considered. Crawford was only twenty-nine; he had had a brilliant military career; and he had been nominated for governor almost without turning a finger. Perhaps a little egotism was natural, or at least understandable.

As the date of the 1866 nominating convention approached, Crawford's bitterest foes and kindest friends agreed that while he was the definite front runner for renomination, his selection was by no means assured. Speer noted that Crawford's friends had begun to "manifest a little anxiety in the matter." He believed that Crawford could be defeated if he did not have a majority of the delegates on the first ballot; he reasoned that many delegates had been instructed to vote for Crawford on the first ballot who actually preferred someone else. George Martin of the Junction City *Union* wrote from Topeka that "the contest for delegates is very close and excited, but the probabilities are, Crawford is a little ahead."[29] Ward Burlingame, writing for the *Conservative* three days before the convention, cautioned that the delegates who had been instructed were generally for Crawford but that the mass of delegates would go to Topeka unpledged. When Burlingame arrived on the scene at Topeka on convention day, he became much more optimistic. He noted that "Mr. Crawford's chances are entirely the best," but Burlingame had been in politics long enough to add a note of caution: "however, King Caucus is often omnipotent, and there is no telling what it may bring forth."[30]

The state Republican convention was called to order at noon

on September 5 by Jacob Stotler. The first test of Crawford's strength came almost immediately. John Speer nominated George Graham of Nemaha for temporary chairman of the convention; he was opposed by Dr. J. P. Root, formerly surgeon of the Second Kansas Cavalry. Dr. Root won by a vote of 47 to 33 and this was considered a Crawford victory. The organizational committees were then appointed and the convention adjourned until 2:00 P.M. Soon after the opening of the afternoon session, a Colonel Pearsall nominated Crawford for governor; D. R. Anthony then nominated Judge Andrew Akin of Morris County. Anthony bitterly charged that Crawford and Thomas Carney had united to control the convention, but his speech got a cool reception. A motion to adjourn was defeated and the balloting for governor began. When the result of the first ballot was announced, Crawford had 64 votes to 18 for Akin. John Speer then made a motion that Crawford be nominated unanimously. The motion carried amid great cheering, and the convention recessed.[31]

At the next session, the other state officials were nominated, including Nehemiah Green of Riley County for lieutenant governor. Sidney Clarke was unanimously renominated for congressman. The Committee of Resolutions recommended a platform which was definitely radical. They condemned the "wickedness which our President has perpetrated . . ." and commended Congress for its "unwavering fidelity to duty . . . in resisting the encroachments of the President." The platform also recommended that the question of impartial suffrage be submitted to the voters at the next election.[32]

At the evening session, short speeches were made by Crawford, Clarke, and A. D. Richardson of the New York *Tribune*. Crawford's speech consisted of little more than denying that he was making a speech:

> Mr. President and Gentlemen: I thank you most kindly for the honor you have conferred upon me. As a guarantee for my future course, I can only point you to my past record.

If I shall be elected I shall endeavor to discharge my duties honestly and faithfully. As for my political record, I am not here to-night to defend it. Ten years in the Republican party, four years in the army, and having commanded a negro regiment for one year, I think is sufficient to establish any man's political character. I am not here to make a speech tonight. Making political speeches is not a part of my official duties. I never made a political speech in my life. I will repeat, I am under many obligations to the members of the convention, and my friends generally. I thank you most kindly.[33]

The margin of Crawford's victory took even his friends by surprise. The Garnett *Plaindealer,* Crawford's hometown newspaper, wrote: "That Gov. Crawford would be renominated was a foregone conclusion, but that he would carry the nomination so triumphantly, over the strong opposition was more than we expected."[34] What factors enabled Crawford to gain such overwhelming support from a party which two months before had been almost hopelessly divided? Perhaps Crawford had made some arrangements with leaders of the various factions. D. R. Anthony charged that Crawford had joined forces with Thomas Carney in order to control the convention. Crawford may have gained the support of the *Conservative* and a large part of the former Lane faction by an arrangement with Ward Burlingame, the editor of the *Conservative* and a former private secretary to both Jim Lane and Thomas Carney, who also became Crawford's secretary in 1867.[35] The evidence that Crawford "bought" support from the Carney or Lane factions is at best only circumstantial. The more likely explanation would follow along these lines: Lane had been the force to which one faction had been attracted and from which the other faction had been repulsed. The result was a sharp cleavage between the factions which are best described as "pro-Lane" or "anti-Lane." When Lane died, the object of the former polarization was desensitized and the two factions were shattered into many smaller factions. Reconstruction was the only issue which could have recreated the split and Crawford, even before Lane's death, had cut the ground out from under the radicals by upholding the congressional reconstruction plan. Crawford, as governor and the nominal leader of the state party, was in the best position to take over party leadership. Many, perhaps a majority, of the delegates came to the convention uncommitted, but with the election of Dr. J. P. Root as temporary chairman, the lukewarm delegates were convinced that opposition to Crawford would be futile. In addition, the bitter attack made on the governor by D. R. Anthony on the floor of the convention may have offended many of the delegates who desired a harmonious convention.[36] Crawford's opposition was vocal, but it was weak because it represented only a minority of the several factions rather than a majority of any one faction.

The opposition organization, the "National Union Party," met in Topeka on September 20 to nominate its slate of candidates. All the candidates were nominated by acclamation; the ticket was headed by James L. McDowell of Leavenworth for governor and Charles W. Blair of Fort Scott for Congress. These two men were postmasters for their respective cities and ardent Johnson supporters. The membership was composed of Republicans who favored Johnson and Democrats who once again decided it would be inexpedient to select their own state ticket. The convention adopted resolutions endorsing the National Union Convention which met at Philadelphia and the conduct of the president: "We heartily endorse the policy of President Johnson in his manly defense of the Constitution and the Union against the assaults of a partisan Congress and a fanatical party. . . ." This was hardly the kind of language which would appeal to radical Kansas, but then they preferred to stand on principle, or perhaps they had other goals. The Leavenworth *Conservative* suggested that the opposition party was motivated by a desire to establish an organization which would become the medium through which the president could channel his patronage and perhaps gain enough seats in the legislature to hold the balance of power in the upcoming senatorial elections. The Republican papers were predicting the defeat of the "Copper[head]-Johnson" ticket by more than ten thousand votes, a prediction which proved to be pessimistic.[37]

The tradition of party regularity has always been a strong force in Kansas politics, and it was never stronger than in the election of 1866. A few short weeks after John Speer had denounced Governor Crawford's "imbecility" he was bowing to the "superior wisdom" of the "representative men of the state" and announcing his "earnest support to the man of their choice." J. P. Greer admitted in print that the ticket was a "strong one." Sol Miller, who had gleefully printed a series of jokes about Crawford's indecisiveness, now explained that Crawford had always been a radical at heart but he had been misled by Lane. Miller put it tersely: "Lane dead and Crawford all right." Even Anthony, who had written that the ball which went through Lane's head had removed Crawford's brains, agreed to support the Republican ticket.[38] The papers which had not opposed Crawford before the convention were unrestrained in their praise. The Atchison *Champion* commended his "eminent faithfulness and honesty," while the *Conservative* proclaimed:

> Tried in the furnace of relentless persecution . . . he has quietly beaten down the malice of his enemies, by the calm dignity of his personal deportment, and the stern, upright consistency of his political conduct. The ides of November will complete his vindication, and the same wave which has submerged his opponents will bear him in triumph on its crest.[39]

According to one account, Crawford was backed by thirty-one of the state's newspapers while only five were in opposition.[40]

Crawford, by his own estimation, was never much of a political speaker. He preferred traveling around the state talking personally with editors and other citizens to making a platform speech. Crawford was prevailed upon to make at least three speeches before the 1866 election, but he always appeared with several other speakers, who did most of the talking. Senator Pomeroy and Governor Crawford spoke before an enthusiastic overflow audience in Price's Hall in Atchison, Pomeroy's hometown, on October 9. Crawford appeared at a meeting in Frazer's Hall in Lawrence on October 26 with Colonel William F. Cloud and T. J. Anderson. The Lawrence *Tribune* said only that "Gov. Crawford spoke in an earnest and effective manner, enlisting the attention of the audience for his plain, practical views." Crawford's last speech of the 1866 campaign was apparently made at Leavenworth on October 30; he appeared there with T. J. Anderson.[41]

Crawford made his newly adopted radical position known to the people of the state through letters and the newspapers. For example, he answered an appeal from Atchison to attend a Soldiers' Convention there by writing them a letter denouncing the president. The letter was widely published. It was extremely radical in tone: "Congress must be sustained, and Andy Johnson rebuked; loyalty rewarded and treason made odious. Tyler's treachery and Buchanan's imbecility are respectable compared with Johnson's treason."[42] The result of the election was never really in doubt, but on November 6, the voters made it official. Crawford received 19,370 votes to 8,152 for his opponent, J. L. McDowell. The remainder of the Republican slate won by a similar margin.[43] Crawford became the first person to be elected twice as governor of the state.

Crawford's election as governor was not the only important event in his life that took place in November. The governor married Isabel Marshall Chase at the Grace Episcopal Church in Topeka on the evening of November 27. Isabel Chase, a member of a pioneer family that had come to Topeka in 1855 from New England, was only eighteen when she married the thirty-one-year-old governor. The bridal party, more than fifty persons strong, left that night on a special railroad car furnished by the Union Pacific, Eastern Division, Railroad. W. W. Wright, the superintendent of the railroad, and J. P. Root visited the party the next morning; after breakfast, Governor and Mrs. Crawford went on to Saint Louis for a few days, and the remainder of the party returned to Topeka. Out of this union would come one daughter, Florence, born July 1, 1868, and one son, George Marshall, born July 10, 1872. Florence later became the wife of Senator Arthur Capper.[44]

6

RAILROADS AND SPECULATORS

The end of the Civil War signaled the beginning of an era in which politics and business were merged on a large scale. Politics became an effective tool in the hands of the speculator and there were few well-defined rules to regulate its use. Consequently, there were a great many instances in which government officials were involved in speculative endeavors which would be considered questionable or even unlawful today. In Kansas, the speculative enterprises centered around the procurement of land and the construction of railroads. Speculators in league with certain politicians attempted to obtain outright government grants of land or bonds for railroad construction or they would attempt to purchase large tracts of valuable land at nominal cost, usually at less than a dollar an acre. Much of the land in Kansas was particularly prized by the speculators because it was Indian land which was not open to preemption or homesteading. This meant that the land could be sold only through some kind of congres-

Cherokee and Osage Indian Land Controversies, 1866-1868

sional action, thus making an alliance between the politicians and the speculators a most lucrative arrangement.

Crawford spent a great deal of time during his administration dealing with problems of land speculation and railroad construction. As the first peacetime governor of Kansas, Crawford found that there were few established laws or precedents to follow in dealing with these problems. The most difficult land problem encountered by the Crawford administration concerned approximately nine million acres in southern Kansas. Here the interests of the settlers, the Indians, and several railroad companies came into conflict. The area in question was fifty miles long from north to south and it extended from the Missouri border on the east to the one-hundredth meridian on the west. The eastern part of this Indian land, consisting of eight hundred thousand acres in an area twenty-five by fifty miles, was known as the Cherokee Neutral Tract. The area beginning at the west edge of the Cherokee Tract and extending westward more than 250 miles was known as the Osage lands. The Osages had taken possession of this land by the treaty of 1825. The twenty-five-mile strip between their eastern boundary and the Missouri line was left as a buffer zone between the Indians and the settlers. In 1835, however, the buffer zone was sold to the Cherokees.[1]

The Cherokee Neutral Tract presented a troublesome problem because of its proximity to Missouri and other white settlements. As early as 1858 some settlers had occupied the Neutral Lands, but they were driven out by federal troops in 1859. When the Civil War broke out, the Cherokees joined the Confederacy, but repealed the arrangement in 1863. After the war, the demand for land became so great that it became almost impossible to keep settlers out of the Indian land.[2]

Crawford believed that the Indians should be removed from the state because "the Indians will neither improve nor cultivate the lands, and their occupancy prevents others from doing it."[3] During his first term as governor, he wrote to Secretary of the Interior James Harlan, asking that a new survey of the Cherokee

Lands be made in the belief that the Indians were holding land to which they were not entitled by treaty. His contention was rejected by the Department of Interior, but Crawford had his own surveyor, G. J. Endicott, make a new survey which coincided with the governor's contention. Crawford presented the whole matter to the 1866 legislature but nothing came of it.[4]

On July 19, 1866, a treaty was concluded between the government and the Cherokees whereby the secretary of interior was empowered to sell the Neutral Lands for the Indians to the highest bidder. A provision was inserted which allowed the entire eight hundred thousand acres to be sold for not less than $800,000 cash. On July 27, Edmund Ross, who had been in the Senate only two days, was able to obtain an amendment which gave *bona fide* settlers, as of the ratification date, a chance to buy not more than 160 acres. The treaty, thus amended, was proclaimed on August 11, 1866. Secretary of the Interior James Harlan withdrew from the Johnson cabinet on September 1, 1866, but before he left he sold the Cherokee Neutral Tract to the American Emigrant Company of Boston. Orville H. Browning, his successor, voided the sale on the ground that the American Emigrant Company had paid only $25,000 while the treaty stipulated that the entire $800,000 should be paid in cash. He was upheld in this contention by Attorney-General Henry Stanbery.[5]

Secretary Browning, after refusing several offers, sold the Cherokee Neutral Tract for one dollar an acre to James F. Joy, a Michigan railroad builder who proposed to build a railroad through southeast Kansas.[6] Kansans wanted their railroads, but they were becoming aroused at the "land grabbing" of the large corporations. By this time, more than five thousand people had moved into the Neutral Tract expecting to obtain government land at the preemption price. They began to send letters and petitions to the governor and the legislature protesting the sale. Crawford answered one of these settlers' letters on January 1, 1868. Crawford stated that he considered the treaty by which the secretary of the interior was authorized to sell the lands to corporations as "an infamous fraud upon the settlers and an insult to the whole state." He proposed to lay the matter before the legislature and ask for a memorial to Congress demanding that the contract between the secretary of the interior and Joy be declared void.[7]

The governor's message of January 14, 1868, decried the sale of the Cherokee Neutral Lands to Joy and recommended that Congress be memorialized to annul the contract and open it to settlers. In the event that Congress should declare the contract void but refuse to open the land to individual settlers, Crawford recommended that the state purchase the land for resale in small tracts. The legislature passed a resolution calling upon Congress to protect the settlers and expressing their belief that the Cherokees had never had a legal title to the land. The resolution received a unanimous vote in the Kansas House of Representatives and passed by an eighteen to five margin in the Senate.[8]

Colonel Kersey Coates, who was identified with the Joy group, answered Crawford in a letter published in the Fort Scott *Monitor*. He contended that Crawford had not read the entire treaty and that the settlers would be cared for by the Joy corporation. Coates had found a weak point in Crawford's argument because Crawford had quoted the treaty in his annual message *without* the amendment which Senator Ross had added providing that actual settlers at the date of ratification would be allowed to purchase their land under preemption laws.[9] The *Monitor*, in commenting on the governor's message, suggested that Crawford was opposing Joy's purchase because it was the popular thing to do and it might get him a few votes for congressman at the next election. The article also implied that Crawford was disappointed because his "ring" had not gained the contract.[10]

Crawford continued to protest the sale of the Cherokee Neutral Lands. On February 20, 1868, he wrote to George W. Julian, the chairman of the House Committee on Public Lands, asking that the settlers be allowed to buy land at not more than $1.25 an acre. He followed this letter with similar letters to other congressmen, but Kansas Senators Pomeroy and Ross and Representative Clarke approved of the sale.[11]

James Joy was not entirely satisfied with the terms of his purchase contract, especially the $800,000 cash requirement. The audacious promoter therefore executed an imaginative scheme to remedy that defect. First, he persuaded the American Emigrant Company to sell its rights to the land for $25,000. Then in order to avoid possible House rejection of the scheme, the Joy group decided to have the earlier agreement reaffirmed and declared valid by using the device of a new treaty with the Cherokees, rather than through a contract between the secretary of interior and the purchaser. Accordingly, the "supplementary treaty" provided that all the land of the Cherokee Neutral Tract not occupied by settlers as of June 8, 1866, would be purchased for one dollar an acre. Only $75,000 was required in cash; the remainder was payable in seven years at 5 per cent interest. Also the arrangement provided that $71,660 of accrued interest on the old American Emigrant Company sale would be cancelled. Joy thus gained these advantages: he did not have to pay cash, possible litigation with the American Emigrant Company was avoided, the sale did not have to be approved by the House, the land which had been settled between the date of the original sale (1866) and the date of the supplementary treaty (1868) would become the property of the Joy group even though it had been improved by the settlers.[12]

The supplementary treaty with the Cherokees was dated April 27, and it was ratified on June 6, 1868. According to Eugene Ware, who claimed to have been present in the Senate chamber, there were no more than three senators present at the night session when the treaty was ratified.[13] It would seem that either of the Kansas senators could have prevented or delayed the action, but they failed to do so.

The supplementary treaty was especially severe upon those settlers who entered the Neutral Tract between 1866 and 1868. They had believed the original contract to be void and that the land would eventually be opened at preemption prices. In addition, even the settlers who preceded the 1866 arrangement found that they had to pay the assessed value averaging almost two dollars an acre rather than the $1.25 government price which they had expected to pay. On July 25, 1868, Crawford wrote to Ross: "If the Cherokee Supplemental Treaty is ratified, it will deprive the State of 47,000 acres of school land, and place thousands of settlers at the mercy of Joy and his Railroad Company. I trust you may be able to defeat it."[14] But Crawford was too late; the treaty had been ratified for more than six weeks.

The Joy organization found that the matter was not entirely settled by the ratification of the treaty. The settlers of the area formed a Land League and began to resist the coming of the Fort Scott railroad by legal and illegal means. On July 4, 1868, the settlers forcibly moved the Cherokee county seat from Baxter Springs to Columbus, asserting that Baxter Springs was a "pro-Joy" town. Railroad surveyors were sometimes fired upon; railroad ties were mysteriously burned; and finally on July 15, 1871, the office of the Girard *Press,* a newspaper allegedly in the employ of Joy, was burned. Federal troops were requested by Crawford's successor, and they remained in the area until 1872.[15]

To the immediate west of the Cherokee Neutral Tract lay the area known as the Osage Lands. Like the Neutral Tract, it was fifty miles wide from north to south; it extended westward past the one-hundredth meridian and contained more than eight million acres of land.[16] By the terms of the treaty of September 29, 1865, which was not proclaimed until January 21, 1867, thirty miles of the eastern end of the Osage Lands were ceded to the United States. Crawford, in his 1868 annual message, asked that Congress be memorialized to open this land to actual settlers. The settlers eventually were allowed to buy this land at $1.25 an acre although there was some litigation with the railroads concerning the land. The great prize, however, was the more than seven million acres extending westward from the ceded lands. The railroad interest of Joy and William Sturges, president of the Leavenworth, Lawrence and Galveston Railroad, joined in an attempt to purchase this land through treaty as had been done in the case of the Cherokee Neutral Tract. The agitation over the Neutral Tract had aroused the public against the treaty-making method of selling land to large corporations. Nevertheless, a group of commissioners came to the Osage Reservation in May 1868 in an attempt to secure such a treaty. Crawford sent his superintendent of public instruction, Peter McVicar, to take part in the negotiations. McVicar and Charles W. Blair of Fort Scott reported to Crawford that threats and intimidation had been used to obtain the Indian assent. It was asserted that the Indians were told that Governor Crawford would raise an army and forcibly eject them if they refused to sign.[17]

The treaty was signed May 27, 1868, and taken back to Washington for Senate approval. According to the treaty, the Leavenworth, Lawrence and Galveston Railroad would pay only about twenty cents an acre for the land. Crawford sent telegrams to Washington opposing the sale of both the Cherokee Neutral Tract and the Osage Lands. Crawford followed his telegram with a letter dated June 9, 1868, addressed to Benjamin F. Wade, the president pro tem of the Senate; Senator Pomeroy, chairman of the Senate Committee on Public Lands; and George W. Julian, chairman of the House Committee on Public Lands. In this letter, he asked that both the Cherokee and Osage treaties be set aside. He wrote: "The Cherokee treaty, and the attempted sale of lands under its provisions, were infamous enough; but the recent treaty with the Osages and the iniquitous manner in which the same was concluded, make the other comparatively respectable. . . ." Crawford said there were more than ten thousand settlers on the land whose rights were being completely ignored by the treaty. The governor also noted that higher bids had been offered for the land but they had been declined. He characterized the whole affair as a "flagrant outrage" and asked that this "scheme which is so full of wrong and outrage to this State and her people" be defeated.[18]

In addition to this letter, Crawford forwarded a memorial signed by the governor, the secretary of state, the auditor, the state treasurer, the attorney-general, and the superintendent of public instruction. The memorial argued that the Osage treaty should be defeated because: the Osages had been induced to conclude the treaty by threats, the price was so low as to constitute a "flagrant robbery" of the Indians, that there was no provision for school lands, and that such a treaty would close nearly one-fifth of the Kansas land available to settlers and thus retard immigration.[19] Crawford also wrote to President Johnson, Senator Henderson of Missouri, and to Ross and Clarke of Kansas. Kansas Attorney-General George H. Hoyt was dispatched to Washington to oppose the treaty.[20]

By this time, the U. S. House of Representatives was thoroughly aroused. It saw the attempt to sell land by treaty as a usurpation of power by the Senate. Kansas Congressman Sidney Clarke, perhaps reacting to the temper of Kansas in an election year, created a great furor in the House. George W. Julian, chairman of the House Committee on Public Lands, introduced a joint resolution which decried the treaty-method of selling land. The uproar over the Cherokee Neutral Tract sale thus paved the way for the defeat of the Osage treaty in the Senate. The defeat of the Osage treaty, in turn, had a great deal to do with the abandonment of the treaty-making policy of disposing of Indian lands.[21]

The land controversy was not ended because of Crawford's vigorous protests. There were many factors, including the struggle between the House and the Senate, which may have been more important than Crawford's actions. His contribution, however, was significant. He used letters, telegrams, resolutions of the legislature, and memorials from the state officers in an attempt to defeat the two treaties. He was unsuccessful in regard to the smaller Neutral Tract but successful in regard to the Osage treaty. Newspaper opinion in Kansas was divided, but Crawford earned the gratitude of the settlers. On August 12, 1868, the Oswego *Register* wrote: "Gov. Crawford . . . is thoroughly identified with the interest [of the settlers] and has done more than any man in the State for the hardy pioneers. We regret that his term of office is so near its expiration."[22] But Crawford was not to completely escape the tag of "railroad tool" himself.

While Governor Crawford deplored the actions of the Joy and Sturges railroad combine, his relationship with the Union Pacific, Eastern Division, was far more friendly. The apparent collusion between the governor and the UPED was in fact the subject of an investigation by a special committee of the Kansas House of Representatives in February 1868. According to the charges made by C. R. Jennison, Crawford had accepted a section of land worth about $10,000 from the railroad in return for "services rendered" during his administration.[23] This charge makes a review of the connection between the UPED and Crawford imperative.

The Union Pacific, Eastern Division, Railway Company was the successor in 1863 of the old Leavenworth, Pawnee and Western Railroad Company. In the same year, John C. Fremont and Samuel Hallett bought a controlling interest in the railroad; and under the guidance of Hallett, construction was begun. Under terms of the Pacific Railroad Act, as amended on July 2, 1864, the first railroad to reach the one-hundredth meridian was in effect given the right of way to connect with the Central Pacific coming from the west. The act also provided that 12,800 acres of land and $16,000 in bonds would be given for each mile of Pacific Railroad construction. The competition between a line crossing Kansas and another crossing Nebraska was great. Hallett got the UPED off to a good start; he expected to open the first forty-mile section in August 1864. On July 27, Hallett was murdered by a disgruntled former employee, and construction was slowed while some questions of ownership were resolved. When construction began again, J. D. Perry, a Saint Louis banker, was in control of the company. It was April 25, 1865, before the UPED felt prepared to ask that the first forty miles be accepted. Meanwhile, the Nebraska line had gained a great advantage.[24]

The procedure followed by the president in accepting the first forty-mile section was to appoint three commissioners to examine the railroad. On April 29, Johnson wrote to Daniel R. Garrison and Henry C. Moore, both of Missouri, and Richard M. Thompson of Indiana, appointing them commissioners to examine the UPED. Thompson, however, declined to serve and Perry wired the Interior Department on May 5 asking that Thomas Carney or Stephen D. Barlow of Missouri be appointed in his place. On the same date, however, a letter had gone out tendering the appointment to Governor Crawford.[25] The commissioners conducted an inspection and made a favorable report to the president. They noted, however, ". . . that although the Law of Congress relating thereto may not have been literally fulfilled in all respects, yet we believe it to have been in all essential particulars."[26]

Between the time the commissioners had been appointed and their report was presented, there had been a change of secretaries of the interior. John P. Usher was replaced by James Harlan on the fifteenth of May. Harlan was from Iowa and he favored the Omaha branch while Usher had been closely identified with the Kansas group.[27] On May 29, Harlan wrote to President Johnson stating that the report of the commissioners had not been sufficiently detailed and recommending that a new board of commissioners consisting of an army engineer, H. D. Scott of Terre Haute, Indiana, and Governor Crawford be appointed to re-examine the railroad. Harlan prepared and forwarded to the president for his signature the necessary appointments, dated June 5.[28] Johnson, however, noted that the necessary information was attainable and after the examination of an engineer's report he suggested that the forty miles could be accepted upon receipt of certain reports and affidavits. On June 19, the president endorsed the acceptance and sent the necessary papers to the secretary of the treasury for payment.[29] On June 22, Crawford wired Senator Lane: "The President has accepted our report on the UPRR and ordered the Board paid."[30]

But Harlan was not defeated yet. On July 1, he informed the president that there were two organizations which claimed to own the UPED. He followed this with a letter dated September 7 which described the conditions on the railroad as less than satisfactory and recommended that the order of June 19 be rescinded and a new examining board be appointed.[31] On September 7, the president ordered a new commission appointed, to be composed of Lieutenant Colonel James H. Simpson, of the Corps of Engineers; Harvey D. Scott of Indiana; and Samuel Crawford. The commissioners arrived on the scene at Wyandotte, Kansas, in early October in spite of the misgivings of the railroad officials, who believed that the commission was loaded against them. Senator Lane, who was apparently associated with the interest of the Kansas railroad, wired the president from Wyandotte on October 3 that Colonel Simpson had arrived there in the morning accompanied by the chief engineer of the Omaha line. He requested that the president suspend the commission for thirty days.[32]

The new examination was apparently made on the third, fourth, and fifth of October 1865. Crawford was for approving the road while Simpson and Scott were opposed. Scott and Simpson asked Crawford to sign a report which Simpson was to work out later, but Crawford refused. He, in turn, wrote a report recommending acceptance of the road which they refused to sign. In this report, Crawford pointed out that the road is "equal to most western roads" and that over one million dollars of private money had been expended. The emphasis of his report was upon the usefulness of the road rather than the details of construction.[33] The majority report, as filed by Simpson and Scott, on the other hand, was filled with detailed reasons for refusing to accept the road. The report contended that the line was not long enough without counting a spur line, that the road bed was too low, that the bridge over the Kansas River was out, and that there were only 2,112 ties per mile of track, which was 284 ties per mile less than the number used by the New York Central.[34]

Crawford countered by sending the president a minority report. The governor conceded that the maximum grade had been understated, but that was a situation easily remedied. Crawford concluded his letter by expressing the hope "that this great National work will not be retarded by mere technicalities." On the same day, October 12, R. M. Shoemaker, the construction contractor for the UPED, wrote to Crawford: "You should write the President at once as governor of Kansas and say to him that the people of Kansas have a vital interest in this enterprise and look to him to do them justice. Your report as commissioner does not say this."[35] Crawford responded by writing to Johnson the next day:

> The early completion of this road is of vital interest to the citizens of Kansas, and they do not believe that the work upon a road of so much importance to their State, as well as to the General Government will be retarded by the action of your Excellency however great the pressure from conflicting interest may be.
>
> As I state in my report, the road for a new one, is as good in all respects as any I have ever passed over in the west. It is eminently sufficient to supply the demands of the country, and I trust your Excellency will not hesitate to accept it, and thereby aid our State in this great enterprise.[36]

Those who favored the construction of the UPED succeeded in obtaining a letter from Major General Sherman recommending acceptance of the railroad on grounds that the army needed a line to Fort Riley and west. Perry made a trip to Washington and on October 26 he promised the president in an interview that he would make the necessary improvements. By this time, the line had been extended several miles farther and the spur line no longer needed to be counted in order to arrive at the necessary forty-mile total. On October 28, Harlan notified the president that he was satisfied the railroad should be accepted.[37] On October 30, President Johnson ended the controversy and accepted the first forty miles of the UPED track. Four days later, John D. Perry, president of the company, was issued bonds in the amount of $640,000.[38]

The Union Pacific, Eastern Division, was not ungrateful to Crawford. By law, the commissioners were to receive ten cents per mile and ten dollars per diem for their expenses. The other commissioners thus received from $300 to $500 for their services. Crawford, however, chose to receive his payment in land. He selected a section near Perryville, Kansas, in which Lane had been interested before his death. The section was bonded to Crawford in July 1866 and deeded to him on March 26, 1867. Some of the newspapers knew about the transaction even before the 1866 election. J. P. Greer, who it will be remembered was a candidate for governor, alluded to the deal in the July 27, 1866, edition of the Topeka *Tribune*. Greer considered the deal dishonest because the governor had been paid too much and because the UPED track was substandard. The *Tribune* reported that no train had passed over a section of the track east of Lawrence for a month. Even the Leavenworth *Conservative,* a Crawford supporter, reprinted a statement from the Springfield *Republican* characterizing the first section of the UPED as "a sham and a fraud upon the public and the Government."[39]

Crawford does not seem to have confined his support exclusively to the UPED. On August 1, 1865, he served as president of the Railroad Convention, which offered a resolution pledging the Atchison, Topeka and Santa Fe aid in the form of county bonds.[40]

The question of regulating railroad rates came before the Kansas legislature of 1867. The UPED management became very concerned about legislation which would hamper their operations and decrease their profits. Judge J. P. Usher, former secretary of the interior and the attorney for the railroad, sent a letter dated February 6 to the governor asking that it be transmitted to the legislature. The letter was read to the House on February 7. In it, Usher pointed out that any interference with the railroad would cause eastern capitalists to be reluctant to invest in the enterprise.

In addition, he stated that the company believed rate regulation to be outside the power of the state government according to the terms of their charter. Crawford transmitted this letter to the legislature with a note advising caution against any actions which might embarrass the railroad company to the detriment of the state while upholding the right of the legislature to tax the railroads.[41]

The 1867 legislature apparently became so angry at the railroad's refusal to admit that the legislature had jurisdiction over rates that they passed a maximum rate bill. As the end of the session neared there were some sober second thoughts and a resolution was passed asking that the secretary return the bill. A controversy arose as to whether this resolution made the original bill void. At any rate, the bill was destroyed and did not become law.[42] Some opponents of the governor said he was responsible for the bill being destroyed.

On February 17, 1868, C. R. Jennison of Leavenworth offered a resolution before the Kansas House of Representatives resolving that a committee of three be appointed to investigate the charges that the governor had been given a section of land by the UPED "in consideration of services rendered." The resolution passed by a 37 to 20 margin and Jennison was made chairman with J. L. Philbrick and R. D. Mobley completing the committee. Of the three, only Jennison had voted with the majority on the resolution.[43] A great many witnesses were summoned, including John Perry and E. M. Bartholow of the UPED and J. B. McAfee. The questions asked indicate that the committee was interested not so much in ascertaining if Crawford had been overpaid for his services as commissioner as in determining if there was any connection between the destruction of the railroad rate bill and the governor's friendship with the UPED. The hearings brought out the fact that Crawford had accepted a section of land in Jefferson County described as section 17, township 11, range 18, located near Perryville on Grasshopper Creek. Railroad officials testified that the land had been given to Crawford "in consideration of services rendered the company." They stated that Crawford had not only served as a commissioner, but that he had made several trips at his own expense on their behalf to Washington, St. Louis, and points in Kansas. Bartholow, the general land agent of the railroad, testified that Crawford had been worth at least two sections of land to the company because he had worked so hard to get the road accepted in 1865 at a time when agents of the Omaha branch were effectively blocking government acceptance. Other witnesses were called to testify as to the value of the land in question. Their estimates varied from $7 to $24 an acre. McAfee, the governor's former secretary, was called. He testified that the governor had been absent "half the summer working for the railroad and soldiers' best interests." McAfee said Crawford told him that he had spent a great deal of money on behalf of the railroad; that it was in the best interest of the state to outstrip the Omaha branch; and that he had paid the railroad more for the land than they had paid for it.[44]

All the witnesses denied having any first-hand knowledge which would indicate that Crawford destroyed the rate bill. S. N. Simpson, however, testified that when the rate bill was before the legislature, Judge Usher had said that he planned to write to the governor and have the bill vetoed. Instead, he decided to go to Topeka himself and "the bill was spoiled, but how it was done I don't know . . . I don't believe that Governor Crawford struck out the words that spoiled this bill."[45]

On February 27, Jennison made a minority report to the House summarizing his findings as a result of the investigations. Jennison found that the governor claimed no more than $1,000 in expenses while the land was worth about $10,000. He concluded that more than $9,000 of the value of the land was a bonus for reporting in favor of accepting the railroad's claim in spite of the fact that Crawford had admitted that the road was not up to standard according to law. Jennison made no charge in connection with the railroad rate bill.[46] The majority report, signed by J. L. Philbrick and R. D. Mobley, found that the governor actually expended in money a greater sum than the land in question cost the railroad company and that he "was justified in accepting the compensation given him." In addition, they agreed that the governor's efforts on behalf of the road, in defeating the Omaha line, "resulted in great and lasting benefit to the company, and ten fold more interest to the state of Kansas."[47]

Perhaps it was fortunate for Crawford that the committee hearings made very few headlines in the Kansas newspapers. A few days before the committee reports were made, the news of the impeachment of President Johnson reached Kansas. This news dominated the headlines for months, but there was still some comment on the hearings in the Kansas press. The Topeka correspondent of the Leavenworth *Conservative* stated that next the Democrats would "raise a committee to ascertain whether the Governor sleeps on his right or left side." The Lawrence *Tribune* carried a story simply stating that a majority and a minority report on the "Governor's Farm" had been submitted. The Atchison *Champion* made no mention of the investigation.[48]

Crawford's later correspondence indicates that he continued to work for the UPED even after the conclusion of the committee investigation. He made a trip to Chicago in May 1868 at the request of John Perry to help Usher represent the railroad before the Chicago Board of Trade.[49]

In 1872, Crawford was accused by a political opponent of having profited to the extent of $20,000 by having helped the railroad during his administration as governor. Crawford then made his first public defense of his relationship with the UPED. He told how he had served as commissioner for almost a year, made two examinations of the road, traveled to Washington, St. Louis, and Chicago in the "line of duty and at my own expense." He remembered that he had made out a bill for $1,130 that the railroad accepted and he added to that $830 with which he purchased eight hundred acres of land in Jefferson County. He reasoned that he thus paid $2.40 per acre for the land which the company had purchased for $1.25 an acre. In addition he spent

$7,000 improving the farm.[50] The records in the Jefferson County Register of Deeds Office show that Crawford bought a section of land from the UPED on March 26, 1867; the consideration listed was $1,000. On March 3, 1870, he sold the section for a total of $22,000.[51]

7

A "LAME DUCK" TERM AND A BID FOR CONGRESS

Governor Crawford began his second term on January 8, 1867. Only thirty-one years old, he had reached the pinnacle of his political power by uniting a political party which had been left leaderless by the death of Jim Lane. Crawford soon found, however, that while it had been a difficult task to unite the party for the 1866 election, it was even more difficult to hold all the factions together through the stress of the events which took place during his second term. Events which were to have some effect upon Crawford's political leadership included: an election of two U. S. senators in 1867; the impartial suffrage election of 1867; the presidential impeachment proceedings and Ross's vote against the charges; the Osage and Cherokee land controversies; the House investigation of Crawford's relations with the Union Pacific, Eastern Division, Railroad, which were discussed in the previous chapter; the difficult problem of Indian depredations, wars, and peace settlements, which will be discussed in a subsequent chapter; and Crawford's bid to unseat incumbent Congressman Sidney Clarke.

The 1867 legislature was organized on January 8 and that body heard the governor's annual message the following day. The governor's secretary read the thirty-page document at the afternoon session. The message included a review of the gains made by the state during the preceding year in education, state building construction, railroads, etc. Crawford repeated his recommendations favoring increased funds to further immigration and the extinction of Indian titles to land in Kansas. He also expressed dissatisfaction with the presidential reconstruction plans, recommended the ratification of the fourteenth amendment to the United States Constitution, and asked that the state constitution be so amended as to allow Negroes to vote in Kansas while disenfranchising those persons who aided the late rebellion.[1]

The governor's message also reminded the legislature that it was their responsibility to elect two United States senators during the 1867 session. The reminder was superfluous because the legislators were thinking of little but the election. The Leavenworth *Evening Bulletin* published a report dated January 19 which indicated that a caucus had been held and Pomeroy's reelection was assured.[2] The big question seemed to be the election of a second senator for a four-year term. The favorite was former Governor Thomas Carney; but Ross, who had received the interim appointment, was conceded a chance. An informal vote taken separately by the House and Senate on January 22 gave Carney a 41 to 29 advantage over Ross. Between the time of the straw vote on the twenty-second and the final ballot on the twenty-third, something happened which enabled Senator Ross to be reelected. Apparently Ross gained powerful support from the UPED and from Perry Fuller, a rich Leavenworth merchant. The joint session of the House and Senate took place at noon, January 23. Only one ballot was necessary to reelect S. C. Pomeroy for the six-year term and Edmund G. Ross for the four-year term. Pomeroy received 84 votes to 25 for A. L. Lee, and Ross beat Carney by a 68 to 40 margin.[3]

Crawford undoubtedly favored Major Ross's reelection, but there is no record which would indicate that he openly used his influence on behalf of Ross. A few days after the election, rumors that the election had been "bought" began to find their way into print. The Leavenworth *Conservative,* which supported Ross and Pomeroy, admitted that "corruption was a factor." In commenting upon a report published in the Garnett *Plaindealer* which reported that $42,000 had been used in one day for election purposes, the *Conservative* conceded that the report was "generally correct" and that corruption had been practiced "on an unprecedentedly large scale."[4]

The rumors of election corruption became so widespread that the legislature ordered an investigation on February 9, 1867. The investigating committee reported on February 25 that they had been unable to obtain testimony sufficient to recommend definite action, but they recorded their convictions that "money has been used for the base purpose of influencing members of the Legislature to disregard the wishes of their constituents, and to vote as money dictated."[5] The legislature of 1872 also appointed a committee to investigate the elections of 1867 and 1871. Testimony from that investigation indicated that Perry Fuller had spent $42,000 to secure the election of Pomeroy and Ross. According to the testimony of William Spriggs of Garnett, Fuller reasoned that the election would have been worth $100,000 to him in order to prevent Thomas Carney's election. According to Spriggs, Fuller feared that he would have to divide his half-million-dollar Indian business with Carney had he been elected to the Senate. Testimony of I. S. Kalloch corroborated Spriggs's testimony. He testified that Fuller had told him that he had enough money to "put a man through" in the 1867 election and the man was Ross.[6]

Whether or not Ross solicited Fuller's support is impossible to prove. That there was a growing awareness of the importance of money in a senatorial campaign was shown in a resolution offered by a member of the House at the next session of the legislature:

> WHEREAS, the landlords and proprietors of the boarding-houses . . . refuse to accommodate the members . . . without "Greenbax."
>
> WHEREAS, at the session of last winter, board was furnished free at the hotels by the candidates for United States Senator. . . .
>
> WHEREAS, a member could get credit at the saloons for refreshments as long as his *thousand dollars* lasted, therefore,
>
> RESOLVED, that senatorial elections are a good thing.
>
> RESOLVED, that if they are a good thing, Kansas needs as much of them as any other state we know of.
>
> RESOLVED, that for the relief of the landlords and land-ladies of Topeka, and in order that the charitable enterprises of said city may prosper, it is necessary that we should have a senatorial election every session. . . .[7]

The 1867 legislature adjourned on March 3 after having considered such diverse items as a resolution "to prevent the throwing of paper balls, etc." in the legislative chamber and the fourteenth amendment to the Constitution. Only the latter was approved.[8] Crawford made his customary trip east after the close of the legislature to sell state bonds and confer with the War Department concerning the Indian problem. He returned in time to accompany a party of excursionists from the East, including Senator Simon Cameron and UPED President John Perry on a trip to Fort Harker. This was followed by a buffalo hunt on the plains of Kansas.[9]

The governor's annual message to the 1867 legislature had advocated the submission to the people of amendments to the state constitution which would allow Negroes to vote and which would disenfranchise enemies of the government during the rebellion. The legislature accepted Crawford's recommendations and added a third amendment which would allow women to vote. The special election on the three amendments was scheduled for November 5. In early April, an impartial suffrage convention was held in Topeka. Lucy Stone Blackwell was present and S. N. Wood, a judge recently appointed by Crawford, was charged with organizing the convention. A state association was formed; Crawford was named president and Wood, corresponding secretary.[10] After Crawford's return from his eastern trip, he answered a request of the Impartial Suffrage Association to take part in a canvass of the state. Crawford replied on May 1 that he might not be able to make an extended canvass, but he assured the association that he was "devoted most earnestly to the success ..." of their cause. The letter was widely published.[11]

In spite of Crawford's support, Lucy Stone's stumping of the state,[12] and a canvass on the part of the Republican state committee, Kansas was not yet ready to accept either woman or Negro suffrage. Kansas, in spite of its reputation as a radical state, was still harnessed with the anti-Negro attitude which was characteristic of the majority of Kansans. The November 5 election results were 10,483 for striking the word "white" from the constitution and 19,421 opposed. A similar margin defeated the attempt to strike the word "male" from Article V, Section 1 of the constitution. The only amendment passed actually decreased the enfranchisement of the state by disenfranchising those who had taken part in the "rebellion." This amendment passed by a 16,860 to 12,165 margin. There was almost no public opposition to allowing the Negroes and women to vote, but the white male voters apparently followed the widely circulated maxim to "talk for it; vote agin it."[13]

Crawford could scarcely be accused of giving only halfhearted support for Negro suffrage. He had gained a great deal of respect for the Negro when he commanded the Second Kansas Colored Infantry during the war. He had often repeated his belief that the

Negro should be allowed to vote; he had urged such enfranchisement in his 1867 annual message; and he served as president of the Impartial Suffrage Association. There is no record of his making a canvass of the state in support of impartial suffrage, but he made very few speeches even on behalf of his own election. In addition, his attention to the details of state, including the recruitment of the Eighteenth Kansas Regiment, left him without time to conduct a canvass.[14]

In August 1867 Thomas J. Anderson resigned his position as adjutant general. Crawford chose his private secretary, J. B. McAfee, to fill this position, which was extremely important in view of the Indian wars of 1867 and 1868. McAfee's position as private secretary was in turn taken by Ward Burlingame, late editor of the Leavenworth *Conservative*.[15] Crawford, still near the peak of his political power in late 1867, was appointed state chairman of the Kansas Republican party on October 5, 1867, by Marcus L. Ward, chairman of the Republican Executive Committee. Crawford later authorized Ross to serve in his place for the December 11 Washington meeting of the National Republican Committee.[16]

Crawford's state chairmanship may well have represented the zenith of his political power, because 1868 was a year in which his political prestige gradually diminished. The legislative investigation of Crawford's connection with the UPED Railroad during February may be taken as an early sign of Crawford's dwindling power. Certain legislators also began to question the governor's pardon policies during the same month. The criticism was so great that Crawford felt constrained to send a message to the legislature explaining his position.[17] The governor was entering his "lame duck" year and governors have traditionally found it difficult to maintain any effective organization during their last year of service. In addition, by early 1868, it was becoming obvious that the party unity which had been maintained through the 1866 election was ending. Crawford and Ross represented one faction while Clarke and Pomeroy were the leaders of the other.

Clarke feared that Crawford would oppose him for his Congressional seat and he found an arrangement with Pomeroy useful. It appears that the Pomeroy-Clarke faction held the upper hand by the time of the March 25, 1868, Republican State Convention. The State Convention endorsed Grant for president and Pomeroy for vice-president. Crawford was not among those chosen as delegates to the National Convention despite the fact he had been serving as state chairman of the Republican party.[18]

But the most damaging blow to Crawford's leadership came not from his enemies but from his friend. Ross's appointment to the Senate had temporarily united the party, but ironically it was destined to divide it once again. On February 24, 1868, the United States House of Representatives adopted a resolution calling for the impeachment of the president. Crawford wasted no time in revealing his position to Senator Ross. Two days after the impeachment resolution, he wired: "The Loyal Republicans of Kansas are a unit on the subject of impeachment. Resolutions endorsing Congress, have passed the House and will pass the Senate. The usurpations of Andrew Johnson have been intolerable. He should be removed."[19]

There were reports circulating in Kansas as early as March that Ross might vote to vindicate the president, but friendly newspapers labeled these assertions "merest fabrications." It was explained that the rumors were reported because of Ross's friendship with Thomas Ewing, Jr., a former chief justice of the Kansas Supreme Court, who was an associate of the president. "That Senator Ross will vote for the impeachment of the President we have not a doubt," wrote the Olathe *Mirror*.[20] If Ross had made up his mind before the actual vote on the impeachment charges, he was keeping his own counsel. May 16 was the day on which the vote on the eleventh article was taken and the wires between Kansas and Washington were busy. D. R. Anthony wired Ross: "Kansas has heard the evidence, and demands the conviction of the President." Ross answered that he had taken an oath to do impartial justice and his vote would not be influenced by such demands. Anthony answered: "Your telegram received. Your vote is dictated by Tom Ewing, not by your oath. Your motives are Indian contracts and greenbacks. Kansas repudiates you as she does all perjurers and skunks."[21]

Later the same day, Senator Pomeroy wired the news to Kansas: "In the vote today Kansas is divided I am sorry and ashamed to say it." Richard J. Hinton, a former Kansas newspaperman wired the *Conservative*: "Judas Ross sold out—voted not guilty on the eleventh article. Impeachment lost."[22] Crawford was apparently the most stunned of all Kansans. He wired Ross the same day: "My God Ross what does it mean. The Telegraph reports you as having voted against impeachment on the eleventh article. If true, for God's sake and the sake of your friends and country don't destroy the party in casting your votes on the other articles."[23]

The newspapers which had consistently praised Ross shared Crawford's surprise and their reaction was vehement. The *Conservative* printed a telegram from Judge L. D. Bailey to Ross which read: "Probably the rope with which Judas hung himself is lost, but the pistol with which Jim Lane committed suicide is at your service." The Topeka *Leader* followed in a similar vein: ". . . the courage which prompted Lane to kill himself is foreign to Ross's nature, for it was a courage born of self respect and Ross has none." The Junction City *Union* carried the story under the heading: "The Infamy of Ross"; while the Emporia *News* spoke of "Judas Ross." The Oskaloosa *Independent* under the title, "The Traitor," placed Benedict Arnold, Jefferson Davis, and Ross on its list of infamous traitors.[24]

The reactions to Ross's vote were not confined to the printed word. On May 19, Ross was burned in effigy in Topeka by former soldiers of the Eleventh Kansas, a regiment to which Ross had belonged. A gathering was held in Chicago during the Republican convention in which about fifty Kansans met to denounce "Ross's betrayal of Kansas." D. R. Anthony was elected chairman of the meeting while J. B. McAfee was elected secretary. Later in

the year, the state nominating convention adopted a resolution:
"Resolved, that the conduct of E. G. Ross, senator from Kansas,
in his votes and associations in Washington against loyalty and
liberty, deserves and meets the disapprobation of all liberty loving
men who are his constituents."[25]

Most of the Kansas papers agreed that Ross had sold out for
money and patronage. Perry Fuller and Thomas Ewing were the
names most often reported as having been responsible for Ross's
vote. The *Conservative* stated that the men who had been responsible for Ross's election boasted that "they carried him in their
pockets." Ross was said to have gone to the White House immediately after he cast his vote. This led to speculation that he had
an arrangement with the president. There was also some speculation that Ross had changed his mind at the last minute because
he discovered that Pomeroy and Clarke were conspiring to turn
all of his friends out of office in Kansas if Benjamin Wade became
president. Ross chose to kill the conspiracy and the impeachment
together.[26] Sol Miller, who never failed to see the humor of any
situation, put it this way:

> When E. G. Ross was chosen United States Senator,
> everybody said he was an honest man who could be de-
> pended upon to vote right every time. When Simon Cam-
> eron was elected for Pennsylvania, many persons said he
> was an old rascal, and would betray the party at the critical
> time. Give us more rascals in Congress, we have enough
> honest men.[27]

It did not take some of Crawford's enemies long to realize
that he could be made to share the responsibility for Ross's action.
The Oskaloosa *Independent* named Crawford as the individual to
whom "the whole evil is traced" because it was Crawford who
had first appointed Ross. But it was Sol Miller again who sum-
marized the whole course of events the most succinctly to Crawford's detriment. He wrote: ". . . it came to pass that Kansas

made Jim Lane, and Jim Lane made Crawford, and Crawford made Ross, and Ross made an ass of himself."[28]

Ross's impeachment vote may have killed any hope Crawford had of obtaining the Republican nomination for congressman. It will be remembered that Clarke had shown more strength at both the 1864 and 1866 conventions than had Crawford. Many of Crawford's supporters were also Clarke supporters and they now had to make a choice and Clarke, as the incumbent, had a definite advantage. A majority of the Kansas newspapermen, including some of Crawford's friends, came out for Clarke. The Topeka *State Record,* for example, professed to like the governor personally but added that experience and seniority dictated that Clarke should stay in Congress. The Topeka *Leader* remained steadfast, contending that Crawford's record of fighting the Indian menace gave him an edge over Clarke. The Burlingame *Chronicle* took a similar view, but an overwhelming majority of the Kansas papers favored the incumbent.[29]

John Speer, who was favoring Sidney Clarke in his Lawrence *Tribune,* reported that the strategy of Clarke's opposition was to offer a multitude of candidates in hopes of preventing Clarke's nomination. Among the candidates listed were Crawford, S. O. Thacher, M. J. Parrott, I. S. Kalloch, and Dr. J. W. Scott. By September 3, just six days before the convention, Speer boasted that Clarke had 55 positive votes, enough to win the nomination. A dispatch from John A. Martin dated the day before the convention reported that there was little excitement about the congressional nomination; the only contest seemed to be between George Crawford and James Harvey for the gubernatorial nomination. The dispatch suggested that Clarke might be nominated on the first ballot.[30] The predictions were surprisingly accurate. When the Republican Convention was called to order on Wednesday, September 9, Clarke was nominated on the first ballot. He polled 55 votes to 12 for Crawford, and approximately 21 other votes were scattered among three other candidates. It took five ballots to secure the nomination of Harvey for governor.[31]

Crawford's attention during the summer and fall of 1868 was not entirely focused upon the congressional seat. His chief concern was the Indian trouble in western Kansas. He had sent and received hundreds of letters concerning the situation and he had persuaded the government to accept a regiment of volunteers to aid the federal troops in dealing with the Indians. On September 14, 1868, just five days after the Republican Convention, Crawford issued a call for volunteers.[32] Crawford apparently did nothing to help elect the Republican ticket in the November election. He may have lost all interest in the party since he was not a candidate for election, or he may have been so preoccupied with the Indian problems that he simply did not have time to aid in the campaign. There is a good deal of evidence that the latter was used an as excuse for the former.[33]

A day or two before the election, it was being rumored that Crawford might personally take command of the newly formed Nineteenth Kansas Regiment in its campaign against the Indians. The November 3 election was an overwhelming Republican victory; Harvey was elected governor and Clarke was reelected to Congress, both by a majority of approximately sixteen thousand votes.[34] The day after the election, Crawford sent the following letter to R. A. Barker, the secretary of state: "For the purpose of accepting the command of the 19th Regiment Kansas Volunteer Cavalry, I hereby resign the office of Governor of this State, to take effect immediately." Lieutenant Governor Nehemiah Green was immediately sworn in as governor for the remaining two months of the term.[35] Crawford and the Nineteenth Kansas left for Indian territory almost immediately.

Crawford thus became the first governor to be elected to two terms in Kansas and the first to resign his office. It is always dangerous to judge men's motives, but perhaps some speculation is justified. His reasons for resigning must have been compelling in light of family considerations. Crawford's twenty-year-old wife had given birth to Florence on July 1. The baby was only about four months old when Crawford left on what promised to be an extremely hazardous campaign. Crawford may have believed a successful campaign against the Indians was the only way to regain his political prestige. If his motives were political, his timing was bad. His resignation received but scant attention in the press, partly because most of the news was concerned with the election results. The Topeka *Leader* placed the story on the "city page" and gave it no heading; the Leavenworth *Evening Bulletin* printed a five-line notice in a column of short items; as might be expected, the White Cloud *Chief* gave it the same treatment but with a little more humor; and the Lawrence *Daily Tribune* did not even mention the resignation for almost a month. These papers were representative of the Kansas papers, most of which hardly mentioned the event.[36]

The timing of the resignation does not rule out the possibility that Crawford hoped to use the campaign to rebuild his political fortunes. Crawford's success in the army during the Civil War had been such that he must have had considerable confidence in his ability as an army commander. The Indian campaign would put him in close touch with such men as General George Custer, General William Sherman, and General Phil Sheridan. This certainly would not hurt his career, especially if the campaign was successful in driving the Indians out of Kansas. Crawford's interest in the Indian situation, however, was not motivated by his election failure. His greatest energies during the last three years of his governorship had been expended in dealing with the problem.

8

CRAWFORD
AND
THE INDIAN
PROBLEM

Crawford's resignation as governor to assume command of the Nineteenth Kansas may have surprised some Kansans, but it came as no great surprise to those who had observed his vigorous measures in dealing with the Indians during his administration. Crawford probably expended more time and energy in dealing with the Indian problem than with any other phase of administration. This apportionment of his time and energy was commensurate with the gravity of the situation during his administration. The Civil War had temporarily checked the movement into western Kansas, but as the war neared an end the great tide of settlers moving west was again unleashed. This movement, combined with the building of a transcontinental railroad, soon brought the Indians into friction with the whites. During the first four years of Kansas statehood, only 74 whites had been killed by Indians in Kansas; while during the nearly four years of Crawford's administration, more than 250 were killed and hundreds more were wounded. The year 1867 represented the peak; that year 128 people were killed in Kansas by Indians. In 1868, the last year of Crawford's administration, 79 whites lost their lives in conflicts with Indians.[1]

Crawford shared the attitude of most frontiersmen toward the Indians. They did not cultivate the land and they prevented others from doing so; they were, therefore, not entitled to hold the land. Crawford consistently advocated the removal of the tribes from Kansas and the transfer of their management from the Interior Department to the War Department.[2] To implement his Indian policy, he advocated driving all the wandering Indians from Kansas by using whatever means might be necessary.

Crawford had to deal with the Indian marauders soon after his inauguration in 1865. The Indians, some of whom had been armed by the Confederacy during the war, attacked travelers on the Smoky Hill and the Santa Fe trails. These attacks were met by assigning several of the Kansas regiments, which had been organized during the Civil War, to western Kansas.[3] When winter came, the Indians returned to their reservations and the number of depredations declined sharply. The following year there were only sixteen whites killed by Indians in Kansas, twenty-one fewer than in the previous year. Perhaps this was because the settlers were becoming more cautious and because the building of the transcontinental railroad had not yet been pushed far enough west to threaten the Indians. In addition, military escorts were provided for stage routes, and wagon travel was restricted to large caravans.[4]

Although 1866 was a comparatively quiet year on the frontier, there was enough activity to clearly establish Crawford's pattern of operation against the Indians. The devices he employed during that year were consistently followed throughout his administration. A complaint from a frontiersman would usually bring the governor or the adjutant general to the scene. Crawford would often organize a local militia to cope with the situation. He would also call upon federal authorities for aid. If protection from the U. S. Army was insufficient, he would offer to raise a regiment of volunteers to be mustered into the army for the defense of the frontier. The governor usually threatened to conduct the militia on a campaign against the Indians if the federal government refused to accept his offer of volunteers. This was an effective threat because a campaign by a state militia would leave the U. S. Army almost powerless to uphold the various treaties with the Indians. The army need not have been so concerned about this threat, however, because the Kansas state government lacked the necessary resources to recruit and provide for any large militia force.[5]

In Crawford's annual message to the legislature in 1867, he reviewed the Indian situation in Kansas and recommended that Congress be memorialized to transfer the management of Indian affairs to the War Department. He also recommended that all liquor traffic be prohibited in Kansas beyond the limits of the organized counties. Crawford contended that the sale of liquor to the Indians had been the cause of much of the trouble. The legislature implemented Crawford's recommendation by passing a law which prohibited liquor traffic in the unorganized portion of the state.[6]

Concerning the transfer of the Indian Bureau to the War Department, the governor, the Kansas legislature, the Kansas press, and the people of the West generally were agreed that the transfer was necessary. Crawford spoke of the Interior Department's handling of Indian affairs as "one of the prolific sources of Indian troubles."[7] He argued that the Indian agents were out to fatten their pocketbooks by selling supplies, including arms, to the Indians at the expense of the frontiersman. This desire for profit, so his argument went, resulted in coddling the Indians, who were doing nothing to improve the West. In Congress, the House of Representatives favored the transfer while the Senate was opposed. The senators managed to effectively block any transfer of the

Indian Bureau throughout Crawford's administration, although they were forced to make concessions to the frontier states which allowed the army to exert more control over the Indian situation.[8]

When Crawford returned from his annual trip to Washington in April 1867, he discovered that "the plains of Kansas were swarming with bloodthirsty Indians." Bloodthirsty or not, 1867 was a year in which more whites were killed by Indians in Kansas than in any other year. The struggle between the whites and the Indians increased in intensity with the coming of spring, perhaps because the railroads and the settlers had pushed farther into western Kansas. Winfield Hancock's attack on the unarmed Indian camp on the Pawnee Fork near Fort Larned in April may also have provoked the Indians. The Indians apparently formed an organization for their mutual defense, thus making them more difficult to disperse.[9]

Crawford received a great many appeals and petitions from the citizens of western Kansas during April and May. They asked to be protected from the Indians who had killed, scalped, outraged, and plundered. Crawford continually harassed the federal authorities in an attempt to obtain more troops for protection of the settlers and the travel routes. The situation became even more serious when the Indians began to attack the workers who were building the Union Pacific, Eastern Division, Railroad, which by midsummer was nearing Fort Hays. R. M. Shoemaker, the general superintendent of the UPED, and John D. Perry, the president of the road, reported that the situation was so grave that the work would have to be abandoned if additional troops were not supplied to protect their workers. On June 22, 1867, Crawford wired Secretary of War Stanton asking for additional arms and ammunition; and then on June 24, he renewed his offer to raise additional troops for federal service. Stanton referred the matter to General Grant, who in turn delegated the decision to his departmental commander, General William T. Sherman. Sherman acquiesced on June 27 and called on Crawford to raise a six- or eight-company regiment; however, he rescinded the order the next day.[10] Sherman, like Crawford, favored a firm Indian policy, and he was also committed to the idea of protecting the transcontinental railroads. He was hesitant, however, about calling for state troops. Sherman believed his regulars capable of handling the situation provided he was not hampered by political considerations. Troops offered by the individual states would be expensive; and, in addition, Sherman had reason to believe that the situation was not so serious as pictured by representatives of the railroads, the stage lines, and the frontiersmen.[11]

When General Sherman recalled his request for volunteers, Crawford was left in a desperate situation. On June 28, he wired Sherman:

> . . . this leaves our frontier settlers, railroad men and all others in western Kansas, exposed, and liable to be murdered and scalped at any moment. What shall be done? I cannot move against the Indians with militia, but will, if desired, furnish the Government with a volunteer force sufficient to put an end to these outrages. The Secretary of War informs me that full power is vested in you and the management of the whole affair committed to your discretion. If so I do earnestly hope you will call out a volunteer force and move against the Indians at once.[12]

Sherman reconsidered, and on July 1, Crawford was authorized to recruit six or eight companies immediately, thus shattering the general's precedent of not calling on the states for volunteers. On the same day, Crawford issued a call for troops.[13]

The activity around the executive office in Topeka must have been extremely feverish during the next two weeks. The conditions under which Sherman had issued the call made the recruitment of the full eight companies almost impossible. The call was issued on Monday and Sherman expected Crawford to have approximately eight hundred mounted men ready to muster by Saturday of the same week. Even with this serious limitation on time, Crawford might have recruited a full regiment had it not been for Sherman's insistence that each man bring his own mount. It was not long until some of Crawford's friends came to the conclusion that Sherman would be just as pleased if the venture failed. Lieutenant Governor Green wired Crawford that he had visited with Sherman and "he would not grieve if you fail."[14]

In spite of these limitations, Crawford managed to recruit four cavalry companies in less than two weeks. During this time, more than one hundred telegrams were sent or received concerning the details of recruitment. Crawford called on his friends around the state, many of whom had served with him in the army, to recruit the necessary men. With the legislature not scheduled to meet for six months, Crawford finally devised a system whereby the state would secure the horses for the individual troopers, but the state would be repaid in monthly installments taken from the soldier's pay. Crawford appealed to Sherman for more time and asked that some of the regiment be mustered without horses. To this Sherman replied on July 10:

> Gov. Crawford I will not change the terms of my first call, and if you cannot mount the men we don't want them. General Hancock will be here the day after tomorrow and although Wednesday was the last day you asked I will have mustered in all full companies that are on the cars en route by the day after tomorrow—none later. Shoemaker has already the infantry Company to guard his construction train and another of black cavalry. Though I assert that Indians have not delayed the progress of the road one hour.[15]

Crawford succeeded in recruiting only four companies (about 350 officers and men) before the deadline. On July 15, the Eighteenth Kansas Cavalry, under the command of Major Horace L. Moore, was mustered into federal service at Fort Harker (near the present Ellsworth, Kansas). During its four months of service, the Eighteenth marched 2,200 miles protecting the settlers and the railroad builders. Two of the companies took part in an engagement known as the battle of Beaver Creek on August 21 and 22. The army force of less than two hundred fought off a war party estimated as high as eight hundred Indians. The remainder of the Eighteenth and a force from the Seventh Cavalry pursued the Indians a few days later and succeeded in scattering the warring tribes. Less dramatic, but more severe to the Kansas Indian fighters was a cholera epidemic which took place soon after their muster. By the time the battalion was mustered out on November 15, about 10 per cent of the regiment had lost their lives.[16]

The original call for a Kansas volunteer regiment had been for six months, yet the Eighteenth was mustered out of the service after a four-month tour of duty. Their service was curtailed because of the coming of winter, and perhaps more importantly because of what Crawford referred to as "a maudlin sentimentality in the East, derived from Cooper's novels and impressed upon the Department by ignorant but well-meaning humanitarians."[17] Crawford was referring to the "soft" peace policy of the Department of Interior as manifested by the appointment of a peace commission in the summer of 1867. The results of the work of the peace commissioners in Kansas became known as the Medicine Lodge treaties of October 21 and 28, 1867.

Congress approved a bill on July 20 which resulted in the appointment of a commission to deal with the Indians. N. G. Taylor, the commissioner of Indian affairs in the Department of the Interior, was selected to head the commission; but General Sherman, representing the army, was also made a member. Sherman, despite his lack of faith in an Indian treaty, ordered his troops to confine their operations to defensive tactics pending the outcome of the treaty negotiations. The commissioners first met in Saint Louis on August 8. From there they planned to go up the Missouri River into Nebraska to deal with the northern Plains Indians and then to southern Kansas to negotiate with the southern tribes.[18] Crawford was anxious to meet with the commissioners to express his ideas on the Indian situation. When he

learned that the commission would be coming to Fort Leavenworth en route up the Missouri River to Nebraska, he sent a wire
to await General Sherman's arrival in Saint Louis; it read: ". . .
When will the peace commission be in Kansas and when can I
meet them." Sherman answered on August 10: ". . . I was just on
the point of asking you to meet the commission at Fort Leavenworth at 12 noon Monday [August 12] or in the evening at the
Planter Hotel. . . ." Crawford met with the commissioners, including Taylor, Sherman, W. S. Harney, John S. Sanborn, and
Samuel F. Tappan, at the appointed time. There are no official
records of the meeting, but the Leavenworth *Conservative* indicated that Crawford would not be satisfied with any attempts on
the part of the commissioners to "buy" peace. The *Conservative,*
like most Kansas newspapers, abhorred the possibility of a soft
peace: "While the Indian is planting his tomahawk into the head
of the white, and with vandal hand is robbing the government
and its citizens, that government is literally begging of him
peace. . . ."[19] This strong statement probably approximated
Crawford's position.

While the commissioners journeyed to the North Platte
River, in Nebraska, to deal with the northern Indians, Crawford's
trouble with the Indians in Kansas continued. The governor continued to receive complaints from Shoemaker and the contractors
on the Union Pacific, Eastern Division, Railroad. On September
21, Shoemaker reported that several of his men had been killed by
Indians on the nineteenth. Crawford made a quick on-the-spot
investigation and then wired Sherman offering to organize another regiment of volunteers. Sherman refused to accept volunteers and advised that Shoemaker be cautioned against pushing his
work parties out too far until the commissioners met with the
Indians.[20]

In early October, the commissioners, minus General Sher-
man, who had been called to Washington, met the Indians at
Medicine Lodge in southern Kansas. Representatives of the
Kiowas, Comanches, Apaches, Cheyennes, and the Arapahoes,

numbering more than five thousand, were lured into meeting with the commissioners by boxes of supplies displayed at the site. The Indians faced the winter without sufficient provisions and they were anxious to deal with the "Great Father."[21]

A party of Kansans, including Governor Crawford and Senator Ross, was invited to participate in some of the council meetings. Crawford came prepared with a three-thousand-word statement detailing the "atrocities committed in Kansas and upon citizens of Kansas." He demanded punishment, not rewards, for the Indians. Crawford believed, as did his fellow Kansans, that the policy of giving supplies to the Indians only encouraged them to commit more atrocities. This policy, he wrote, "is virtually paying the Indians—and they so understand it—a reward for every scalp taken and a premium for every woman and child captured."[22]

The Indians generally opposed the white settlement of the Plains and the building of the western railroads, while the commissioners insisted upon opening large areas for settlement and railroad construction. There were occasions when discussions became so heated that an Indian massacre of the commissioners was feared. Milton W. Reynolds, a reporter in attendance at the peace council, later wrote:

> On one occasion we came very nearly being gobbled up by the Indians, and probably would have been but for the presence of two old Indian fighters—Gov. Sam Crawford and General Harney. It was a dull, dreary day. Listlessly and lazily the drops of rain drizzled all day long. Towards evening the Indians became restless; they moved about sullenly, sluggishly, and also, they would not come into council. Governor Crawford called General Harney's attention to the unpleasant signs, which to his practiced eye were plainly visible. The General drew up his troops in a hollow square, placing the commission in the center, and turned a Gatling gun straight upon the camp of the Indians; and the massacre

at the lava beds in California was not repeated upon the virgin bosom of southern Kansas.[23]

After a few anxious hours, the commissioners resumed their meetings with the Indians. On October 21, the Kiowas, Comanches, and Apaches came to terms and a week later the Cheyenne and Arapahoe tribes agreed to the commissioners' conditions. According to the treaties, the Indians agreed to allow the construction of the Pacific railroads and to the relinquishment of their claims between the Platte and Arkansas rivers. In return, they received reservations in Indian Territory, the right to hunt south of the Arkansas River, and a guarantee against white settlement in the area between the Arkansas River and the southern border of Kansas for three years. In addition, they carried away with them the $10,000 worth of presents which has been displayed at Medicine Lodge with the promise of additional food and supplies. At the conclusion of the peace treaty, General Sherman ordered his army to cease hostilities against the Indians; and they, in turn, generally observed the treaty during the winter of 1867–68. Subsequent events indicate that the season of the year had more to do with the coming of peace than did the great Medicine Lodge treaty.[24]

The uneasy peace in Kansas was broken in June 1868 by a Cheyenne raid on the Kaw reservation near Council Grove. Major E. S. Stover, who had served with Crawford in the Second Kansas Cavalry, was the agent for the Kaws and he called upon the governor for help. Crawford received the message from Stover about seven in the evening, but he had no troops immediately available. The governor was still a soldier at heart; he recruited three of his friends and they traveled the sixty miles in an all-night ride in hopes of reinforcing the Kaws. When they arrived, the Kaws had succeeded in driving the raiding party away, but the incident makes Crawford's resignation to head the Nineteenth Cavalry later the same year less surprising.[25]

As the Cheyennes withdrew from their engagement with the

Kaws, they pillaged a number of Kansas communities. The young bucks of several other tribes were also becoming restive by the summer of 1868. They had been promised supplies, which they assumed included arms, by the terms of the Medicine Lodge treaty. The army generally refused to supply them with weapons for potential warfare against the soldiers and settlers. Early in August, however, the Indians succeeded in persuading General Alfred Sully at Fort Larned that they only wanted guns with which to hunt on their way back to their reservation. A few days after the distribution of the guns, messages began to pour into Crawford's office detailing the atrocities of the Indians. Parties of Indians raided up the Smoky Hill valley and northward into the Saline, Solomon, and Republican valleys. Houses were pillaged and burned, settlers were killed, women ravaged, and women and children carried away, according to the reports.[26]

Crawford followed the same procedure that he had found effective in previous years. He first visited the scene of the raids, organizing some local makeshift militia companies. He then returned to Topeka and fired off a letter to President Johnson. In a letter dated August 17, 1868, he told the president that men, women, and children had been murdered indiscriminately by the Indians and he asked for more protection. Once again he offered to furnish volunteers for service against the Indians. The president referred the matter to General Phil Sheridan, who had become the commander of the Department of Missouri in March. Sheridan wrote Crawford on the twenty-first assuring him that he had ordered the building of block houses for the protection of the settlers in the Saline, Solomon, and Republican valleys. Crawford addressed the president again on August 22. Once again he appealed for more protection and asked that the Indians be driven from Kansas. He vehemently concluded his letter:

> If the Government cannot protect its own citizens, let
> the fact be made known, that the people may endeavor to
> protect themselves, or if volunteers are needed we will fur-

nish the Government all that may be necessary to insure a permanent and lasting peace. The Peace Commission is a mockery and their policy a disgrace to the nation. I trust, therefore, that you will keep the Commissioners at home, and stop issuing arms, ammunition and supplies to hostile Indians while they are robbing, murdering and outraging a defenseless people.[27]

Crawford continued to make personal visits to the areas which had suffered Indian raids, and he also continued to pressure the federal officials for more protection. General Sheridan was apparently given a free hand in dealing with the Indians, and he wrote to Crawford on September 10 that he proposed to send troops south of the Arkansas River to attack the families and stock of the raiding Indians. He hoped, thereby, to force the raiding parties to return to their camps in Indian Territory. The governor may have felt this indirect method was too slow to afford any immediate protection for the settlers. He decided to organize a battalion of state militia, providing the government would furnish the necessary supplies. In response to Crawford's inquiry, Sheridan immediately agreed to furnish the necessary carbines and accouterments. Sheridan apparently saw this as a splendid opportunity to release several of his regular companies for duty elsewhere. Two days later, Sheridan wired that he would also authorize rations for as many as five hundred men for two months' service.[28]

On September 10, 1868, Governor Crawford issued the call for troops which would bring into existence the First Frontier Battalion. The call requested five companies of eighty to one hundred men each. The enlistees were told that they would be furnished arms and rations but would be required to supply their own mounts, and any pay they might receive would have to await the next meeting of the legislature. The lack of assurance of pay and the necessity that each soldier provide his own horse apparently did little to hamper the fast recruitment of the militia battalion. Letters poured in asking for recruiting commissions and in two weeks' time the governor was able to send a company off to the southwest to aid Sheridan. Five companies, the number authorized, were completed and placed on duty guarding the frontier. Judged by the decrease in Indian depredations during their sixty-day tour of duty, the First Frontier Battalion was a success. Only one raiding party was able to break through their lines, killing four men.[29]

Crawford's recruitment of the Frontier Battalion had stabilized the Indian situation in Kansas, at least temporarily, but the Indian question in the West was far from settled. As the Indian wars continued, the public in general, and the Congress and its appointed peace commissioners in particular, came to the conclusion that stronger military action against the Indians was necessary. One result of this change in attitude was the recruitment of the famous Nineteenth Kansas Cavalry.

General Sherman had been dubious about the chances of "buying" peace even before the Medicine Lodge treaties. He had agreed to the treaties, however, because they were in keeping with his overall strategy against the Indians. Sherman was anxious to see the Omaha and Kansas branches of the Pacific railroad completed and the area in between settled as a permanent dividing line between the northern and southern Indians. Once this was accomplished, he would have the Indians divided and he could push them farther and farther away from the central states into the extreme northern and southern territories. When the Indians started their raids in the summer of 1868 he began to give General Phil Sheridan and his other officers more power to deal with the Indians as they saw fit. The Chicago meeting of the peace commissioners held on October 7, 1868, confirmed and enlarged Sherman's powers. There the peace commissioners voted to allow the army to drive the Indians back to their reservations. They even suggested that the Indian Bureau be placed back under the jurisdiction of the War Department.[30]

General Phil Sheridan, as the commander charged with dealing with the situation in the field, chose to adopt the strategy of defending the settlers in the summer and massing his forces for all-out attacks upon the Indian villages in the winter. "Little Phil," as he was affectionately called, reasoned that the Indians must be made to realize that they would suffer extinction unless they remained on their reservations. Sheridan now saw the advantage of accepting the offer which had been repeatedly tendered by Governor Crawford; he agreed to accept a full regiment of Kansas volunteer cavalry. This time the army agreed to furnish everything, including horses, and to allow the officers and men the same pay and privileges as received by the regulars. Perhaps Sheridan realized that the experience gained in organizing the Eighteenth Cavalry and the Frontier Battalion, plus the militant feeling in Kansas, would bring speedy results.[31]

Governor Crawford issued a call for troops for six months' service on October 10, 1868. In spite of the obvious fact that the soldiers would be exposed to all the discomforts of a winter campaign, the response to the call was tremendous. After two other similar experiences, Crawford had an efficient recruiting machine running throughout the state. His militia under the command of Adjutant General McAfee, together with the help of his old friends from Civil War days, made it an easy matter to organize the twelve full companies (about thirteen hundred men) in a little over three weeks.[32]

Sheridan's overall strategy was to launch a three-pronged attack upon the Indians. Columns coming from Fort Bascom, New Mexico, and Fort Lyon, Colorado, were to confine the Indians while the main force, under the personal command of General Sheridan, would march south from Kansas into Indian Territory, expecting to encounter the enemy villages along the Washita River. Sheridan's personal command consisted of the Nineteenth Kansas Volunteer Cavalry, eleven troops of the Seventh United States Cavalry, and a battalion of five companies of infantry. The Nineteenth Kansas was ordered to rendezvous with the regulars at a place called Camp Supply in Northwest Indian

Territory. Camp Supply was located about one hundred miles south of Fort Dodge at the confluence of Beaver and Wolf creeks.[33]

The Nineteenth Kansas Volunteer Cavalry was organized and mustered at Camp Crawford, which was a farm rented for that purpose about one mile outside of Topeka. The regiment was mustered on November 4, the same day in which Governor

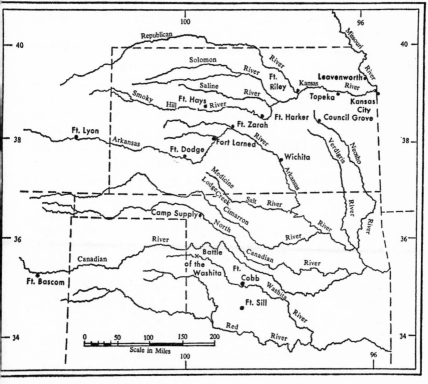

Kansas and Indian Territory, 1868-1869

Crawford resigned his office to accept the command of the new regiment. Crawford's move had been anticipated by the men, and they were apparently pleased with their new commander. One of them wrote in his diary: ". . . Governor Crawford has resigned and will command our regiment. He has the reputation for being a very fine gentleman, kind to all who meet him in any way."[34]

The Nineteenth Kansas broke camp on November 5; two troops were sent by rail to Fort Hays, hence to Camp Supply on escort duty, while the remaining ten troops headed cross-country for the same destination via Camp Beecher (present-day Wichita). Crawford and the main body of his regiment reached Beecher in seven days without incident. At Camp Beecher, Colonel Craw-ford expected to receive supplies for the next ten days, but upon arrival he found that the garrisoned troops had consumed half of the rations. Crawford was faced with a formidable task. He was expected to cross two hundred miles of uncharted country with 1,100 new recruits and 1,300 animals on five days' rations and three days' forage. The snows had not yet begun, but they were an ever-present danger. Sheridan was expecting Crawford at Camp Supply by about November 20, so Crawford felt constrained to go ahead without waiting for additional supplies.[35]

At Camp Beecher, James R. Mead, an Indian trader, previ-ously castigated by Crawford for allegedly selling arms to the Indians, told Crawford that he could not cross the unknown country without a good guide. Mead offered to furnish such a guide; but, by his own account: "the Colonel replied in language too forcible to repeat that Sheridan had furnished him these [two] guides, and they had to take him through; that he had no authority or money to employ other guides." According to Mead, it was only a six-day trip when led by a competent guide. He later referred to Crawford's course of action as a "stupendous blunder."[36] Sheridan had furnished Crawford with guides named Apache Bill Simpson and Johnny Stillwell. Neither the guides nor any of Crawford's men had even been over the proposed route to Camp Supply. They could only rely on the sun, their compass, and their knowledge of that general area.

The Nineteenth Cavalry left Beecher on November 14; by November 17 the regiment had passed beyond the timber and grass. The first incident occurred near sundown on November 18. A greenhorn trooper tied a lariat which had been placed around his horse's neck to his dismounted saddle. The horse moved and was frightened by the consequent movement of the saddle. The horse then ran off, pulling the saddle and frightening the other grazing horses. Perhaps as many as 450 horses ran away. The regiment spent the next day tracking them down. Finally, all but about one hundred were returned. The train was thereby slowed down because about one hundred men were without horses; in addition, the rations ran out about the same time. Hunting became a time-consuming necessity.[37]

As the regiment continued over extremely rough country, subsisting on buffalo meat, another hazard appeared. A norther, or snowstorm, began about the twenty-first and in forty-eight hours piled up ten inches of snow. As the situation became more critical, Crawford and his officers began to demand more exact information from their scouts. From the point of view of the scouts, the officers were making unreasonable demands of them, expecting them to "know to a gnat's heel the location of every stream and little old blind spring in the country penetrated." To the Kansas militia, on the other hand, the scouts "appeared bewildered" and seemed to be lost.[38] As the snow continued and no buffalo were in sight, the Nineteenth made camp on Sand Creek on November 22. The only food available was six barrels of coffee sugar in the officers' stores. Crawford ordered every man issued his share of sugar cubes. At this juncture, he decided to send Captain A. J. Pliley with fifty men in search of Sheridan and an anticipated relief party. When the snow let up, buffalo was again available and the men were reasonably well fed, but the lack of forage took a great toll among the animals. Crawford ordered that the animals not be mounted without special permission.[39]

By November 24, the regiment had reached the Cimarron hills, which made passage even more difficult. Crawford decided to make camp there for all those without horses strong enough to continue. On the twenty-fifth, he took approximately half of the regiment and pushed on toward Camp Supply, leaving the other men at what they chose to call "Camp Starvation." Crawford's segment of the regiment found Camp Supply on November 28; there they learned that Captain Pliley had arrived in camp three days previously and Sheridan had sent a relief expedition after the remaining men. The entire regiment finally was reunited at Camp Supply on December 1. Miraculously no men were lost, but approximately seventy-five horses had died and many others were too weak to mount.[40]

General Phil Sheridan had arrived at Camp Supply on November 21 with plans to start the campaign immediately, but he found the Nineteenth Kansas "unaccountably absent." Rather than wait for Crawford's regiment, he sent the Seventh Cavalry, under the command of Brevet Major General George A. Custer, on a scout. On the morning of November 27, Custer succeeded in surprising Black Kettle's sleeping village. The battle of Washita was a great victory for Custer. He reported that more than a hundred braves had been killed and the enemy routed, while his losses were reported as only nineteen men. Sheridan had wanted to follow Custer's victory with an immediate pursuit of the Indians, but Crawford's cavalry was in no condition to travel for several days after their arrival at Camp Supply.[41]

In General Sheridan's memoirs, written twenty years after the event, Sheridan stated that Crawford had been given competent scouts and that he had become lost because he refused to follow their advice. Crawford, on the other hand, remembered that the scouts were incompetent and that General Sheridan had been pleased with the conduct of the Nineteenth Kansas in the face of such hardship. Sheridan, according to Crawford, had been misinformed by the scouts, "whose reputations and wages depended largely on their skill as liars." Sheridan in a letter to General Sherman, written the day after the arrival of the last segment of the Nineteenth at Camp Supply, said: "The boys, I mean the 19th Kansas are doing pretty well, better a great deal than could have been expected." According to James A. Hadley, one of the members of the Nineteenth: "It is the cold, hard fact that the weather and the absurd lack of stores were the causes of the catastrophe . . . the universal ignorance of the country, including that of Sheridan himself, was at the bottom of it all."[42] Sheridan was understandably disappointed that he was not able to start his campaign on schedule, but he must have realized that delay would be one of the likely hazards of a winter campaign. The remainder of the campaign, under his personal command, was to suffer many of the same difficulties experienced by Colonel Crawford and his men.

Sheridan combined the able-bodied men of the Nineteenth Kansas and Seventh U. S. Cavalry into a force of about eighteen hundred men and broke camp on December 7. He led the army southward toward Fort Cobb located in West-Central Indian Territory. The snows continued and the temperature was often below zero. On December 12, the army set out from its camp of the previous night, only to be forced back to the same site. On December 17, the expedition overtook the Kiowas, who presented a letter from General W. B. Hazen, commander at Fort Cobb, which said that they were friendly Indians. Sheridan insisted that the Indians accompany him into Fort Cobb. Most of the Indians wandered off, however, and Sheridan arrested Chiefs Satanta and Lone Wolf, threatening them with hanging if the members of their tribe did not return. The threat was successful and the Kiowas and soon thereafter several other tribes came into camp. During the eleven-day campaign from Camp Supply to Fort Cobb, the Nineteenth Kansas lost an additional 148 horses by exposure to the extreme weather.[43]

Sheridan stayed at Fort Cobb several days to be sure that the

Indian tribes were placed on their reservations. Only the Cheyennes were missing and Custer was sent to track them down. The Nineteenth Kansas journeyed south to Fort Sill. On February 5, 1869, Sheridan ordered the Nineteenth Cavalry to relinquish their good horses to the Seventh Cavalry. On February 12, Crawford resigned his commission. The command of the Nineteenth Kansas fell to Colonel Horace L. Moore, who had commanded the Eighteenth Kansas and had been second in command to Crawford in the Nineteenth. The Nineteenth pursued the Cheyennes and suffered additional hardships before their tour ended and they were mustered out on March 23, 1869. The Kansas regiment took part in no important battles during their tour, but they suffered almost every conceivable discomfort resulting from blizzards, short rations, and the lack of horses. The men of the Nineteenth could boast of having formed an important segment of a campaign which forced the Kiowas, Comanches, Cheyennes, and Arapahoes onto their reservations. The Indian troubles in Kansas were not ended, but they were greatly diminished by their campaign. The total casualty list for the Nineteenth Kansas Volunteer Cavalry was four who died of disease, one wounded on duty, one killed by accident, and ninety who deserted.[44]

The timing of Crawford's resignation has led to some speculation concerning the cause of his leaving the Nineteenth. A letter written by George W. Martin, secretary of the Kansas State Historical Society on August 29, 1908, to E. C. Manning, a former fellow soldier with Crawford in the Second Kansas Cavalry, indicates that the whole story may never have been told:

> I found your note on my table. Now this is confidential. Tear this letter up because I wouldn't reflect on Crawford for the world. Ever since I read the story of the 19th Kansas I have suspicioned why Crawford resigned. I see the same strikes you. I asked Col. Lindsey the question, and his response was "I think he was asked to." Crawford says himself that he resigned in order to go home and attend to

the pay of the men. The loss of those horses caused the suspicion. Crawford always makes light of that march and suffering. Mead has talked to me about this for years. He is very sore about it. At one time I intended printing all he said, but at the last concluded to cut it out. He complains that at that time he was a State Senator, and all the men interested knew of his experiences on the border and in that particular direction, and he never was consulted about anything. Crawford refused to take his guide because he said he had two furnished him, and no money to pay another. But Mead offered to furnish him one for nothing, you see this is only suspicion, and if you go to work with him help him out as best you can. I hope he doesn't need any help, I mean in straightening up a suspicion. . . .[45]

Exhaustive research has produced little information which would indicate exactly what it was that Martin suspected or any substantiation that Crawford was asked to resign. Neither the official reports nor the personal memoirs of Sherman or Sheridan indicate that Crawford was asked to resign. The diary of David Spotts, who was a trooper in the Nineteenth, indicates that Crawford and Sheridan were, in fact, good friends. Colonel Moore, Crawford's successor, stated simply that Crawford received a leave of absence of twenty days on February 12 after which his resignation took effect. Crawford's version as presented in his memoirs was to the effect that the campaign had been brought to an end by the internment of a majority of the Indians. He was also concerned that the pay of the men might be delayed and he determined to go to Washington if necessary to secure the required appropriation before the scheduled muster out of the regiment. Crawford apparently called upon the secretary of war and secured the necessary funds from the War Department Contingent Fund.[46]

If Crawford was forced to resign, or if there was some kind of skullduggery involved, it was certainly a well-kept secret.

When Crawford resigned, David Spotts wrote in his diary: "He is going home to see if he can get the War Department to pay us for we have not seen the color of money since we left Kansas." Spotts added: "He may have to go to Washington, but he has our best interest at heart and will do all he can for us." The next day's entry indicates that Crawford and Sheridan left with the same escort for Topeka. Dispatches to the Leavenworth *Evening Bulletin,* a paper generally unfriendly to the former governor, tell how the men of the Nineteenth passed a series of resolutions "highly complimentary to the Colonel as an officer and soldier," upon the occasion of his departure. The correspondent to the Junction City *Union* reported that Crawford's resignation "was a source of regret to all."[47]

In retrospect, Crawford's handling of the Indian situation in Kansas was the most successful aspect of his administration. He was a true son of the frontier in that he shared the settler's attitude of displacing the Indians. He implemented this attitude by repeatedly applying to the federal government for military support; by consistently protesting any attempted "soft" peace; and by organizing a recruiting machine which produced the Eighteenth Kansas Cavalry, the Frontier Battalion, and the Nineteenth Kansas Cavalry, each on short notice and in spite of great obstacles.

9

A DECADE
OF
DEFEAT

Ex-Governor Crawford, a seasoned veteran of numerous military and political campaigns at age thirty-three, returned home in March 1869.[1] He could review the events of his adult life with considerable pride. From his small law practice in Garnett, he had been catapulted into the mainstream of politics in Kansas. In rapid succession, he had been elected to the legislature, commissioned a colonel in the Union Army, and twice elected governor of the state. The next ten years of his political career were destined to be in sharp contrast to the easy successes of the previous decade.

Crawford remained in Topeka about six months seeking suitable employment. When none was forthcoming, he decided to move to Emporia. There he became a partner with J. M. Steele in the firm known as Crawford, Steele and Company, Real Estate. Crawford was not entirely without resources. On March 3, 1870, he sold the section of land located near Perryville, which had been the subject of the legislative investigation in 1868, for $22,000.[2]

As the state elections of 1870 approached, Crawford once again became involved in the political situation. His name was generally associated with a loose-knit group which came to be called the "purifiers." This reform group wanted to unseat incumbent Congressman Sidney Clarke, who had defeated Crawford in the 1868 convention. They believed their chances were enhanced when the number of convention delegates was more than doubled, presumably making it more difficult to buy a nomination. Crawford was not a candidate for Congress, but he placed himself squarely with the anti-Clarke faction. Some bitter words between Clarke and Crawford resulted. Clarke charged that Crawford, as governor in 1866, had allowed the Price raid claims to "go by the board." Crawford's countercharge was to the effect that Clarke as the state's "sole representative" had allowed the bill to be defeated so that "agents of rings could be sent out to buy up the scrip at less than half its real value."[3]

Clarke's opponents made effective use of political posters and cartoons in which he was accused of taking bribes from land speculation companies. When the Republican State Nominating Convention met at Topeka on September 8, Clarke found that he had a serious opponent in D. P. Lowe of Fort Scott, a city adjacent to the area of the Cherokee Neutral Land treaty. The first informal ballot showed Clarke leading Lowe 77 to 58 with 63 votes scattered among seven other candidates. Lowe, however, gained a sufficient number of the previously scattered votes on the first formal ballot to gain the nomination.[4]

With incumbent Senator Edmund G. Ross discredited because of his vote in the presidential impeachment trial, and Sidney Clarke defeated in a party convention, Crawford saw his chances of gaining the 1871 senatorial nomination as good. On October 15, he wrote to Judge James Hanway:

My Dear Judge

Friends in different parts of the state are using my name in connection with the Senatorial question. Don't know what my chances for election may be but from letters rec'd and such other information as I have I am led to believe that they are at least no worse if not better than other candidates. . . .

If there is no other candidate whom you would prefer, I should be very glad to have your support. If you can spare the time to look after the matter for me in your county— Miami and Linn and such other places as you think necessary, I will return the favor if an opportunity is ever offered. . . .[5]

With Clarke defeated in the convention, the state general election of November 8, 1870, was a lackluster affair. D. P. Lowe easily defeated his Democratic opponent 40,368 to 20,950. Governor James Harvey, who had been renominated by the Republicans, defeated Isaac Sharp by an almost identical margin. The election of the state representatives and senators who would choose a United States senator at the next legislative session caused some excitement, but the results showed that no majority of legislators was pledged to any one senatorial candidate. Crawford believed he had sixteen pledged supporters in the House and two in the Senate as a result of the election.[6]

As the year neared an end, the names of three senatorial candidates were being prominently mentioned. They were former Governor Thomas Carney of Leavenworth, Sidney Clarke, and Crawford. On November 25, the Emporia *News,* which was supporting Crawford, quoted an article from the Garnett *Plaindealer* (Crawford's former hometown newspaper):

Gov. Crawford, of Emporia, undoubtedly has the inside track for U. S. Senator. He will have as many votes on the first ballot as any other man, and after that first

rush of excitement cools down, we believe he will *draw*
well. When the shysters and . . . political hacks and wire-
pullers are played out, the large majority of the legislature
will turn and cry with one acclaim "Give us Sam Crawford." The people have not lost their faith in honest men.
Not by any means.[7]

When the legislature convened on January 10, 1871, Crawford
had many reasons to be optimistic. Persons whom he believed to
be his supporters organized the House of Representatives and
elected B. F. Simpson, a staunch Crawford supporter, to the
Speakership. The race seemed to be narrowing to Crawford and
Clarke. Crawford's supporters were heartened by the response to
an article which appeared in the Oswego *Register*. This article,
which was widely discussed, asserted that Clarke was really supporting the James Joy land speculative interests and not the settlers
and that the Republican Convention's rejection of Clarke had
shown his unpopularity with the people. On the other hand, the
article pointed out that Crawford was the true friend of the frontiersman, as he had shown by fighting Indians and opposing the
Joy land grabs. By January 12, Crawford's friends could boast
that he had "positive strength" of no less than forty votes, more
than any other candidate.[8]

Optimism in the Crawford camp reached its zenith about
January 13. On that day, Jacob Stotler, the editor of the Emporia
News and a veteran politician, wrote that Crawford's chances
were getting better every day. "It is thought now by many shrewd
political observers that he cannot be beaten," he wrote. Stotler
believed Clarke's strength to be only about twenty-three votes and
he had heard rumors that Carney had withdrawn from the contest. The difficulty was, however, that an election law passed in
1866 had set the date for election of U. S. senators for the "second
Tuesday after the meeting and organization of the Legislature,"
in this case January 24. This delay, according to Crawford's

memoirs, gave the "boodlers" time to buy the votes of the legis-lators.[9]

Late in December, powerful business interests centered in Leavenworth had decided to support Alexander Caldwell for the senatorial seat. As a former Democrat, a virtual newcomer to Kansas, and an inexperienced politician, he was not generally taken seriously as a candidate. On January 13, however, Thomas Carney, also of Leavenworth, announced that he would not be a candidate for the Senate. The Leavenworth *Evening Bulletin,* which was supporting Caldwell, announced that the Carney men would unite on Caldwell; it thus became obvious that Caldwell was a serious contender. By January 17, the Leavenworth forces had established an effective organization in Topeka. Caldwell had arrived in the state capital and had set up headquarters in the Tefft House; Governor Carney was "working very zealously in the interest of Caldwell"; and the delegation from Leavenworth was optimistic.[10] This turn of events, which made the contest a three-way race, was a blow to the Crawford forces who had hoped for a clear-cut battle between Crawford and Clarke.[11]

On Tuesday, January 24, the day on which the balloting for U. S. senator could legally begin, there was a great deal of excite-ment. There was considerable discussion as to the use of money in the election. Thomas P. Fenlon offered a resolution calling on each member of the House to take an oath which read: "You, and each of you, do solemnly swear, before Almighty God, the searcher of all hearts, that you have not received, and will not receive, any money or other valuable thing to influence or control your vote on the senatorial question." The resolution carried the House and the Speaker and thirty-two of the legislators took the oath.[12] Thereafter, the House and Senate, meeting separately, took in-formal ballots to determine their preference for U. S. senator. The Senate gave Caldwell 8 votes, Clarke 6, and Crawford 5; while in the House, Caldwell received 29, Clarke 21, and Crawford 22. This made the totals of both houses read: Caldwell 37, Clarke and Crawford 27 each; the remaining votes were scattered. Approximately 63 votes would be needed in a joint session to elect. The House and Senate adjourned after scheduling the joint session to elect a U. S. senator for noon the next day.[13]

"King Caucus" was given complete reign on the eve of the election. The "purifiers" and other anti-Caldwell factions held a number of caucuses. They were about fifty strong, but they were unable to unite on a candidate. About midnight, a messenger representing Sidney Clarke approached this group and asked that Clarke be allowed to address them. The caucus refused but appointed a committee to meet with Clarke's supporters. The two groups were unable to agree on any candidate and the meeting broke up. According to Stotler, one of Clarke's agents later approached Crawford and offered to turn over twenty votes, but "the conditions were such that Crawford could not have accepted them and preserved his manhood." At about 5:00 A.M., the Clarke supporters held another caucus and decided to support Caldwell in preference to Crawford or any of the so-called purifiers. The Clarke forces were bitter because of the preelection Crawford-Clarke fight, and they were much more disposed to support Caldwell if no compromise candidate could be elected. In addition, a Caldwell representative agreed to pay Clarke's "expenses," which totaled from $12,000 to $15,000.[14]

At noon the next day, the Senate joined the House in its chambers for the joint session. The president of the Senate assumed the chair, and the election proceedings began. S. M. Strickler, who had nominated Sidney Clarke on the previous day, was the first to make a speech. He said that Clarke's supporters had been willing to unite upon a compromise candidate, but that "the gentlemen professing to be opposed to both Clarke and Caldwell were unwilling to compromise." The friends of Clarke were therefore forced to choose between Crawford and Caldwell and they had chosen Caldwell. He asked that Clarke's name be withdrawn and that Caldwell be elected. H. P. Welch, of Franklin County, then formally nominated Caldwell. Next to speak was James D. Snoddy of Mound City, who gave a brief review of

Crawford's military and political history and placed his name in nomination. A seconding speech was made by B. F. Simpson, the Speaker of the House. Elijah Sells of Douglas County made a speech favoring Crawford. J. M. Morris, of Riley County, described contemptuously by the *Bulletin* as one of the "original purifiers," alleged that votes were being purchased. He said his children (thirteen of them) would not be ashamed to look him in the face because he had taken no bribes and he would support Crawford. The galleries, according to the *Bulletin,* an opposition newspaper, gave the pro-Crawford speakers "encouragement by thundering applause." Speeches on behalf of Caldwell by James Legate, T. L. Bond, J. H. Snead, and B. H. McEckron were made in an effort to neutralize the effect of the pro-Crawford speeches. On motion of Legate, each member was required to rise and state his vote for U. S. senator. When the roll call was completed, Caldwell had beaten Crawford by an 87 to 35 count.[15]

Crawford came out of the senatorial contest with a reputation for honesty. An opposition newspaper, while admitting his honesty, alluded to his incompetence to hold a Senate seat. The Emporia *News* noted that Crawford had "spurned, throughout the fight, all dishonorable offers to withdraw, or combine."[16] On the other hand, charges to the effect that Caldwell had bought the election began to be made almost immediately after the election. On February 2, 1871, the Lawrence *Democratic Standard* printed the following story under the title "Sale of the Senatorship":

> The future historian of our State will class the 24th day of January, 1871, among the dark days of her history. . . . The naked fact is, that the election of Alexander Caldwell was the triumph of *money* over every other consideration. . . .
>
> We say then . . . that the election of Alexander Caldwell is the most disgraceful event in our political history, and that the Senatorship for this State has been put up and sold to the highest bidder, for cash, in the same manner as was the Roman Empire put and sold by the Pretorean guards.

> A powerful corporate interest situated beyond the borders of our State—the Pennsylvania Central Railroad Company—have with their money and through their agents, entered the political arena, and in combination with the Kansas Pacific Railroad Company, they have pressed the election of Mr. Caldwell, and he goes to the Senate of the United States not to represent the interest of our State, but to represent the interest of those corporations.[17]

The *Standard,* on January 17, 1872, published a list of nineteen legislators who were said to have been offered no less than $1,000 each for their votes in the senatorial election. The next day a resolution was introduced in the Kansas legislature calling for an investigation. Testimony was taken from January 30 to February 23 by a joint committee of investigation, but the committee was hampered by the unavailability of certain key witnesses such as Thomas Carney, who had suddenly left the state. James McDowell was called, however, to testify that some kind of written agreement between Carney and Caldwell existed. McDowell had made a copy of the agreement, but he was unable or unwilling to produce the document. Sidney Clarke was also called and he testified that he had been approached by Caldwell, who offered to pay "the legitimate expenses that I had incurred in the canvass." The committee collected enough information to make a report dated February 24, 1872. The unanimous report concluded that Thomas Carney had come to Topeka to support Caldwell's election because of some "confidential relation with Caldwell" for which a written agreement had been made. The report also stated that agents of the Kansas Pacific Railway Company had promised to contribute $30,000, as its share of Caldwell's election expenses. The report concluded that Alexander Caldwell had used "bribery and other corrupt and criminal means . . . to secure the election of 1871."[18]

As a result of the Kansas legislature's investigation of Caldwell's election, the U. S. Senate began its own investigation in

May 1872. The Senate committee called James McDowell, who produced a copy of an agreement between Carney and Caldwell which read:

> I hereby agree that I will not, under any condition or circumstances, be a candidate for the U. S. S., in the year 1871, without the written consent of A. Caldwell, and in case I do, to forfeit my word of honor, hereby pledged. I further agree to bind myself to forfeit the sum of fifteen thousand dollars, and authorize the publication of this agreement.
>
> *Thomas Carney*

The agreement was dated January 13, 1871, the same date on which Carney had announced his withdrawal from the senatorial race. Carney was called and admitted that the copy of the agreement was authentic and that he had also agreed to go to Topeka to help gain the election for Caldwell.[19]

The committee published its report on February 17, 1873. It found that Len T. Smith, in behalf of Caldwell, had made an agreement with Carney whereby the latter would step aside for $15,000 and that an arrangement had been made on behalf of Caldwell to pay Clarke's expenses, estimated at from $12,000 to $15,000. The committee also reported that Carney and Clarke had testified that Caldwell had told them that the election cost him $60,000. The Kansas Pacific Railroad Company was said to have contributed $10,000 on January 23, 1871, toward the election of Caldwell. The committee therefore: "*Resolved,* that Alexander Caldwell was not duly and legally elected to a seat in the Senate of the United States by the legislature of the State of Kansas." Caldwell resigned his Senate seat on March 24, 1873.[20]

Crawford returned to Emporia after his defeat in the senatorial campaign of 1871. He felt that he had campaigned using "principles not money," and when money was the apparent winner, his faith in the legislators must have been shaken. Perhaps this was one of the reasons for his break with the regular Republican party in 1872. Many of the same persons who were in the "purifiers" camp, from which much of his support had come, were involved in the organization of the Liberal Republican party in Kansas. Crawford may have also noted that the election of a state Liberal Republican ticket in 1872 would place him in a strong position to succeed Senator Pomeroy, whose term would end in March 1873. Whatever his reasons, Crawford placed himself squarely in the Liberal Republican camp when on April 4, 1872, he wrote Alois Thoman, one of the leaders of the new party, a widely published letter wishing the new party success.[21]

On April 10, 1872, a Liberal Republican Convention was held in Topeka for the purpose of completing the state organization and selecting delegates to the national convention at Cincinnati. The meeting was called to order by Marcus J. Parrott and an election of convention officers was the first order of business. Former Governor Samuel J. Crawford was chosen as convention president. The group was addressed by Governor B. Gratz Brown of Missouri, who would subsequently be nominated for vice-president at the national convention. The convention named more than one hundred delegates to the Cincinnati convention including Crawford.[22]

Republican party defectors in Kansas have traditionally been subject to the most vitriolic abuse at the hands of the Republican newspapermen, and Crawford was no exception. The Atchison *Champion,* in recording that Crawford had been elected president of the Liberal Republican Convention, expressed the belief that his defection from the Republican party was "good riddance." They charged him with having been a "wooden man" as governor for Lane. "He is as weak as he is vain, and as stupid as he is corrupt . . . he is thoroughly played-out." The only surprise, according to the *Champion,* was that he had not joined "this mournful funeral procession of defunct politicians long ago." Sol Miller commented that the Liberal Convention must have been a big thing because it was presided over by a "Big Nothing."[23]

Crawford's defection also precipitated a break with Jacob

Stotler, editor of the Emporia *News* and Crawford's caucus manager in the 1871 senatorial contest. Under the title "Another Recruit," Stotler chastised Crawford for leaving the party which had done so much for him. It had made him governor and put him in a position to make $20,000 by accepting a gift of a section of land from a railroad company. Stotler said that Crawford had recently applied for several positions through the Republican party but had failed:

> The logical deductions from his present conduct are that having made up his mind that he can get no more offices nor twenty thousand dollar land jobs, he has concluded to raise his hands in holy horror and let his honest soul revolt at the horrible spectacle presented by its great corruptions (?)

Crawford answered in kind in "An Open Letter to Jacob Stotler," printed in the Emporia Democratic paper. In the lengthy letter he answered the charges made against him and accused Stotler of having extorted money from various political candidates. When the next issue of the *News* came out, Stotler took four columns of small print to "expose" Crawford's political record. The indictment was all encompassing: he had been made governor by Lane; his letter of acceptance of the 1864 nomination had been rewritten for him; the pamphlet on immigration he had written was "incredible"; he was paid to use his influence to get Pomeroy and Ross elected in 1867; he had accepted a section of land from the Union Pacific, Eastern Division; he had offered to make Stotler the postmaster at Emporia in return for his help in the 1871 election; he had lost the senatorial contest because of his stupidity; and Clarke "actually had a spy staying in the same room with him" during the senatorial race. Stotler denied that he had accepted any bribes, as Crawford had charged, and he concluded, "Besides, if someone is buying, someone is selling."[24]

The Liberal Republican Convention met in Cincinnati on

May 1 and nominated Horace Greeley and B. Gratz Brown to head the national ticket.[25] Crawford apparently did not attend the national convention, but he strongly supported its nominees. In a letter addressed to J. F. Warwick, chairman of a Liberal Republican "ratification" meeting held in Council Grove, Crawford characterized the Cincinnati ticket as "one that every honest man can afford to support." Commenting upon the state and national situation, Crawford charged that there was great corruption in the Grant cabinet; that Grant's administration was a "no policy" government; that James Joy was attempting to take the "homes of 20,000 people in Kansas" with the connivance of officials of the U. S. government; and that "all over the state you can point to men who have sold their votes as often as they have been members of the legislature . . . and they are Grant supporters."[26]

The regular Republican party was the first to hold its state nominating convention. The delegates met in Topeka on September 4 and after ten ballots chose Thomas A. Osborn as their gubernatorial candidate. The Democrats and the Liberal Republicans scheduled their meetings for the same day, September 11, the Liberals meeting at Union Hall and the Democrats at Representative Hall in Topeka. Crawford's support was solicited by a number of candidates, but he advised them not to make a fight before the convention. He apparently believed that the important thing was to select any "good ticket" while disappointing as few people as possible. He was optimistic, believing that a good ticket, plus a determined fight, would carry the state.[27]

The two conventions met in Topeka as scheduled. The Liberal Republicans appointed a committee to confer with the Democrats for the purpose of nominating a common ticket. Crawford was a member of this committee, which after a conference with the Democrats, reported back to the full convention that an agreement had been reached whereby the Liberal Republicans would nominate a candidate for governor and for two congressional seats. The Democrats were to select the lieutenant governor and one congressman. The conventions adopted a joint

platform and they both endorsed Greeley and Brown for president
and vice-president. Thaddeus H. Walker of Topeka was given
the nomination for governor while Robert B. Mitchell, W. R.
Laughlin, and S. A. Riggs were chosen as congressional nominees.[28]

The charges of corruption, which had been widely circulated
during the year 1872 after the legislative investigation of Caldwell's election, seem to have had little effect upon the voters of
Kansas. They chose a Republican governor, all three congressmen, and the presidential electors by a margin of two to one.
Osborn beat Walker 66,715 to 34,608 in the gubernatorial contest.[29]

If a Senate seat was Crawford's goal, he might have been
better advised to have remained in the Republican party. In 1873,
as a result of legislative and congressional investigations and a
sensational maneuver by the opponents of Pomeroy, the two U. S.
senators from Kansas were removed from office. The most start-
ling of these events was connected with the senatorial election of
1873. Incumbent Senator Pomeroy was expected to be easily reelected when state Senator A. M. York, on January 29, during the
joint session to elect a senator, arose and made this speech:

> I visited Mr. Pomeroy's room in the dark and secret re-
> cesses of the Tefft House, on Monday night, and at that in-
> terview my vote was bargained for, for a consideration of
> $8,000; two thousand dollars of which were paid to me on
> that evening, five thousand dollars the next afternoon, and
> a promise of the additional one thousand when my vote had
> been cast in his favor. I now, in the presence of this honor-
> able body, hand over the amount of $7,000 just as I received
> it, and ask that it be counted by the secretary.[30]

The outcome of this speech was a furor which resulted in the
election of John J. Ingalls, a man who had had only one vote on
a previous informal ballot. Had Crawford stayed in the party,
while continuing to be identified with the reform group, he might

conceivably have received the Senate seat. The other Senate seat became vacant on March 24 of the same year, when Alexander Caldwell was forced to resign as a result of the investigations into the 1871 election. Governor Osborn appointed Robert Crozier to the Senate seat and the next legislature, meeting in 1874, chose former Governor James Harvey for the seat. Since this investigation made it clear that Crawford had been defeated by money in 1871, it seems entirely possible that he might have been able to ride a wave of righteous indignation into a Senate seat for himself had he only stayed in the Republican party.

The years 1873 to 1876 mark a period of political inactivity for Crawford. He had received crushing blows in the elections of 1871 and 1872, and his defection from the Republican party left him without an effective vehicle on which to carry his political ambitions. Another factor affecting his temporary retirement from politics was a financial one. Crawford was hard hit by the Panic of 1873; he lost his real estate business, his savings, and even his home. Even after selling his home, he had to pay his debtors on a *pro-rata* basis. After his real estate business was closed, Crawford joined a law firm called Watson, Crawford and Graves in an attempt to recover his losses.[31]

In 1874, many of Crawford's friends who had been associated with the Liberal Republican movement in 1872, together with many persons who would join the "Greenback" movement in 1876, formed an Independent Reform party. Crawford's name was mentioned as a possible Independent Reform candidate for congressman, but he was not nominated. Privately, he urged the defeat of Grant and the Republican party, but he took no active role in the canvass of the party. The effects of the depression plus the coming of great hordes of grasshoppers to Kansas in 1874 caused some uneasiness among the Republicans. But Governor Osborn called a special session of the legislature to meet two weeks before the election for the purpose of passing legislation to alleviate the situation. The tactic worked, and Osborn defeated James C. Cusey, the Independent Reform candidate, by 48,594 to

35,301. However, J. R. Goodin, the Independent Reform candidate from the Second District, was able to capture one of the three congressional seats.[32]

In 1876, Crawford was the Independent Greenback candidate for Congress from the Third District. A letter written to the Emporia *Globe* on December 4, 1874, shows that his Greenback ideas had been forming long before his candidacy:

> For fourteen long, weary months the people have been dragging themselves slowly through the mire of a financial panic, such as the world has seldom witnessed. . . . Already it has created wide-spread distress, and unless relief is afforded by the present Congress, financial ruin is inevitable. . . .
>
> They [Congress] cannot say, let the people go to work, because there is no work to be done and no money with which to do it. The laboring people are willing to work, but who can employ or pay them . . . nobody, until Congress moves in the right direction.
>
> While the Government undertakes to furnish a circulating medium, let it furnish an amount sufficient to meet the demands of trade. The contraction policy, whether dictated by Wall Street or otherwise, has been tested, and the result, so far, is general stagnation under a fourteen months' panic, with the end still in an uncertain future. Coupled with this contraction policy has been another no less detrimental to the interest of the people. Millions of dollars have been collected by the Government annually and applied to the payment of bonds not due for many years, under the frivolous pretext of keeping up the credit of the country.

Crawford continued his letter by suggesting that the government halt the prepayment of bonds and use the money thus diverted to build up the transportation system in the West. The great resources, thus tapped, would more than repay the country, and it would also help to end the economic depression.[33]

Crawford apparently took no active part in the organization of the Independent Greenback party on the state level. The Greenbackers called an "Independent Reform Convention" in Topeka on July 27. They nominated M. E. Hudson for governor and endorsed the National Greenback candidates for president and vice-president, Peter Cooper and Newton Booth. The Democrats met in Topeka on August 23 and nominated John Martin for governor and endorsed the Democratic presidential nomination of Samuel J. Tilden. A resolution was passed appointing a committee to confer with the Greenbackers to see if a union against the Republican party could be effected. The attempt was made but no agreement was reached concerning a gubernatorial candidate and any possible fusion with the Greenbackers for congressmen was left to the congressional districts concerned. Meanwhile the Republicans met in Topeka and endorsed Rutherford B. Hayes for president and nominated George T. Anthony for governor.[34]

Crawford was involved in a serious attempt to fuse the Independent Greenback and the Democratic tickets in the Third Congressional District. The Greenbackers met on Thursday, August 24, in Emporia and nominated Crawford for Congress. Crawford went before the Democratic convention, which was held in Emporia the next day, and agreed to support Tilden if Cooper seemed to have no chance of being elected. According to some reports, he also agreed to support whomever the convention might nominate for Congress. There was still considerable hope among many Greenbackers and Democrats that a union could be made on the congressional level. The Emporia attempt was regarded as a test case to see if fusion could be accomplished. Crawford and Thomas L. Davis, a Democrat, were placed in nomination by the Democratic convention. There was considerable political and personal bitterness exchanged between the Crawford and Davis supporters. Crawford supporters alleged that the handsome Mr. Davis had made an insulting request of a lady in an Emporia hotel, while Davis's friends alleged that Crawford was not a polished enough speaker to meet Thomas Ryan, the Republican nominee, on the stump. The Democratic convention chose Davis. Crawford, according to the *Commonwealth,* agreed to accept the situation and make no canvass on his own behalf.[35]

During the month of September, there were some reports that the Greenbackers in the Third District wanted to get Crawford back in the race, but Crawford remained silent. In mid-October, however, there was an event which put Crawford back in the contest. The St. Louis *Globe Democrat* published a series of letters which Davis had written to a young widow. Davis, who had a wife and three children, had met the young lady in question during a train trip to St. Louis. He had asked her permission to write to her and there was an exchange of letters and pictures. The affair apparently never got beyond the letter writing stage, but when the young lady made some discreet inquiries and found that her correspondent was married, she was persuaded to allow the publication of his letters. Davis had admiringly written of her "lovely beautiful sad face, with golden hair and heavenly eyes," hardly the sort of thing which, when published, would enhance his congressional chances.[36]

On October 17, two days after the publication of the letters in Kansas, Davis withdrew from the race, leaving the Democrats without a candidate. Crawford's friends, including former Senator Ross, C. V. Eskridge, and C. K. Holliday, quickly made arrangements for a vigorous Crawford campaign. On October 20, Crawford opened his rejuvenated campaign by making a speech at the courthouse at Emporia. His speech was largely concerned with money matters. He spoke of the coming election as a test to determine "whether this is to be a government of the people, and administered in the interest of all, or whether it is to be and remain subverted and used for the benefit of a monied aristocracy." He accused the federal government of having brought on an unnatural panic by its money policy. Specifically, he opposed the 1866 and 1869 contraction policy of the government, the demonetizing of silver in 1873, and the Specie Resumption Law of 1875.

The latter, according to Crawford, "was wicked in its inception, and hellish in its design." Crawford contended that there simply was not enough gold in the world to do business in the age of steam power. Gold, he asserted, "is a relic of barbarism, and can no more be compared to our national greenback currency as a circulating medium than can be compared the speed of a jackass to the lightning streaks of electricity." Crawford demanded of Congress a "uniform national currency, issued by the government direct, and made a full legal tender for all debts, public and private . . ." which would be "convertible into a low interest bearing bond, at the pleasure of the holder." The proposed system, he declared, would destroy the present monopoly in money and allow the expansion or contraction of currency "in proportion as the business interest of the country demanded." Referring to the "bloody shirt" policy of the Republicans, Crawford noted that the war was over insofar as the soldiers were concerned, "but not so with bondholders, public jobbers and Wall Street gamblers."[37]

Crawford's speech came only eighteen days before the November election and the campaign began to move at a feverish pace. The day after the Emporia speech, the Democratic central committee met and accepted the withdrawal of Thomas L. Davis, while endorsing the candidacy of Crawford. Two days later, the Kansas City *Times* strongly endorsed Crawford, characterizing him as one who "has not enriched himself at the public crib"; one who is experienced in public affairs; and one who is "certainly preferable to Ryan, who in this race is but the creature of a combination formed to dispose the spoils." Crawford carried his campaign to nine cities between October 31 and November 4. In spite of Davis's withdrawal, the Republican candidate, Thomas Ryan, administered a crushing defeat to Crawford. The election count showed Ryan with 25,171 votes to 11,634 for Crawford. The Republicans also won the other two congressional seats and Republican George T. Anthony easily won the three-way contest for governor, polling 69,173 votes to Democrat John Martin's 46,204, while Greenbacker M. E. Hudson got only 6,020 votes.[88]

During the years 1875 and 1876, Crawford had begun to extend his law practice to include considerable work in Topeka and Washington, D. C. In 1876, at the request of Governor Thomas A. Osborn, he seems to have done some preliminary work in Washington concerning the state's claims against the federal government. In 1876 or early 1877, Crawford established himself in a law partnership with his brother-in-law in Topeka, George S. Chase. His name stopped appearing in the "Attorneys-at-Law" directory in the Emporia *Ledger* with the January 4, 1877, issue. Crawford moved his family to Topeka at approximately the same date.[39]

When the 1877 legislature met, the Republicans had an overwhelming majority. After six joint sessions and sixteen ballots were taken to choose Preston B. Plumb of Emporia for the U. S. Senate, the legislature returned to its routine business. On February 9, 1877, state Senator Almerin Gillett, a Republican from Emporia, introduced Senate bill 179, a bill to appoint a state claims agent in Washington. The bill went through the normal legislative channels without much comment. The Senate passed the bill by a 23 to 4 vote on February 24 and the House approved on March 3 by a 73 to 5 vote. The bill was signed by the governor on the same day and two days later, Governor George T. Anthony sent several appointments to the Senate for confirmation. Among those appointments were the directors of the normal schools at Emporia, Leavenworth, and Concordia, and "S. J. Crawford, of Topeka, to be State agent for the prosecution of State claims, under the law of March 3, 1877." All the appointments were approved without incident. The confirmation seems to have been accomplished without much comment on the floor of the House or Senate or in the newspapers.[40] Thus Crawford, who had denounced George Anthony and the Republicans during the campaign of 1876, was appointed state agent by Governor Anthony and confirmed by a Republican state Senate.

Crawford enjoyed considerable success in his new job as state claims agent in Washington during the Anthony administration, but he had not yet completely given up his political ambitions.[41] In 1878, he made his last attempt to secure an elective office when he announced that he would be an Independent candidate for congressman-at-large. This time Crawford was running for a nonexistent congressional seat. After the regular nominations for the three congressional districts had been completed, Crawford announced on September 24 that he felt that Kansas deserved more than three congressmen, and he proposed to place his name on the ballot for congressman-at-large in the hope that the House would admit him. His argument was that Kansas had a population in 1878 of 825,000 and only three congressmen while Maryland, for example, had only 780,000 population and six representatives. He contended that Congress would see the validity of his claim and admit him if the people of Kansas gave him a large vote. Crawford's announcement also made it clear that he had not given up his Greenback ideas, although he placed the emphasis of his campaign upon the idea of an additional seat in Congress.[42]

The idea of Kansas obtaining an additional congressional seat struck a responsive chord among many Kansas editors, Republican and Democratic. The Topeka *Commonwealth* endorsed Crawford in spite of his "wild Greenback ideas" and placed his name on its masthead under the names of the three regular Republican nominees for Congress. Editorially, the *Commonwealth* pointed out that this would be an aid in prosecuting the state claims in Washington while assuring its readers that the "Greenback Craze" would soon end. The Emporia *Ledger* followed suit and agreed that Kansas was entitled to a larger representation in Congress. The *Ledger* admitted to disagreeing with Crawford on the money question, but it endorsed him as a "straightforward conscientious man, [who] can and will do the State good service if elected and admitted to a seat in Congress." A Democratic paper, the *Western Spirit,* also endorsed Crawford and concluded that "Crawford has really been the only Representative Kansas has had in Congress the past two years."[43]

Not everybody in the Republican party, however, was convinced that Crawford's election would be a good thing. The Atchison *Champion,* in an editorial dated October 4, pointed out that if the House were organized by the Democrats and the next presidential election should be thrown into the House of Representatives, where each state voted as a unit, and if one of the three Kansas congressional seats should go to the Democrats, the House might vote to admit Crawford in an attempt to neutralize the Kansas vote by splitting it two and two. The *Champion,* therefore, called upon the Republican central committee to meet and select a man to run against Crawford. Crawford was, after all, a Democratic "Fiatist" who had gone "with Greeley and stayed." On October 5, the Republican central committee accepted the suggestion and appointed J. R. Hallowell from Cherokee County as their candidate for congressman-at-large. The *Ledger* and the *Commonwealth* dutifully hoisted Hallowell's name to their masthead as the approved Republican slate, but the *Commonwealth* continued to place Crawford's name immediately below the list which included Hallowell.[44]

Hallowell made an active campaign, but Crawford seems to have confined his activity to occasional speeches in the Topeka vicinity. When the election results were announced, Crawford once again learned the power of party regularity in Kansas. He was defeated 73,978 to 60,158. Crawford's vote totaled about the same as the combined Democratic and Greenbacker votes for governor. The Republican candidates from the three congressional districts were also victorious, but Hallowell was never seated.[45]

The 1878 campaign was Crawford's last. The decade beginning in 1868 had been marked by repeated defeats. As a Republican he had been unsuccessful in his attempts to obtain a seat in the United States House of Representatives in 1868 or in the Senate in 1871; as a Liberal Republican in 1872, his ambitions were thwarted when the regular Republican party succeeded in organizing the Kansas legislature; and he was decisively beaten when he ran as an independent Greenback in 1876 and 1878 for congressman. Republican party defectors were seldom successful political candidates during the first score of years of Kansas statehood.

10

A
NEW
CAREER

Samuel J. Crawford was confirmed as state agent on March 5, 1877; it was a position which he would occupy until March 15, 1891. His commission was issued on the sixth and delivered to him on the ninth, although he did not post the necessary bond until the nineteenth of March. The authority for the appointment was Chapter 176, Kansas Laws of 1877, which included four sections. Section one provided for the types of claims to be prosecuted against the federal government. It included a percentage of the proceeds from the sale of public lands disposed of by the United States in Kansas; these were the so-called five per cent claims. Another category was called the "school lands"; this was based upon a provision which provided that sections 16 and 36 of the public lands should be set aside for school purposes. Since some of these sections had already been sold, the state claimed indemnity for their loss. Another major category for which the state made claim was that which had to do with the money spent by the state in organizing troops for military service both in the Civil War and in the Indian wars. Section one also contained a provision which required money recovered to be paid directly to the state treasurer rather than to the agent. Section two required the posting of a $20,000 bond by the state agent.[1]

Sections three and four concerned the amount and method of compensation to the agent. These sections stipulated that the governor, auditor, and attorney-general of the state would make an agreement with the agent, who was to be paid no more than 10 per cent of the money or land recovered. The agent was to bear all of his own expenses and his compensation was not to be taken from any source other than that received by the state from claims prosecuted by the agent. The provision concerning the recovery of land was subsequently changed by the legislature, making the payment in money rather than land.[2] The actual contract between Crawford and the state was not completed until October 3, 1877. It allowed Crawford 10 per cent of money and land recovered, the maximum allowed by the statute.[3]

On May 30, 1877, soon after his arrival in Washington, Crawford wrote to his Topeka law partner concerning his progress in prosecuting the claims of the state. He pointed out that the military claims, specifically the Price raid claims, could not be paid without an act of Congress because the law dealing with such matters had expired on January 1, 1876. Missouri, Kentucky, and Minnesota had been paid similar claims but Kansas had failed to collect because they had had no state agent. Crawford described to his partner the "immense amount of work" necessary to prepare the claims for the next meeting of the Congress. He had compiled and bound every act of Congress relating to Kansas since 1854, together with laws relating to the military and Indian claims. He wrote: "I deemed it best to take every precautionary step to secure success in the end, and sooner or later will succeed with every claim presented, because they are right. . . ." Turning to the matter of compensation for his work, he professed to be "somewhat embarrassed by the small per cent paid by Kansas as compared with what is paid by other states." None of the states, he maintained, paid less than 20 per cent on the amount secured, and Indiana paid 25 per cent. Yet, he quickly added, "I shall exert every effort to the extent of my ability, and exhaust every resource, and trust to the legislature to do what, in its judgment may be deemed right."[4]

On June 30, 1877, Crawford presented the state's claim for "five per centum" before J. A. Williamson, commissioner of the General Land Office. The claim was based upon section three of the act admitting Kansas to statehood. The act provided: "that five per centum of the net proceeds of sales of all public lands lying within said state, which shall be sold by Congress . . . shall be paid to said state." Crawford followed this up with a detailed statement concerning the military claims of the state. This argument took the form of a statement signed by Governor George Anthony and dated October 20, 1877. During the same year, Crawford asked for indemnity school lands in lieu of sections 16 and 36, which had been sold by the federal government. The school lands claim was adjusted almost immediately in favor of the state. In a ruling by the commissioner of the General Land Office, dated August 14, 1877, and confirmed by the secretary of interior on August 18, Kansas was allowed to choose indemnity lands of more than 267,000 acres. The state also received a favorable decision on the "five per cent" claims, but the actual appropriation was delayed until action was taken on March 3, 1881, by Congress.[5]

In 1879, a constitutional question arose in regard to the payment of the state agent. The legislature asked the attorney-general of the state to give an opinion as to the validity of paying Crawford 10 per cent out of the school funds he had recovered. Attorney-General Willard Davis ruled that the state constitution held that the school fund was perpetual and "shall not be diminished." He therefore gave his opinion that section four (allowing the agent 10 per cent of lands recovered), Chapter 176, Laws 1877, was void. To avoid this constitutional difficulty, the legislature voted to pay Crawford in cash for the lands recovered, the money to be taken from the general fund. Crawford received about $56,000 by the authority of the 1879 legislature.[6]

In 1883, George W. Glick became the first Democratic governor in the history of the state. Soon after the beginning of his administration, the legislature approved an act which gave Crawford additional responsibilities. He was authorized to investigate "all matters pertaining to grants of land made by Congress to aid in the construction of railroads within the state of Kansas." Crawford soon gathered evidence that many of the railroads in Kansas were claiming land to which they had no right and causing certain land to be withheld from the market. Crawford first attacked the claims of the Atchison, Topeka and Santa Fe Railroad Company. By August, he had prepared a brief and presented it to Commissioner of the Land Office N. C. McFarland and Secretary of Interior Henry M. Teller. Crawford soon received a ruling which opened to settlement the lands previously withdrawn on behalf of the Santa Fe Railroad in Kansas. Crawford simultaneously acted as attorney on behalf of a number of private citizens who were interested in the land withdrawn for the railroads, thus making his investigation of the railroad grants doubly profitable. He later broadened his attack to include the Kansas Pacific and other railroads in Kansas.[7]

Crawford's term as state agent seems to have been very rewarding both from the standpoint of personal satisfaction and financial gain. He served under five different governors, representing both the Republican and Democratic parties. In 1882, Milton Reynolds, whom Crawford had denounced as a "Copperhead" during his administration, filed the following dispatch from Washington:

. . . These State claims have by an act of the Legislature been placed in the hands of Ex-Governor S. J. Crawford for adjustment and collection. For five years he has worked with a diligence, fidelity, and ability worthy of the highest praise, and his success has been the much merited and honorable reward of consummate tact and skill. His standing with the heads of departments is such as only reflect the highest honor upon the State. Prudent, conservative, careful and cautious in statement, he has presented no claim that was not honest and justly due the State.[8]

By the time of Crawford's retirement from the position in 1891, he had succeeded in recovering 276,000 acres of land for the state, plus about $1,200,000. In addition, he had been largely responsible for the return of 850,000 acres of public land to the market.[9]

Crawford invested his earnings into diversified interests. Among his holdings by 1891 were the $75,000 Crawford building in Topeka, numerous sections of land scattered around the state, and almost half of the capital stock of the *Kansas Farmer*. He and his family were able to enjoy long summer vacations at Nantucket and other resort areas. Crawford's only son, George, was sent to Yale University. His only daughter, Florence, was often mentioned in the "society columns" of the Topeka newspapers. Her marriage, on December 1, 1892, to Arthur Capper, a popular writer for the Topeka *Capital* who later became Kansas governor and United States senator, was the social event of the season.[10]

Crawford's tenure as state agent was marked by a decline in the amount of his political activity and by his return to the Republican party. His political activity was largely confined to personal letters and an occasional "letter to the editor" for publication. His name was mentioned on several occasions as a possible candidate for governor or senator, but he apparently never gave such speculation any encouragement. His 1878 attempt to obtain a congressional seat was his last divergence from the Republican party until after he left his position as state agent. His return to the party was emphasized by a speech he made at Pomona on October 5, 1880. In this speech, he admitted that he had been in favor of the triple standard (gold, silver, and greenbacks), but, he reasoned, the people had decided otherwise. Resumption had been accomplished; the route taken was longer than the one he had favored, but it had been traveled nonetheless. Crawford characterized the Democratic presidential aspirant, Winfield S. Hancock, as a gallant soldier, but one who would be "used." James A. Garfield, on the other hand, was pictured as a "statesman." Crawford also gave his support to the state Republican ticket. His comparison of the two major parties confirmed his orthodoxy. The Republicans were the party that saved the union, passed the homestead act, made agricultural colleges possible, built the railroads, and was responsible for the phenomenal growth of Kansas. The Credit Mobilier and the "salary grab" were insignificant when compared to the crimes of the Democrats. The bill of particulars against the Democrats made them responsible for the spoils system, the war with Mexico, the breakdown of the Missouri Compromise, the "rape of Kansas," the Civil War, the empty treasury, treason, and the evils of reconstruction in the South.[11]

Crawford was allowed to continue as state agent during the administration of Democratic Governor George W. Glick (1883–85). Fortunately for Crawford, his success in recovering land and money for the state had been so marked that the Democrats not only allowed him to continue, but they added new authority to his job. They authorized him to represent the state in attempting to reopen some of the railroad lands for public sale. He prepared several briefs which were supplied to the proper government officials and the newspapers. He generally received bipartisan support although there was some Republican dissatisfaction. Crawford's vigorous prosecution of the state's case, contending that as much as eight hundred thousand acres of previously withdrawn land should be opened for sale, won him praise from many newspapers. In addition to many Kansas papers, the Chicago

Tribune, Kansas City *Times,* and New York *Truth* had words of praise for Crawford's work.[12]

The favorable publicity may have been responsible for some embarrassing speculation in regard to Crawford's being the Republican candidate for governor at the next election. Such talk, more than a year before the election, was not only premature but it could have cost Crawford his job during a Democratic administration. The speculation stemmed from an article in the Kansas City *Journal,* printed in mid-October.

> There is a new gubernatorial boom on now, which is in the very first stages of incipiency, and hasn't been very much talked about as yet. The movement is in favor of Hon. Samuel J. Crawford as the Republican gubernatorial nominee of 1884, the idea being that he will take well with the antimonopolist reformers. . . .[13]

Crawford wasted no time in denying the accuracy of the story. His reply was dated Washington, September 25:

> To the Editor of the *Commonwealth*
>
> I see in your paper of Saturday an article clipped from the Kansas City *Journal* of recent date, to the effect that a movement is on foot to make me the Republican candidate for Governor in 1884. . . .
>
> The article, of course, is mere newspaper gossip, and ordinarily I should take no notice of it, but in view of the work I have in hand and to which I intend to adhere until the end is reached, it is perhaps best for you to say that there is no truth in the article referred to.
>
> I am not a candidate, and under no circumstances would I accept the position mentioned.[14]

Crawford's letter seems to have put an end to any "Crawford for Governor" boom which may have been budding.

Meanwhile, in Washington, Crawford's case in regard to the

railroad lands had been heard and a decision was forthcoming. On October 22, 1883, he telegraphed Governor Glick:

> All indemnity lands heretofore withdrawn from the Santa Fe road, and not certified, are restored to the market. This opens to settlement over a million acres of land between Larned and the west line of the State.

To this Glick replied on the same day: "Your dispatch received. In the name of the State of Kansas I thank you." Six days later Crawford wired:

> Land Commissioner McFarland today signed an order cancelling a list of fifty one thousand acres of indemnity land of the Santa Fe railroad company, and ordered the same restored to market. This land lies west of Nettleton, and is an addition to the million acres restored last week.[15]

During the next several years, Crawford continued to press for further adjustment of the railroad grants. He received some satisfaction from the commissioner of the General Land Office and the secretary of the interior, but their decisions often required implementation by the Congress. Crawford, therefore, often appeared or presented arguments to the House Committee on Public Lands concerning the adjustment of the land grants. Crawford's vigorous actions on behalf of the state kept his name before the public and prompted continued speculation as to his political future. In the January 23, 1885, edition of the Wichita *Daily Beacon,* there appeared an editorial suggesting that Crawford should replace John J. Ingalls as United States senator from Kansas. The editorial reasoned that Crawford had done more for the state than the entire Kansas delegation in Congress. The *Beacon,* however, did not follow the editorial with any campaign and the legislature reelected Ingalls by an overwhelming majority.[16]

Republican Congressman from the Fifth District John A. Anderson was one of those who shared Crawford's views that the grants to the railroads had been excessive. Accordingly, he was one of Crawford's chief supporters in Washington. When the Republican nominating committee met at Concordia in 1886, it did not renominate Anderson. Whereupon, Crawford charged that the railroad interests had "tried to get to John in Washington and they couldn't so they came home to do it. . . ." He warned that "it is not John Anderson alone that the railroads are striking, but at every man who cannot be used or controlled by them." Crawford expressed the hope that Republicans from Anderson's congressional district would condemn this "political trickery and fraud." The result was that there were two Republicans on the ballot; but in spite of this division, Anderson won rather handily. The final count showed Anderson with 19,240 votes to A. S. Wilson, also a Republican, 3,856, and J. G. Lowe, Democrat, 12,751.[17]

Crawford quietly continued his claims work for the next four years without becoming involved in any political disputes. In 1890, however, he became embroiled in an argument with certain members of the Farmers Alliance; this feud may have been one of the factors which caused him to resign as state agent in 1891. Crawford started the dispute with a letter dated July 18, 1890, to the editor of the Topeka *Daily Capital*. In this letter, he noted that L. L. Polk, president of the National Alliance, was "out in Kansas, telling the farmers what they ought to do politically, and otherwise." Crawford charged that Polk's aim was to split the Republican party, thus enabling the Democrats to win. According to Crawford: "If the farmers were left free from the pernicious advice and hellish influence of such men as Polk . . . they would be happy, contented, and prosperous." Crawford contended that the farmers were not really as downtrodden as they believed. If they would figure the aggregate value of their farms, stock, etc., and compare this to their indebtedness, they would see that there was no truth in "the wild, reckless statements which have been put in circulation by these designing, wicked montebanks, for selfish and political purposes."[18]

The Alliance, in the midst of organizing a political party in

Kansas, could scarcely allow this attack to go unanswered. The Topeka *Advocate,* the official paper of the Farmers Alliance, answered on July 30. The editors of this paper took sixteen pages to present a comprehensive biography of Crawford. They pointed out that Crawford had joined the Liberal Republicans in 1872, and the Greenback party in 1876 and 1878. During this time, he was said to have supported many of the reforms which the Alliance later sponsored. They totaled Crawford's compensation as state agent for the period 1879 to 1887; the amount came to $152,236, which they implied was the price of Crawford's return to the Republican party. Crawford's reply was dated August 10; he conceded that he had supported the Greenback movement but he argued that the resumption act had destroyed the reason for the existence of the Greenback party. In addition, he charged that the South's adoption of the "nullification and shot-gun policy" was a threat to the nation more serious than the economic situation. "Under such a state of affairs, I had no difficulty in finding where I belonged," i.e., in the Republican party. The Democratic party, in Crawford's view, was still suspect because the "nullifiers of the south and the anarchists of the north, without exception, vote the Democratic ticket." Crawford concluded that "many Kansas farmers are so busy having conventions that they spend all their money and don't do any farming." As the dispute continued, the attacks from both sides became more personal. The Alliance characterized Crawford as "the cringing tool of a domestic and foreign plutocracy," while Crawford spoke of the "political tramps, croakers, and animated gasbags" who "discourage, distract and keep the farmers from their work."[19]

During the 1890 campaign, Crawford also became involved in a dispute with William A. Peffer. Crawford owned more stock than any other individual in the *Kansas Farmer*. Peffer was the editor and he aligned the paper with the Alliance. Crawford wrote to Peffer telling him to "talk more crops and less politics." But Peffer obtained the backing of a majority of the stockholders, enabling him to continue his policy of supporting the Alliance despite Crawford's opposition.[20]

The People's or the Populist party as it came to be called, consisted of the members of the Farmers Alliance, the Union Labor, and the former Greenback parties. In Kansas in 1890, they nominated a complete ticket and refused to fuse with the Democrats. Their failure to join the Democrats in the November 4 election probably cost them the control of the state administration; nonetheless they had phenomenal success in electing members of the state legislature and the Congress. They elected 92 of the 125 members of the Kansas House. There were, however, enough carry-over Republicans in the Senate to prevent the Populists from gaining complete control. They captured five of the seven Kansas seats in Congress, including one for the famous Jeremiah ("Sockless") Simpson.[21]

After the election results were known, Crawford asked Governor Lyman Humphrey to accept his resignation as state agent. Humphrey asked Crawford to continue until the new session of the legislature met to confirm a new appointment. The 1891 meeting of the legislature proved to be a stormy one. The Populists organized the House while the Republicans were in control of the Senate. P. P. Elder, a Populist, was elected as Speaker of the House. On January 28, the Populists were able to elect William Peffer to the United States Senate replacing John J. Ingalls, who had been associated with the "money powers" in the view of the Populists. Since Governor Humphrey had made known Crawford's wish to retire as state agent, the Populists were deprived of an opportunity to force his resignation. They did find, however, that they could cause him some embarrassment by failing to approve an appropriation to compensate him for the money and land he had recovered for the state. The Senate passed Senate bill 283, which provided about $17,000 for Crawford's payment, on February 18. The bill came to a vote in the House on March 9 and 49 votes were cast for the bill as against 36 opposed. Speaker Elder, however, ruled that the bill had failed because of "a lack of a constitutional majority." The Republican Senate countered by including Crawford's payment in a miscellaneous appropriation bill. As the session neared an end, the Populists were left with a choice of approving the entire bill or allowing some necessary appropriations to go unpassed. They finally approved the miscellaneous money bill on the last day of the session. On the next to the last day of the legislative session, the Senate confirmed the appointment of William Wallace Martin of Fort Scott to replace Crawford as state agent.[22]

Crawford's tenure as state agent ended on March 15, 1891. Several motives for his resignation may be suggested. Probably the most important factor was his feud with the Populists. Although they did not have complete control of the legislature, they could easily make it difficult for him to collect his fee. Even though he had a contract with the state, no money could be delivered without an appropriation act. Another potential source of harassment would likely have been the newly elected attorney-general. J. N. Ives was the only Populist state official elected in 1890, and he believed that a contract with a state agent was unconstitutional. When Crawford's successor attempted to enter into the required contract with the governor, auditor, and attorney-general, Ives refused to sign. Subsequently, the Supreme Court declared the act creating a state agent unconstitutional. Yet another contributing factor may have been that Crawford had already secured most of the state's claims, leaving little to be gained by continuing in that position.[23]

The position of state agent was the last official position Crawford ever held. It was a position which enabled him to gain fame and fortune. Seven different legislatures over a period of fourteen years voted him compensation totaling more than $200,000. During the same period he handled land cases on behalf of certain Indian tribes which netted him a similar amount. He also had an extensive private practice.[24]

Crawford returned to Washington to continue his practice after his resignation as state agent. Soon after his return certain investors in Boston inquired of Crawford concerning the safety of their investments in view of the emergence of the Alliance in Kansas. Crawford's answer was published in the Boston *Herald,* the St. Louis *Globe Democrat,* and the Chicago *Times.* He assured the investors that there were still good farmers and good crops in Kansas in spite of the publicity given to a few agitators. He contended that certain speculators were using the Alliance to frighten investors into selling at a discount. Crawford urged his inquirer not to sell his securities at a sacrifice "on account of false reports put in circulation by schemers, croakers, agitators, demagogues and political montebanks."[25] When Crawford returned to Topeka in August 1891 he was interviewed by a reporter from the *Capital.* His answers indicated that his ideas largely coincided with those of the Republican party. When asked what he thought of the idea of an Alliance bank and warehouse in each county, he replied that the idea was only another scheme doomed to failure. The successful farmer, he argued, needs no scheme to know how to build and when to sell, because the basic qualities needed are simply "individuality and self reliance." In answer to a question concerning the McKinley tariff, he defended it as protecting labor against the pauper labor of foreign countries, increasing the domestic market for farm goods and as providing a necessary source of government income.[26]

Kansas Senator Preston B. Plumb died on December 20, 1891. Once again Crawford's name was connected with the speculation as to who the new senator would be. The St. Louis *Globe Democrat* reported that some of Crawford's friends had suggested his name to Governor Humphrey. Crawford, according to the dispatch, had declined to be considered as a candidate but certain of his friends believed that he might serve the remaining year of the term out of deference to his friend Plumb and "in the interest of the state." The governor ended this line of speculation when he appointed Bishop Waldo Perkins of Oswego on January 1, 1892, to fill out the unexpired senatorial term.[27]

After Crawford vacated the position as state agent, he found himself gradually becoming dissatisfied with the policies of the Republican party. Perhaps the panic of 1893 set him to thinking on money matters again. On June 15, 1895, he penned a letter to Chairman Thomas H. Carter of the National Republican Committee. He wrote:

> The Republican Party received a slap square in the face for stopping the coinage of silver in 1873.
>
> The Democratic Party blotted itself out of existence by repealing the silver purchasing act and giving nothing in lieu thereof. And now it remains for the Republican Party to either follow the wake of Democracy and go down and out, or heed the demands of the country and establish itself in the hearts of the people.
>
> Gentlemen who are trying to commit the Republican Party to a single gold standard should consider well what they are doing, because, if they succeed, they will wreck the party just as certain as the election takes place in November.[28]

Crawford apparently went along with the party in 1896 in spite of its refusal to accept his advice, but the outbreak of the Spanish-American War and the beginning of what he considered imperialism was more than he could take. In September 1898 he laid down a barrage of letters opposing the policy of territorial expansion. In his view, the country was caught up in a "whirl of midsummer madness." He felt that the country could not bear the additional burden which would be imposed by the annexation of Cuba, Puerto Rico, and the Philippines. Such territorial acquisitions would necessitate an increase in the army and navy and other "proposed wildeyed schemes such as the $100,000,000 Nicaraguan canal." Not only that, but Crawford warned that the "new fangled colonial empire schemes" would cost thousands of lives unless the "tramps, jingoes, and yellow journalists" were stopped.[29]

By the time of the election of 1900, Crawford had become so disillusioned with the Republican party that he openly supported William J. Bryan. The reelection of McKinley, in his view, would mean expensive colonies, a prohibitive tariff, a large standing army, trusts, monopolies, sacrifice of lives, higher taxes, and higher prices. The Democrats were allowed to use one of his anti-imperialism letters as a piece of campaign literature. It was entitled: "Folder No. 52, A Veteran's Letter Giving Sound Reasons Why Union Soldiers and Everybody Else Should Vote the Democratic Ticket in 1900, Views of Hon. S. J. Crawford, Ex-Governor of Kansas."[30]

Over a period of the next decade, Crawford continued to oppose imperialism, the tariff, and the trusts. "These things called the Big Stick, colonial empire and world-wide power, are the sheerest of rot," he wrote. The tariff, in his view, had "not only spawned upon the country a brood of avaricious trusts, but it has destroyed competition by making it possible for the trusts to monopolize the business of the country." He advised Kansas stockmen to form an organization and swear not to ship any beef to the stockyards until "beef trusts" began paying a reasonable price.[31]

As Crawford grew older, he began to attract some attention in Washington as a storyteller. His appearance, described as "tall, soldierly, and straight, with snow white hair and a military mustache," added to this reputation. From time to time, the Washington *Post* would carry stories about Crawford's exploits in the Civil War or as governor of the state. About 1905, he became interested in obtaining the Medal of Honor as some of his friends were doing. He found that most of his companions were dead so he called upon the Kansas State Historical Society to furnish him with the newspaper accounts of his exploits during the Civil War. When Secretary George Martin was unable to produce much corroborating information, Crawford seems to have given up the idea. Soon thereafter, Henry W. Blair, a close friend of Crawford's and a Washington attorney, wrote to Martin suggesting that Crawford be given an honorary degree from the University of Kansas, Martin sent the letter along to Frank H. Hodder of the History Department. Hodder, however, replied that the university had a long-standing policy against giving such degrees.[32]

Although Martin was unable to assist Crawford in either obtaining a Medal of Honor or an honorary degree, he did encourage him to contribute a paper concerning his administration to the *Kansas Historical Collections*. Crawford did extensive research himself and hired additional work done at the historical society in 1905. He used the letter books from his administration, the commission books from the office of the secretary of state, newspapers, the adjutant general's records, and other manuscripts. A part of this research may have gone into an article by Edwin Manning entitled, "A Kansas Soldier." Martin made it a practice to get someone to "father" articles written about the various administrations, although they were generally written by the former governors themselves. Crawford seems to have kept most of the material, however, and about 1910 he began to work on an autobiography. The result was a book called *Kansas in the Sixties,* published in August 1911. The four-hundred-page book is clear evidence that, although his memory was not always accurate, his mind was still very much alert. In addition, his style was interesting and the book generally received good reviews.[33]

About 1900, Crawford had purchased a farm on Spring River near Baxter Springs, Kansas. He loved to spend his time there on his "model" farm experimenting with new farming methods. Although he continued his Washington practice until about 1911, he spent progressively less time in Washington and more on his farm during his last years. He believed that the farm was the ideal place to live; "the poorest and most improvident of the farmers live better, have better health, see less trouble, and are happier than the most wealthy of the millionaires."[34]

Crawford was seventy-eight years old on April 10, 1913. He spent his last summer on his farm near Baxter Springs. The heat there in August weakened him and he was brought to Topeka. On October 21, 1913, he died at his home at Fifth and Harrison. Tributes came in from all over the country. He was remembered as a gallant soldier of the Civil War; the youngest governor in the history of the state; the leader of an expedition against the Indians; and as the successful claims agent for the state.[35]

In retrospect, Crawford's political career may be divided into three distinct phases. During his first decade in Kansas, Crawford rose from country lawyer to governor of the state. His courageous conduct during the Civil War, combined with a unique political situation in Kansas, enabled him to become governor at age twenty-nine. Two years later, the death of Senator James H. Lane placed Crawford in a position from which he was able to assume leadership of the Republican party in Kansas. During his "lame duck" second term, however, his power began to wane. His unsuccessful bid for a congressional seat in 1868 signaled the end of his leadership of the party in Kansas. After his defeat, he resigned as governor and accepted command of the Nineteenth Kansas Cavalry on an expedition against the Indians. Perhaps he hoped to refurbish his political career with another successful war campaign.

The next phase of his political career was marked by a decade of frustration and defeat. He represented three political parties in four attempts to obtain a seat in the United States Congress. The political climate was such that his easy victories of the sixties were replaced by repeated defeats in the seventies. It was a decade in which Kansas politics was dictated by certain business interests. Votes were bought and sold and Crawford would not or could not join in the bidding.

The third phase of his career began with his appointment as state claims agent. This position enabled him to gain security and a measure of independence. He was never again a serious candidate for an elective position, but he was always quick to express his political views.

Crawford was not a genius, but he was capable of careful

reasoning. He was not an exceptional speaker, but he was able to present an argument effectively. He was sometimes deliberate and sometimes impulsive. The flush of his sudden rise to fame may have left him a little brash, but the subsequent series of failures, followed by renewed success, left him self-assured but unassuming. The force of his personality made no great impression upon the development of the state or the nation, and yet his contribution was not insignificant. He helped to guide the state during its infancy by displaying the qualities which the frontiersmen admired: courage, hard work, honesty, and tenacity.

NOTES

CHAPTER 1

1. *United States Census Report, 1860,* I, 166; Daniel W. Wilder, "Where Kansans Were Born," *Kansas Historical Collections,* IX (1905–06), 507.

2. Nathaniel Thompson Allison, ed., *History of Cherokee County, Kansas and Representative Citizens* (Chicago, 1904), 215. Other general biographies consulted include: Frank W. Blackmar, *Kansas, A Cyclopedia of State History,* 2 vols. (Chicago, 1912), I, 475–76. William E. Connelley, *A Standard History of Kansas and Kansans,* 4 vols. (Chicago, 1918), III, 1202. Thomas L. Harris, "Crawford, Samuel Johnson," in the *Dictionary of American Biography* (New York, 1946), IV, 523–24. [Edwin C. Manning], "Samuel Johnson Crawford," *Kansas Historical Collections,* XII (1911–12), 271–73. Charles R. Tuttle, *A New Centennial History of the State of Kansas* (Madison, 1876), 673–76.

3. Samuel J. Crawford, *Kansas in the Sixties* (Chicago, 1911), 1. This autobiography is a valuable document on the life of Crawford, but it must be used with caution. It was written more than forty years after many of the events it describes and it is often inaccurate. Crawford was seventy-six at the time of publication, yet from the context of this book it is obvious that his mind was still very alert. The book includes a great many documents and he obviously used many others in its preparation. This work will hereafter be cited as: Crawford, *Kansas.*

4. *Ibid.,* 1–2.

5. Daniel W. Wilder, *The Annals of Kansas* (Topeka, 1875), 198–201. Hereafter cited as: Wilder, *Annals.*

6. G. Raymond Gaeddert, *The Birth of Kansas* (Lawrence, 1940), 12.

7. O. E. Learnard, "Organization of the Republican Party," *Kans. Hist. Coll.,* VI (1897–1900), 313; Martha B. Caldwell, "When Horace Greeley Visited Kansas," *Kansas Historical Quarterly,* IX (May 1940), 121–23. The *Kansas Historical Quarterly* will hereafter be cited as *KHQ.*

8. Atchison, *Freedom's Champion,* May 28, 1859. According to Connelley's *A Standard History of Kansas and Kansans,* III, 1202, Crawford attended both the Osawatomie organization meeting and the Republican State Convention in 1859. I can find no verification for this. The above article in the *Freedom's Champion* does, however, mention that there was an attempt to seat six delegates from Anderson County rather than three. It was finally decided to seat them all but allow only the prescribed number to vote.

9. Gaeddert, *Birth of Kansas,* 34–35.

10. Quoted in Wilder, *Annals,* 215. The anti-Negro, antislavery attitude of the Kansas Republicans is explained in Eugene H. Berwanger, *The Frontier Against Slavery: Western Anti-Negro Prejudice and the Slavery Extension Controversy* (Urbana, Illinois, 1967), 97–118.

11. Gaeddert, *Birth of Kansas,* 56–57.

12. Wilder, *Annals,* 201, 225–35.

13. *Ibid.,* 238–46.

14. Gaeddert, *Birth of Kansas,* 22–25.

15. Crawford, *Kansas,* 8.

16. Wilder, *Annals*, 253–58.
17. Gaeddert, *Birth of Kansas*, 96–97.
18. William E. Connelley, ed., "Some Ingalls Letters," *Kans. Hist. Coll.*, XIV (1915–18), 121.
19. Gaeddert, *Birth of Kansas*, 100.
20. David E. Ballard, "The First State Legislature," *Kans. Hist. Coll.*, X (1907–08), 235.
21. John Speer, *The Life of Gen. James H. Lane* (Garden City, Kan., 1897), 224.
22. Gaeddert, *Birth of Kansas*, 102–03.
23. *Ibid.*, 104–06.
24. Wilder, *Annals*, 261.
25. Photostat of the tally sheet of J. J. Ingalls included in Gaeddert, *Birth of Kansas*, 108–09.
26. *Kansas House Journal* (1861), 76.
27. Crawford, *Kansas*, 20–21.

CHAPTER 2

1. Crawford, *Kansas*, 21–22.
2. James G. Blunt, "General Blunt's Account of His Civil War Experiences," *KHQ*, I (May 1932), 213–14.
3. *Official Military History of Kansas Regiments During the War for the Suppression of the Great Rebellion* included in a volume entitled *Report of the Adjutant General of the State of Kansas, 1861–'65* (Topeka, reprinted 1896), 11. This work will hereafter be cited as *Kansas Regiments*.
4. Crawford, *Kansas*, 27.
5. *Kansas Regiments*, 12–13; *The War of the Rebellion: Official Records of the Union and Confederate Armies*, 128 vols. (Washington, 1880–1902), 1 ser., III, 48. Hereafter cited as *Official Records*.
6. *Ibid.*, 72, 106.
7. Crawford, *Kansas*, 37–39; *Kansas Regiments*, 14–15.
8. Muster Roll of the Second Kansas Cavalry from the files of the Kansas adjutant general's office, on microfilm at the Kansas State Historical Society. Crawford had actually reached his twenty-seventh birthday five days before the official muster.
9. *Kansas Regiments*, 20.
10. *Ibid.*; Blunt, "Civil War Experiences," *KHQ*, I, 218.
11. Crawford, *Kansas*, 53, 85; *Kansas Regiments*, 20, briefly describes Lane's role in the organization of the Twelfth Infantry. The best description of the political maneuvering in Kansas during the war is in Albert Castel, *A Frontier State at War: Kansas, 1861–1865* (Ithaca, N.Y., 1958).
12. *Official Records*, 1 ser., XIII, 324–26.
13. This account of the battle is taken from the reports of Generals Blunt and Cooper in *ibid.*, 324–27, 332; Edwin C. Manning, "A Kansas Soldier," *Kans. Hist. Coll.*, X (1907–08), 421–22. The campaign is described in William J. Willey, "The Second Federal Invasion of Indian Territory," *The Chronicles of Oklahoma*, XLIV (Winter, 1966–1967), 420–30.
14. *Official Records*, 1 ser., XIII, 327–28, 331.
15. Crawford, *Kansas*, 57–58.
16. Manning, "A Kansas Soldier," *Kans. Hist. Coll.*, X, 423–24; Crawford, *Kansas*, 66–67. Both of these accounts were written more than forty years after the event in question. *Kansas Regi-*

ments, 25, confirms that Crawford was at least given such an assignment.

17. *Official Records,* 1 ser., XXII, 41–45; Thomas L. Snead, "The Conquest of Arkansas," in Robert Underwood Johnson and Clarence Clough Buel, eds., *Battles and Leaders of the Civil War,* 4 vols. (New York, 1887–88), III, 447–49.

18. *Ibid.,* 449–50; *Official Records,* 1 ser., XXII, 70–77. The battles of Cane Hill and Prairie Grove are ably described in Stephen B. Oates, *Confederate Cavalry West of the River* (Austin, 1961), 85–112.

19. *Ibid.,* 77, 93, 95.

20. Blunt, "Civil War Experiences," *KHQ,* I, 235–36.

21. Crawford, *Kansas,* 102; Crawford and twelve other officers of the Second Kansas to Bassett, January 4, 1863, in Records of the War Department, Office of the Judge Advocate General, Record Group No. 153, "Court Martial of Lt. Col. Owen A. Bassett, 2d Kansas Cavalry" (No. 48, Inventory Entry 18, The National Archives, National Archives and Records Service, General Service Administration, Washington, 1960). Documents concerning the court martial are on microfilm at the Kansas State Historical Society.

22. *Ibid.*

23. Bassett to Cloud, March 15, 1863; General Curtis order for court martial, dated March 28, 1862; "Charges and Specifications Preferred Against Lieutenant Colonel Bassett," n.d.; the court martial proceedings for July 10, 11, 13, and 14, 1863; all in *ibid.; Kansas Regiments,* 31, also contains a brief summary of the proceedings.

24. Castel, *Frontier State at War,* chap. 6; Blunt, "Civil War Experiences," *KHQ,* I, 242–43.

25. This account is based upon material from: Blunt, "Civil War Experiences," *KHQ,* I, 242–47; Crawford, *Kansas,* 95–102; *Kansas Regiments,* 32; and *Official Records,* 1 ser., XXII, 597–99, 601–608.

26. Crawford, *Kansas,* 102.

27. *Ibid.,* 104.

28. *Ibid.,* 106–08.

29. *Ibid.,* 109–117; *Official Records,* 1 ser., XXXIV, pt. 1, 743–46. For a more complete account of the role of the Negro in the war see: Dudley Taylor Cornish, *The Sable Arm: Negro Troops in the Union Army, 1861–1865* (New York, 1956).

30. *Kansas Regiments,* 258.

31. *Ibid.;* Crawford, *Kansas,* 118–34; *Official Records,* 1 ser., XXXIV, pt. 1, 757–58, 698. The "gallantry" of Crawford and his Negro troops is described in Edwin C. Bearss, *Steele's Retreat from Camden and the Battle of Jenkins' Ferry* (Little Rock [1967]), 132–35, 139–44. A more general account of the campaign is Ludwell H. Johnson, *Red River Campaign: Politics and Cotton in the Civil War* (Baltimore, 1958).

32. Crawford, *Kansas,* 134–38.

CHAPTER 3

1. Castel, *A Frontier State at War,* 166–77; Wilder, *Annals,* 378–79.

2. Leavenworth *Daily Conservative,* September 9, 1864; Wendell

Holmes Stephenson's, *The Political Career of General James H. Lane,* Publications of the Kansas State Historical Society, III (Topeka, 1930), 146, describes Lane's August political tour of Kansas.

3. Leavenworth *Daily Conservative,* September 10, 1864; Topeka *Commonwealth,* February 25, 1886.

4. Leavenworth *Daily Conservative,* September 10, 1864; Leavenworth *Times,* February 14, 18, 1886.

5. E. C. Manning, "Kansas Politics in the Early Days: How Governor Crawford was Nominated," a clipping in the Samuel J. Crawford Scrapbook, 3 vols. (Kansas State Historical Society), III. The Kansas State Historical Society will hereafter be cited as KSHS.

6. Leavenworth *Daily Conservative,* September 10, 1864.

7. *Ibid.;* Leavenworth *Times,* February 14, 1886. Wilder in the *Annals* reports Crawford's nomination on the sixth ballot. The *Conservative* reporter considered the first ballot taken at the afternoon session as an "informal poll," thus the discrepancy in the two accounts. There are other discrepancies as to the exact total number of votes cast for each candidate and the number of army delegates voting, but the difference is never more than three.

8. "Who Nominated S. J. Crawford?" Topeka *Commonwealth,* February 25, 1886. It should be noted that most of the testimony on this question came more than twenty years after the event. The occasion was the quartercentennial of Kansas statehood. The Kansas City *Times* started the controversy by publishing a history of the Kansas governorship. In its article on Craw-

ford's administration, it included a subheading, "Crawford Made Governor by Lane." Whereupon the Kansas newspapermen, particularly those who had been participants in the 1864 convention, rushed into the fight and offered testimony. See Kicking Bird [Milton W. Reynolds], Kansas City *Times,* January 24, 1886.

9. E. C. Manning, "Kansas Politics in the Early Days: How Governor Crawford was Nominated," from an undated newspaper clipping, Samuel J. Crawford Scrapbook (KSHS), III.

10. Crawford to James H. Lane, January 14, 1865, Governor Crawford Copybook (Archives, KSHS).

11. Anthony's testimony is found in the Leavenworth *Times,* February 14 and 18, 1886; Leavenworth *Daily Conservative,* September 10–16, 1864.

12. Eldorado *Republican,* February 26, 1886.

13. Wichita *Daily Eagle,* February 16, 1886.

14. Quoted in Kansas City *Times,* February 24, 1886.

15. M. M. Murdock to Governor Crawford, March 14, 1865, Governor's Correspondence (1865–1868), General Correspondence (Archives, KSHS); Crawford to M. M. Murdock, February 16, 1867, Governor Crawford Copybook (Archives, KSHS); "An Open Letter to Jacob Stotler, Esq." dated April 15, 1872, from the Emporia *News,* n.d., Crawford Scrapbook (KSHS), II; Crawford to Hon. Lyman Trumbull, February 21, 1867, Governor Crawford Copybook (Archives, KSHS); Crawford to Senator Fessenden, n.d., Gover-

nor Crawford telegrams copied (Archives, KSHS).

16. [Jacob Stotler], "Session of 1865," Emporia *Weekly Globe,* January 20, 1887, Kansas Legislative Clippings Scrapbook (KSHS), I; John Speer, *Life of Gen. James H. Lane* (Garden City, Kan., 1897), 300; Web Wilder wrote a letter to the Leavenworth *Times,* October 7, 1864, denouncing Lane; the Leavenworth *Evening Bulletin,* September 6, 1864, published the report on Clarke's candidacy.

17. *Official Records,* ser. 1, XXXIV, pt. 1, 757.

18. Crawford, *Kansas,* 134.

19. *Ibid.,* 138.

20. Compare the letters published in the Leavenworth *Daily Conservative,* October 20, 1864, and the Lawrence *Kansas Tribune,* August 28, 1866. See chap. V for further analysis of the issue.

21. Crawford, *Kansas,* 142.

22. Wiley Britton, "Resume of Military Operations in Missouri and Arkansas, 1864–65," in Johnson, *Battles and Leaders of the Civil War* (New York, 1887–88), IV, 374–77; Wilder, *Annals,* 380.

23. Crawford, *Kansas,* 143; *Official Records,* ser. 1, XLI, pt. 1, 484.

24. *Ibid.,* 471, 475.

25. *Ibid.,* 484; Britton, "Resume of Military Operations in Missouri and Arkansas, 1864–65," in Johnson, *Battles and Leaders of the Civil War,* IV, 374–77.

26. This story was hard to substantiate although it was accepted by William E. Connelley in *The Life of Preston B. Plumb, 1837–1891* (Chicago, 1913), which gives a statement of Charles Waring, a member of Curtis's band, as authority. Waring said he followed

Curtis out to the "six-mile house" on the road to Leavenworth (fn 189). The contents of page 190 indicate that Connelley used Crawford's memoirs, published only two years earlier, for his source, although there is no reference to Crawford. Jay Monaghan, *Civil War on the Western Border: 1854–1865* (Boston, 1955) accepts the story of the midnight mutiny without reservation, 331–32.

27. *Official Records,* ser. 1, XLI, pt. 1, 484–85.

28. Leavenworth *Daily Conservative,* October 22, 1864.

29. James G. Blunt, "General Blunt's Account of His Civil War Experiences," *Kansas Historical Quarterly,* I (May 1932), 285–89. There is no reason to believe that Blunt would have withheld information about such an event had it occurred. At the time of his report he was ". . . now freed from the restraints of army regulations" (*ibid.,* 213) and he admitted countermanding or disobeying Curtis's orders on many occasions. If Blunt had been responsible for forcing the battle of Westport he would certainly have taken credit for it.

30. Crawford, *Kansas,* 152.

31. *Official Records,* ser. 1, XLI, pt. 1, 485–86.

32. *Ibid.,* 491–95.

33. *Ibid.,* 601–06; Crawford, *Kansas,* 154.

34. *Ibid.,* 159.

35. *Ibid.,* 160–61; Oskaloosa *Independent,* April 27, 1867; Fort Scott *Monitor* quoted in the Olathe *Mirror,* November 5, 1864. The *Mirror* carried the story of the heroism of Crawford and others at Mine Creek despite the fact it was sup-

porting Crawford's opponent for governor, a rare occurrence in early Kansas journalism.

36. *Official Records,* ser. 1, XLI, pt. 1, 479, 491–99, 501, 520.
37. McDowell Collection (KSHS).
38. Robinson Papers (KSHS).
39. White Cloud *Kansas Chief,* September 15, 1864. Lane's friend and biographer concluded some years later that only the Price raid made the Lane party successful in 1864; Speer, *Life of Gen. James H. Lane,* 334.
40. Leavenworth *Daily Conservative,* September 10, 1864.
41. Bloss joined the Leavenworth *Times* and became an outspoken opponent of the "Lane ticket."
42. Leavenworth *Daily Conservative,* September 16, 17, and October 2, 1864.
43. Oskaloosa *Independent,* October 1, 1864.
44. Atchison *Freedom's Champion,* September 15, 1864.
45. White Cloud *Kansas Chief,* September 22, 1864.
46. Leavenworth *Times,* October 21, 1864; See Chapter II for the story of the capture of the Confederate paymaster.
47. *Ibid.,* October 22–October 26, 1864.
48. *Official Records,* ser. 1, XLI, pt. 1, 465–71; Wilder, *Annals,* 380; letter from Charles Robinson to his wife, October 9, 1864, Robinson Papers (KSHS).
49. Leavenworth *Conservative,* October 8, 1864.
50. *Ibid.,* October 11, 1864.
51. Charles Robinson to his wife, October 16, 1864, Robinson Papers (KSHS).
52. *Official Records,* ser. 1, XLI, pt. 1, 471.

53. Leavenworth *Times,* October 19, 20, 1864.
54. Leavenworth *Daily Conservative,* October 20, 1864.
55. *Ibid.,* October 21, 22, 23, 1864.
56. John Speer, *Life of Gen. James H. Lane,* 300.
57. Leavenworth *Daily Conservative,* October 27, 1864.
58. Leavenworth *Times,* October 26, 29, 1864.
59. Charles Robinson to his wife, October 30, 1864, Robinson Papers (KSHS).
60. Leavenworth *Daily Conservative,* November 3, 1864.
61. *Ibid.;* Leavenworth *Times,* November 5, 6, 1864; Lawrence *Kansas Tribune,* November 8, 1864. It is possible, of course, that Crawford's friends did not want him to speak. It seems strange that the *Conservative* made no mention of him in its writeup the day after the scheduled meeting in Leavenworth. The *Times* remarked: "Crawford did not make his appearance. Lane, as usual, said he was sick. He will be a lot sicker after the election."
62. Wilder, *Annals,* 384.
63. White Cloud *Kansas Chief,* November 24 and September 29, 1864.
64. Thomas Murphy to Lane, October 25, 1864, Lane Collection (Kansas University). Thacher, Crawford's opponent, was willing to fight fire with fire. In a letter to James McDowell, September 9, 1864, McDowell Collection (KSHS), he wrote: "It may be wise to conciliate—Guthrie if possible—since he is one of the Board of State Canvassers and no one can tell what complication may rise in

that, we shall need a majority of that board. This will be especially true with respect to the soldiers' votes. They will, doubtless try to reject parts of their votes or per-

haps foist fraudulent ones on to us."

65. Charles Robinson to his wife, November 11, 1864, Robinson Collection (KSHS).

CHAPTER 4

1. Leavenworth *Evening Bulletin,* January 13, 1865.

2. Crawford, *Kansas,* 226.

3. This statement is based upon a survey of virtually every Kansas newspaper published in 1865 which has been preserved in the Kansas State Historical Society or at the University of Kansas. Even the Leavenworth *Times,* Crawford's most outspoken critic during the election campaign of 1864, felt constrained to tone down or delete some of its correspondents' dispatches which were critical of Crawford. See especially January 13, 1865.

4. *Kansas House Journal* (1865), 16–23.

5. This account is taken from the Leavenworth *Evening Bulletin,* January 14, 1865, and Edwin C. Manning's "The Kansas State Senate of 1865 and 1866," *Kans. Hist. Coll.,* IX (1905–06), 364.

6. *Ibid.,* 365; *Kansas House Journal* (1865), 58, 123.

7. Manning, "The Kansas State Senate of 1865 and 1866," *Kans. Hist. Coll.,* IX (1905–06), 361; Wilder, *Annals,* 424; Leavenworth *Evening Bulletin,* February 10, 1865.

8. Topeka *State Record,* February 22, 1865.

9. See Notaries Public 1865 and Correspondence, General, 1865, in Governor Crawford Papers, and Secretary of State, Commissions,

September 7, 1863, to June 1, 1866, all in Archives, KSHS.

10. *Ibid.;* Crawford, *Kansas,* 207; Seneca *Nemaha Courier,* March 2, 1865.

11. *Kansas House Journal* (January 11, 1865), 19.

12. *Ibid.* (January 10, 1866), 21; the *United States Census, 1860,* I, 162, reports only 627 Negroes living in Kansas in 1861.

13. *Kansas House Journal* (January 20, 1865), 232–33; *Report of the Adjutant General of the State of Kansas for the Years, 1862, 1865, 1866, 1867, and 1868* (Topeka, 1902), 1865, Report 7. Hereafter cited as *Kansas Adjutant General's Report (1865).*

14. Telegram from James B. Fry, Provost Marshal General, Washington, D.C., to Capt. Sidney Clarke, Acting Assistant Provost Marshal General, Leavenworth, dated January 23, 1865, in the Leavenworth *Evening Bulletin,* January 24, 1865.

15. Crawford to Hon. Sidney Clarke, February 1, 1865, Governor Crawford Copybook (Archives, KSHS).

16. Printed as a footnote to Edwin C. Manning, "The Kansas State Senate of 1865 and 1866," *Kans. Hist. Coll.,* IX (1905–06), 368–71.

17. Leavenworth *Times,* February 7, 1865.

18. *Ibid.,* February 19, 1865.

19. Crawford, from Leavenworth, to

Stanton and Crawford to Lane, both sent February 22, 1865, Crawford Telegrams (Archives, KSHS).

20. Leavenworth *Conservative,* February 23, 1865.

21. Leavenworth *Evening Bulletin,* January 24, 1865, Leavenworth *Times,* March 3, 1865.

22. *Kansas Adjutant General's Report (1865),* 6–9; Crawford, *Kansas,* 210; Crawford, Washington, to Secretary McAfee, Topeka, March 20, 1865, Crawford Telegrams (Archives, KSHS).

23. Leavenworth *Daily Conservative,* March 16, 1865; Leavenworth *Evening Bulletin,* March 15, 1865; Leavenworth *Times,* March 16, 28, 1865.

24. Crawford, *Kansas,* 210, 215–17; Governor Crawford's Message, *Kansas House Journal* (January 11, 1866), 22–24.

25. Crawford, *Kansas,* 210–11.

26. Leavenworth *Times,* April 22, 1865.

27. Atchison *Daily Champion,* August 8, 1865.

28. Leavenworth *Daily Conservative,* June 3, 1865.

29. Crawford, *Kansas,* 229, 243–44; *Kansas House Journal* (January 11, 1865), 21; Oskaloosa *Independent,* October 26, 1866.

30. Crawford, *Kansas,* 215, 224; Reprint of Crawford's "Annual Message" (1867), 6; Crawford, New York, to McAfee, Topeka, May 26, 1866, Crawford Telegrams (Archives, KSHS); Jacob Stotler in his Emporia *News,* April 26, 1872.

31. *Kansas House Journal* (January 10, 1866), 24–25.

32. Crawford to McAfee, April 25, 1866, Crawford Copybook (Ar-chives, KSHS). Sidney Clarke, Washington, to Crawford, June 29, 1866, Crawford Telegram (Archives, KSHS).

33. *Kansas Adjutant General's Report (1866),* 14–17.

34. From reprints of Crawford's "Annual Message" (1867), 6–7 and "Annual Message" (1868), 6–7. A history of the Price raid claims is given in note 11 of James Humphrey's "The Administration of George W. Glick," *Kans. Hist. Coll.,* IX (1905–06), 411–12.

35. *United States Census* (1860), I, 162; Census Report in *Kansas Senate Journal* (January 18, 1867), 104; *United States Census* (1870), I, 336.

36. The governor's annual messages for 1865–68 in the *Kansas House* or *Senate Journals.*

37. [S. J. Crawford], *The State of Kansas, A Home for Immigrants* (Topeka, 1865); also printed in German as *Der Staat Kansas* (Leavenworth, 1866).

38. Leavenworth *Daily Conservative,* November 8, 1865. Other favorable comments were published in the Junction City *Union,* May 6, 1865; the Seneca *Nemaha Courier,* April 27, 1865; and a number of unidentified clippings found in the Crawford Scrapbook, I (KSHS).

39. The criticism of Crawford was published in the Lawrence *State Journal* and quoted in the Leavenworth *Daily Conservative,* February 15 and 23, 1866, and the Leavenworth *Times,* March 2, 1866. The favorable comments are found in the Leavenworth *Daily Conservative,* February 15 and 23, 1866.

40. Leavenworth *Times,* February 27,

1867; a reprint of Crawford's "Annual Message" (1867), 21.

41. The land was not so free or cheap as many of the immigrants had been led to believe. See Paul Wallace Gates, *Fifty Million Acres: Conflicts over Kansas Land Policy, 1854–1890* (Ithaca, N.Y., 1954), *passim*.

42. Crawford, *Kansas,* 230, and Crawford's annual messages for 1867 and 1868.

43. Wilder, *Annals,* 422–23; Lane, Leavenworth, to Crawford, Topeka, January 8, 1866, Crawford Telegrams (Archives, KSHS); White Cloud *Kansas Chief,* June 20, 1866.

44. Atchison *Free Press* quoted in Leavenworth *Evening Bulletin,* March 12, 1866. A check of the other leading papers indicates that only the Lawrence *Tribune* (edited by John Speer, Lane's longtime political associate), the Leavenworth *Daily Conservative* (the Lane organ), the Leavenworth *Times* (Thomas Carney's paper), and the Atchison *Daily Champion* (John A. Martin's paper) hesitated to condemn the president. See Martha B. Caldwell, "The Attitude of Kansas toward Reconstruction before 1875" (Ph.D. dissertation, University of Kansas, 1933) for a more complete survey of Kansas's "radical" opinions.

45. Leavenworth *Evening Bulletin* quoted in Atchison *Daily Champion,* April 15, 1866; Leavenworth *Evening Bulletin,* March 17 and April 23, 1866; Wilder, *Annals,* **437.**

46. Crawford, Topeka, to General J. G. Blunt, Washington, D.C. (n.d., but the contents indicate it was written in late March), Crawford Copybook (Archives, KSHS).

47. *Congressional Globe,* 39th Congress, 2nd Session, 1799–1804; Leavenworth *Evening Bulletin,* April 23, 1866; Crawford, *Kansas,* 234–35.

48. Crawford, Washington, D.C., to J. B. McAfee, Topeka, April 25, 1866, Crawford Copybook (Archives, KSHS).

49. Ward Burlingame, Leavenworth, to J. H. Lane, Washington, D.C., May 18, 1866, James Henry Lane Collection, Kansas Room, University of Kansas Libraries. Items found at the University of Kansas Libraries will hereafter be cited as KU.

50. Carney, Western Hotel, Washington, to Crawford, Saint Nicholas Hotel, New York, May 25, 1866, and Lane and Carney, Washington, to Crawford, Saint Nicholas Hotel, New York, May 26, 1866, Crawford Telegrams (Archives KSHS).

51. Leavenworth *Evening Bulletin,* June 4 and June 29, 1866; Wilder, *Annals,* 439.

52. Olathe *Mirror,* June 14, 1866.

53. *Ibid.*

54. Leavenworth *Evening Bulletin,* June 9, 15, 29, 1866; White Cloud *Kansas Chief,* June 14, July 5, 1866.

55. Leavenworth *Daily Conservative,* June 9, 1866; Leavenworth *Times,* June 10, 1866; Lawrence *Kansas Daily Tribune,* June 12, 1866.

56. Ward Burlingame to J. H. Lane, May 18, 1866, James Henry Lane Collection (KU); Lane and Carney to Crawford, May 26, 1866, Crawford Telegrams (Archives, KSHS); Leavenworth *Evening Bulletin,* June 4, 1866.

57. Burlington *Kansas Weekly Patriot,* August 18, 1866.
58. Leavenworth *Evening Bulletin,* June 15, 1866; White Cloud *Kansas Chief,* June 14, 1866.
59. *Ibid.,* July 5, 1866.
60. Topeka *Leader,* June 28, 1866; Wilder, *Annals,* 439; Oskaloosa *Independent,* July 7, 1866; Leavenworth *Daily Conservative,* July 12, 1866.

61. Osborn, Leavenworth, to Crawford, Topeka, July 2, 1866; John Speer, Lawrence, to Crawford, July 2, 1866; Insley and Osborn, Leavenworth, to Crawford, July 2, 1866; J. W. McCall, Leavenworth, to Crawford, July 7, 1866; J. B. McAfee, Topeka, to Crawford, Garnett, July 12, 1866. All found in Crawford Telegrams (Archives, KSHS); Topeka *Weekly Leader,* July 19, 1866.

CHAPTER 5

1. Chicago *Tribune,* July 17, 1866.
2. *Ibid.*
3. *Ibid.;* Topeka *Tribune,* August 24, 1866; Burlington *Kansas Patriot,* July 28, 1866.
4. C. W. Adams, Lawrence, to Crawford and John Speer, Topeka, July 17, 1866; Smith, Washington, to Crawford, Topeka, July 17, 1866; Insley and Smith, Washington, to Crawford, Topeka, July 19, 1866, Crawford Telegrams (Archives, KSHS); telegram from J. B. Henderson, dateline Washington, July 18, printed in the Leavenworth *Daily Conservative,* July 20, 1866; the Topeka *Tribune,* July 20, 1866, alleged that Speer had been promised the appointment.
5. Secretary of State, Commission Book, Commission Number 397 (Archives, KSHS); Leavenworth *Daily Conservative,* July 20, 1866; Topeka *Record,* July 20, 1866.
6. R. W. Ludington, John Hutchings, C. S. Eldridge, Lawrence, to Crawford; James M. Hendry, Eugene Lakin, O. A. Bassett, Lawrence, to Crawford; "Many Names in Lawrence" to Crawford; C. W.

Adams, Lawrence, to Crawford; all telegrams were dated July 19, 1866, Crawford Telegrams (Archives, KSHS).
7. Crawford, *Kansas,* 236.
8. Crawford to Ross, March 15, 1865, Edmund Gibson Ross Collection (KSHS).
9. This story is taken from Edward Bumgardner, *The Life of Edmund G. Ross: The Man Whose Vote Saved a President* (Kansas City, Missouri, 1949), 56–57.
10. Crawford, *Kansas,* 236.
11. Ross was sworn in as United States senator on July 25; Congress adjourned three days later, see *Congressional Globe,* 39 Cong., 1 Sess., 4133. An expanded account of Ross's appointment may be found in my "Governor Crawford's Appointment of Edmund G. Ross to the United States Senate," *KHQ,* XXVIII (Summer 1962), 145–53.
12. Leavenworth *Daily Conservative,* July 21, 1866; J. W. Wright and Ward Burlingame, Leavenworth, to Crawford, Topeka, July 19, 1866, Crawford Telegrams (Archives, KSHS).

13. White Cloud *Kansas Chief*, July 26, 1866.

14. Burlington *Kansas Patriot*, July 28, 1866.

15. White Cloud *Kansas Chief*, August 2, July 26, 1866.

16. Leavenworth *Evening Bulletin*, July 21, 1866.

17. Lawrence *Daily Tribune*, July 21, 1866.

18. Topeka *Tribune*, July 27, 1866.

19. Lawrence *Kansas Tribune*, July 21, 1866.

20. Junction City *Union*, July 28, 1866.

21. Olathe *Mirror*, August 16, 1866; Oskaloosa *Independent*, July 28, 1866; Topeka *Tribune*, August 31, 1866.

22. Olathe *Mirror*, August 16, 1866; Anthony's accusation was in the Leavenworth *Evening Bulletin*, August 31, 1866.

23. Leavenworth *Daily Conservative*, October 20, 1866; Burlington *Kansas Patriot*, August 18, 1866.

24. A more exact comparison of the letters may be made by referring to the letter published by the Junction City *Smoky Hill and Republican Union*, November 5, 1864, or the Leavenworth *Daily Conservative*, October 20, 1864.

25. Lawrence *Kansas Tribune*, August 28, 1866.

26. The best collections of this paper are at the University of Texas and the University of Arkansas libraries. I am indebted to Mr. S. J. Park of Texas and Miss Georgia Clark of Arkansas for checking their files of the *New Era* for me. The Arkansas collection is on microfilm.

27. Emporia *News*, April 26, 1872.

28. Atchison *Freedom's Champion*, November 24, 1864.

29. Lawrence *Kansas Tribune*, September 5, 1866; Junction City *Union*, September 1, 1866.

30. Leavenworth *Daily Conservative*, September 5, 1866.

31. This account is taken from *ibid.*, September 6, 1866; the Topeka *Tribune*, September 7, 1866; and Wilder, *Annals*, 442.

32. *Ibid.*

33. Lawrence *Kansas Tribune*, September 9, 1866. One might question the accuracy with which John Speer transcribed Crawford's speech in view of Speer's hatred for Crawford.

34. Quoted in Leavenworth *Daily Conservative*, September 16, 1866.

35. *Ibid.*, September 6, 1866; Crawford, *Kansas*, 246.

36. This is suggested by the Leavenworth *Daily Conservative*, September 8, 1866.

37. Wilder, *Annals*, 443–44; Oskaloosa *Independent*, September 22, 1866; Leavenworth *Daily Conservative*, September 21, 1866.

38. John Speer in Lawrence *Kansas Tribune*, September 7, 1866; J. P. Greer in Topeka *Tribune*, September 14, 1866; Sol Miller in the White Cloud *Kansas Chief*, September 27, 1866; the report of Anthony's reversal is in the Leavenworth *Daily Conservative*, September 8, 1866.

39. Atchison *Daily Champion*, September 7, 1866; Leavenworth *Daily Conservative*, September 8, 1866.

40. *Ibid.*, September 11, 1866. A survey of the available newspapers indicates that the *Conservative's* ratio was approximately correct.

41. *Ibid.*, October 12, 31, 1866; Lawrence *Kansas Tribune*, October 27, 1866.
42. White Cloud *Kansas Chief*, September 27, 1866.
43. Wilder, *Annals*, 446.

44. The Topeka *Tribune*, December 7, 1866; Topeka *Leader*, November 29, 1866; Crawford, *Kansas*, 239–43; Family Bible of Isabel Marshall Chase Crawford on deposit at KSHS.

CHAPTER 6

1. Eugene F. Ware, "The Neutral Lands," *Kans. Hist. Coll.*, VI (1897–1900), 147–48 (hereafter cited as Ware, "Neutral Lands"); Anna Heloise Abel, "Indian Reservations in Kansas and the Extinguishment of their Title," *ibid.*, VIII (1903–04), 77.
2. Ware, "Neutral Lands," 149.
3. Reprint of Crawford, "Annual Message" (1866), 10.
4. Crawford to Harlan, August 3, 1865; J. M. Edmunds to Harlan, August 31, 1865; Crawford to G. J. Endicott, September 15, 1865; G. J. Endicott to Crawford, n.d., all in *ibid.*, 10–15.
5. *Journal of the Executive Proceedings of the Senate of the United States of America* (Washington, 1887), XIV, 1171–72; Ware, "Neutral Lands," 153–54; Lula Lemmon Brown, *Cherokee Neutral Lands Controversy* (Girard, Kansas, 1931), 9; *U.S. Statutes at Large*, XIV, 804–05.
6. Gates, *Fifty Million Acres* contains the best discussion of the maneuvering connected with the Cherokee Neutral Lands and the Osage Lands in chapters five and six. For a contemporary account see "The Neutral Lands," in the Lawrence *Tribune*, November 22 and 25, 1868.
7. Crawford to James Sloan, Baxter Springs, Kansas, January 1, 1868,

Crawford Copybook (Archives, KSHS).
8. Reprint of Crawford's "Annual Message" (1868), 22–23; Resolution of February 3, 1868, in *Kansas Session Laws* (1868), 66–68.
9. Coates's letter was dated February 8, 1868, printed in the Fort Scott *Monitor*, February 19, 1868; Crawford, "Annual Message" (1868), 23; *U.S. Statutes at Large*, XIV, 805, 808.
10. Fort Scott *Monitor*, January 22, 1868. See also Craig Miner, "Border Frontier: The Missouri River, Fort Scott & Gulf Railroad in the Cherokee Neutral Lands, 1868–1870," *KHQ*, XXXV (Summer 1969), 105–29.
11. Crawford to Julian, February 20, 1868, in Crawford, *Kansas*, 312; Gates, *Fifty Million Acres*, 178–79.
12. *Ibid.*, 164–70.
13. Ware, "Neutral Lands," 158.
14. Crawford, *Kansas*, 313.
15. Ware, "Neutral Lands," 156, 168.
16. Gates, *Fifty Million Acres*, chapter VI.
17. Crawford, *Kansas*, 300–03.
18. A letter to B. Wade, President of the Senate, S. C. Pomeroy, Chairman, Committee on Public Lands, and Geo. W. Julian, House Committee on Public Lands, June 9, 1868, found in Crawford Telegrams (Archives, KSHS).
19. The memorial is dated June 9,

1868, and it is printed in Crawford, *Kansas,* 304–06.

20. *Ibid.,* 306; Abel, "Indian Reservations in Kansas and the Extinguishment of Their Title," *Kans. Hist. Coll.,* VIII (1903–04), 107.

21. *Ibid.;* Gates, *Fifty Million Acres,* 201, 210.

22. Oswego *Register,* August 12, 1868, from a clipping in Crawford Scrapbook, I, 4, KSHS.

23. *Kansas House Journal* (1868), 835. This is the same Charles R. Jennison who led the feared "Jayhawkers" during the slavery controversy.

24. This account is taken from Alan W. Farley, "Samuel Hallett and the Union Pacific Railroad Company in Kansas," *KHQ,* XXV (Spring 1959), 1–13.

25. Andrew Johnson to Daniel R. Garrison, Henry C. Moore, and Richard M. Thompson, April 29, 1865; Johnson to Crawford, May 5, 1865; telegram from John D. Perry, May 5, 1865, all in Records of the Interior Department (Railroads and Wagon Roads), Natural Resources Division, National Archives (from microfilm copies at the University of Kansas Libraries). Hereafter cited as: *Interior Department Report.*

26. Report of Garrison, Moore, and Crawford to the President, May [11], 1865, Crawford Copybook (Archives, KSHS). The report was received in Washington, May 25, 1865.

27. Usher, in fact, was a director of the UPED even before he was succeeded by Harlan. See the list of directors published in the Leavenworth *Daily Conservative,* April 4, 1865. After Usher left Washington, he became the legal counsel, in addition to his directorship, of the UPED. For a more complete account of the Usher-Harlan fight see Elmo R. Richardson and Alan W. Farley, *John Palmer Usher, Lincoln's Secretary of the Interior* (Lawrence, 1960), 79–91.

28. Harlan to Johnson, May 29 and June 5, 1865, *Interior Department Report.*

29. "Report of the Secretary of the Interior," *House Exec. Docs.,* 39 Cong., 1 Sess., No. 1 (Serial 1248), 961-62.

30. Crawford to Lane, Lawrence, June 22, 1865, Crawford Telegrams (Archives, KSHS).

31. "Report of the Secretary of the Interior," *House Exec. Docs.,* 39 Cong., 1 Sess., No. 1 (Serial 1248), 962–63.

32. *Ibid.;* Lane, Wyandotte, to President Johnson, October 3, 1865, telegram in *Interior Department Report.*

33. The report addressed to Johnson which Simpson and Scott would not sign, dated October 5, 1865, is found in Crawford Copybook (Archives, KSHS).

34. "Report of the Secretary of the Interior," *House Exec. Docs.,* 39 Cong., 1 Sess., No. 1 (Serial 1248), 966–73.

35. Minority Report of Commissioners on 1st Section of UPRRED, Wyandotte, Kansas, to President Johnson, October 12, 1865, Crawford Copybook; R. M. Shoemaker, Wyandotte, to Crawford, October 12, 1865, Crawford Telegrams, both in (Archives, KSHS).

36. Crawford to President Johnson, October 13, 1865, Crawford Copybook (Archives, KSHS).

37. "Report of the Secretary of the

Interior," *House Exec. Docs.*, 39 Cong., 1 Sess., No. 1 (Serial 1248), 975–77.

38. Wilder, *Annals*, 428; Leavenworth *Daily Conservative*, November 8, 1865.

39. The summary of facts concerning the sale by the UPED of a section of land to Crawford may be found in [Mrs. Frank Montgomery], "Chronology" in the *Union Pacific Railroad* (typewritten copy in KSHS Library), 35; the deed was recorded in the Jefferson County Register of Deeds Office, Oskaloosa, Kansas, and it is dated March 26, 1867, the consideration was listed as $1,000; the Topeka *Tribune*, July 27, 1866, and the Leavenworth *Daily Conservative*, July 18, 1866, carried stories about the poor quality of the UPED track.

40. Leavenworth *Times*, August 1, 1865.

41. *Kansas House Journal* (1867), 468–74.

42. Leavenworth *Daily Conservative*, April 10, 1867.

43. *Kansas House Journal* (1868), 575–76.

44. Testimony of S. N. Simpson, E. M. Bartholow, Wilson Shannon,

Jr., John D. Perry, J. B. Johnson, H. S. Walsh, and J. B. McAfee, *Kansas House Journal* (1868), 850, 858.

45. Testimony of S. N. Simpson, *ibid.*, 851.

46. Minority report of C. R. Jennison made on February 27, 1868, *ibid.*, 835–36.

47. Majority report of J. L. Philbrick and R. D. Mobley, February 27, 1868, *ibid.*, 847–48.

48. Leavenworth *Daily Conservative*, February 19, 1868; the Atchison *Champion*, February 10 to March 1, 1868; Lawrence *Kansas Tribune*, February 28, 1868.

49. John Perry, St. Louis, to Crawford, May 5, 1868; Crawford to J. B. McAfee, May 8, 1868; and Crawford to Mrs. Crawford, May 9, 1868; all in Crawford Telegrams (Archives, KSHS).

50. Emporia *News*, April 12, 1872; "An Open Letter to Jacob Stotler," dated April 15, 1872, but not published in the *News*, the clipping may be found in Crawford Scrapbook, II, KSHS.

51. Jefferson County Recorder of Deeds, Record Book J, Oskaloosa, Kansas.

CHAPTER 7

1. *Kansas House Journal* (1867), 38–68.

2. Leavenworth *Evening Bulletin*, January 19, 1867.

3. Olathe *Mirror*, [January 24] 1867; Leavenworth *Evening Bulletin*, January 19, 1867; *Kansas House Journal* (1867), 235–40.

4. Leavenworth *Daily Conservative*, February 7, 1867.

5. Wilder, *Annals*, 457, 459.

6. Testimony of William Spriggs and I. S. Kalloch, *Report of Joint Committee of Investigation, Kansas Legislature, 1872* (Topeka, 1872), 243, 239.

7. *Kansas House Journal* (1868), 323–34.

8. Topeka Correspondent, dated February 25, 1867, in the Leavenworth *Times*, February 27, 1867; Wilder, *Annals*, 459.

9. Crawford's trip east was described in the Leavenworth *Daily Conservative*, April 28, 1867; the report of the excursion was printed in the Leavenworth *Times*, June 5 and 6, 1867.

10. Accounts of the suffrage convention may be found in Wilder, *Annals*, 460; Topeka *Tribune*, April 5, 1867; Leavenworth *Daily Conservative*, April 5, 1867. See also Sister Jeanne McKenna, "With the Help of God and Lucy Stone," *KHQ*, XXXVI (Spring 1970), 13–26.

11. *Ibid.*, May 26, 1867; Leavenworth *Times*, May 21, 1867; Crawford to S. N. Wood, Topeka, May 1, 1867, Crawford Copybook (Archives, KSHS).

12. The story of Lucy Stone's campaign for equal suffrage in Kansas is detailed in Alice Stone Blackwell's *Lucy Stone Pioneer of Woman's Rights* (Boston, 1930), 206–10.

13. Wilder, *Annals*, 461, 467, 471.

14. A discussion of the recruiting of the Eighteenth Kansas is included in the next chapter.

15. Leavenworth *Daily Conservative*, August 20, 1867.

16. Ward to Crawford, October 5, 1867, and Crawford to Ross, December 2, 1867, Crawford Copybook (Archives, KSHS).

17. Junction City *Union*, February 22, 1868.

18. Wilder, *Annals*, 481.

19. Crawford to Ross, Washington, February 26, 1868, Crawford Telegrams (Archives, KSHS).

20. Wilder, *Annals*, 480; Olathe *Mirror*, March 12, 1868.

21. D. R. Anthony and thousands of others to Ross, May 16, 1868; Ross to Anthony, May 16, 1868; Anthony and others to Ross, May 16, 1868; all telegrams printed in Oskaloosa *Independent*, May 23, 1868.

22. S. C. Pomeroy to George T. Anthony and others, May 16, 1868; R. J. Hinton to W. W. Wilder, editor, *Conservative*, May 16, 1868; both printed in Leavenworth *Daily Conservative*, May 17, 1868.

23. Crawford to Ross, May 16, 1868, Crawford Telegrams (Archives, KSHS).

24. L. D. Bailey to E. G. Ross, May 16, 1868, printed in Leavenworth *Daily Conservative*, May 17, 1868; Topeka *Leader*, May 21, 1868; Junction City *Union*, May 23, 1868; Emporia *News*, May 29, 1868; Oskaloosa *Independent*, May 23, 1868.

25. The report of the effigy burning was in the Leavenworth *Daily Conservative*, May 21, 1868; the Chicago meeting was reported in the Emporia *News*, May 29, 1868; the state convention resolution was reported in the Fort Scott *Monitor*, September 16, 1868.

26. The Emporia *News*, May 29, 1868; Leavenworth *Daily Conservative*, May 17, 1868; Burlington *Patriot*, June 20, 1868; Junction City *Union*, May 23, 1868.

27. White Cloud *Kansas Chief*, May 21, 1868.

28. Oskaloosa *Independent*, May 23, 1868; White Cloud *Kansas Chief*, quoted in the Olathe *Mirror*, May 28, 1868.

29. Topeka *State Record*, August 26, 1868; Topeka *Leader*, August 20 and 27, 1868; Burlingame *Chronicle* as quoted in *ibid.*, August 27, 1868.

30. John Speer in the Lawrence *Tribune*, August 29, and Septem-

ber 3, 1868; John A. Martin in the Atchison *Champion and Press,* September 9, 1868.

31. Accounts of the convention may be found in Wilder, *Annals,* 487; and the Olathe *Mirror,* September 17, 1868.

32. A broadside found in Crawford Scrapbook, I (KSHS Library).

33. Even the Junction City *Union,* usually one of Crawford's staunch supporters, found fault with Crawford for his lack of interest in the November election. See the November 7 edition.

34. See A. L. Runyon, "A. L. Runyon's Letters from the Nineteenth Kansas Regiment," *KHQ,* IX (February 1940), 61; for the election returns see Wilder, *Annals,* 491–92.

35. Atchison *Champion and Press,* November 6, 1868.

36. Topeka *Leader,* November 5, 1868; Leavenworth *Evening Bulletin,* November 5, 1868; White Cloud *Kansas Chief,* November 5, 1868; Lawrence *Tribune,* December 3, 1868.

CHAPTER 8

1. The casualty figures are based on statistics gathered by Louise Barry from documents at the Kansas State Historical Society. Miss Barry was kind enough to allow me to use the year-by-year summary.

2. Crawford, "Annual Message" (1866), 10; Marvin H. Garfield, "The Indian Question in Congress and in Kansas," *KHQ,* II (February 1933), 37.

3. Crawford, *Kansas,* 223–24.

4. Marvin H. Garfield's "Defense of the Kansas Frontier," *KHQ,* I (November 1931 and August 1932), 50–62, 326–44, includes a good study of the Crawford administration's handling of the Indian problem. This study will hereafter be cited as Garfield, "Defense of the Kansas Frontier."

5. *Ibid.,* 327; Crawford, *Kansas,* 232.

6. Crawford, "Annual Message" (1867), 20; Garfield, "Defense of the Kansas Frontier," 328.

7. Crawford, "Annual Message" (1867), 20.

8. Garfield, "The Indian Question in Congress and in Kansas," *KHQ,*

II (February 1933), 29–40; the Leavenworth *Daily Conservative,* February 26, 1867, reported that both Pomeroy and Ross voted against the transfer of the Indian Bureau on a vote taken February 23, 1867.

9. Crawford, *Kansas,* 251. Hancock's decision to burn the Indian camp is ably discussed in Donald J. Berthrong, *The Southern Cheyennes* (Norman, 1963), 266–279.

10. Most of the important dispatches to and from Crawford's office during May and June may be found in Crawford, *Kansas,* 252–58.

11. Garfield, "Defense of the Kansas Frontier," 332–34; Sherman to Crawford, June 24, 1867, Crawford Telegrams (Archives, KSHS).

12. Crawford to Sherman, June 28, 1867, *ibid.*

13. Crawford's call for state troops was dated July 1, 1867, Crawford Copybook (Archives, KSHS).

14. Crawford to Sherman, July 3, 1867; Green to Crawford, July 5, 1867, in Crawford Telegrams (Archives, KSHS).

15. Crawford to Colonel Thomas Moonlight, Leavenworth, July 5, 1867, Crawford to J. A. Martin, Atchison, July 8, 1867; W. T. Sherman to Crawford, July 10, 1867; all in *ibid*.

16. Lonnie J. White, "Warpaths on the Southern Plains: The Battles of the Saline River and Prairie Dog Creek," *Journal of the West*, IV (October 1965), 500, concludes that the battle known as Beaver Creek was fought on Prairie Dog Creek in northwestern Phillips County, Kansas. Accounts of the campaign of the Eighteenth Kansas Cavalry may be found in: James Albert Hadley, "The Nineteenth Kansas Cavalry and the Conquest of the Plains Indians," *Kans. Hist. Coll.*, X (1907–08). 428–56; Horace L. Moore, "The Nineteenth Kansas Cavalry," *ibid.*, VI (1897–1900), 5; George B. Jenness, "The Battle of Beaver Creek," *ibid.*, IX (1905–06), 443–52; Leavenworth *Times*, August 27, 1867; Lawrence *Kansas Tribune*, November 28, 1867; and Crawford, *Kansas*, 259–62.

17. *Ibid.*, 263.

18. Leavenworth *Times*, July 24, 1867; Garfield, "Defense of the Kansas Frontier," 341.

19. Crawford to Sherman, August 5, 1867; Sherman to Crawford, August 10, 1867, both in Crawford Telegrams (Archives, KSHS); and Leavenworth *Daily Conservative*, August 11 and 13, 1867.

20. Garfield, "Defense of the Kansas Frontier," 341.

21. Robert G. Athearn, *William Tecumseh Sherman and the Settlement of the West* (Norman, Okla., 1956), 183.

22. Crawford, *Kansas*, 264–70; Douglas C. Jones, *The Treaty of Medicine Lodge: The Story of the Great Treaty Council as Told By Eyewitnesses* (Norman, Okla., 1966), 56–64.

23. A letter from Milton W. Reynolds written about 1888 and printed in T. A. McNeal, "The Indians Agree to Abandon Kansas," *Kans. Hist. Coll.*, VI (1897–1900), 345–46. Among the other reporters at Medicine Lodge was Henry M. Stanley, who later became famous for locating Dr. David Livingston in Africa. Reynolds described Stanley as ". . . undoubtedly the biggest liar of the newspaper crowd," *ibid.*, 344. Stanley's dispatches to the St. Louis *Daily Missouri Democrat* may be found in "A British Journalist Reports the Medicine Lodge Peace Councils of 1867," *KHQ*, XXXIII (Autumn 1967), 249–320.

24. Garfield, "Defense of the Kansas Frontier," 343; Sherman's Order Number 10 ordering his troops to cease hostilities against the Indians was printed in the Leavenworth *Daily Conservative*, November 6, 1867.

25. Crawford, *Kansas*, 288–89.

26. The alleged atrocities are detailed in, U.S. Army, Military Division of Missouri, *Record of Engagements with Hostile Indians within the Military Division of Missouri, from 1868 to 1882, Lieutenant General P. H. Sheridan, Commanding* (Chicago: Headquarters Military Division of the Missouri, 1882), 9–11; Wilder, *Annals*, 486; many letters on file in a folder entitled "Indians, 1867–68," Governor Crawford Correspondence (Archives, KSHS); Salina *Herald*, August 16, 1868, in Crawford Scrapbook, I, KSHS Library.

27. Crawford's letter to the president, dated August 17, 1868, and Sheridan's dispatch to Crawford, August 21, 1868, are found in Crawford, *Kansas,* 291–93; the August 22 letter was printed in the Topeka *Leader,* August 27, 1868.

28. Topeka *State Record,* August 26, 1868; Sheridan to Crawford, September 10, 1868; Crawford to Sheridan, September 11, 1868; Sheridan to Crawford, September 11, 1868; Sheridan to Crawford, September 13, 1868; Sheridan-Crawford Correspondence in Crawford, *Kansas,* 296–97.

29. *Ibid.,* 421–22, 298; "Indians, 1867–68" in Governor Crawford Correspondence (Archives, KSHS).

30. Athearn, *Sherman and the Settlement of the West,* 223, 227–28.

31. P. H. Sheridan, *Personal Memoirs of P. H. Sheridan* (New York, 1888), II, 297–99; Sheridan to Crawford, October 9, 1868, in Crawford, *Kansas,* 319–20.

32. Crawford's call for troops, October 10, 1868, is found in *ibid.,* 426; correspondence concerning the detail of recruiting the Nineteenth is found in "Indians, 1867–69," Governor Crawford's Correspondence (Archives, KSHS).

33. Sheridan, *Personal Memoirs,* II, 307–08; U.S. Army, *Record of Engagements with Hostile Indians . . . from 1868 to 1882,* 16–17.

34. David L. Spotts, *Campaigning with Custer and the Nineteenth Kansas Volunteer Cavalry on the Washita Campaign, 1868–'69* (Los Angeles, 1928), 45.

35. Detailed accounts of the campaign of the Nineteenth Kansas, written by the participants, are found in: James Albert Hadley, "The Nineteenth Kansas Cavalry and the Conquest of the Plains Indians," *Kans. Hist. Coll.,* X (1907–08), 428–56 (hereafter cited as Hadley, "The Nineteenth Kansas Cavalry"); Spotts, *Campaigning with Custer;* Horace L. Moore, "The Nineteenth Kansas Cavalry," *Kans. Hist. Coll.,* VI (1897–1900), 35–45 (hereafter cited as Moore, "The Nineteenth Kansas Cavalry"); Crawford, *Kansas,* 317–36.

36. James R. Mead, "The Little Arkansas," *Kans. Hist. Coll.,* X (1907–08), 13–14. Selling arms to the Indians had been legal at the time of Crawford's chastisement of Mead because the Indian tribes in question were not at war with the United States.

37. Spotts, *Campaigning with Custer,* 56–57; Hadley, "The Nineteenth Kansas Cavalry," 436.

38. George W. Brown, "Life and Adventures of George W. Brown," *Kans. Hist. Coll.,* XVII (1926–28), 106; John McBee, "Account of the Expedition of the Nineteenth Kansas," *Kans. Hist. Coll.,* XVIII (1926–28), 362.

39. Crawford, *Kansas,* 322–23; Hadley, "The Nineteenth Kansas Cavalry," 437; Spotts, *Campaigning with Custer,* 59.

40. Hadley, "The Nineteenth Kansas Cavalry," 439–41; Moore, "The Nineteenth Kansas Cavalry," 39; Luther A. Thrasher, "Diary, October 15 to December 31, 1868," *Kans. Hist. Coll.,* X (1907–08), 662.

41. Sheridan, *Personal Memoirs,* II, 321. Custer's strike against Black Kettle is described in William H. Leckie, *The Military Conquest of the Southern Plains* (Norman, Okla., 1963), 98–105. Custer's

regular army rank in 1868 was lieutenant colonel.

42. *Ibid.;* Crawford, *Kansas,* 324; Sheridan to Sherman, December 2, 1868, quoted in Athearn, *Sherman and the Settlement of the West,* 272; Hadley, "The Nineteenth Kansas Cavalry," 435.

43. This account was synthesized from: *ibid.,* 444–45; Moore, "The Nineteenth Kansas Cavalry," 42–44; *U.S. Army, Record of Engagements with Hostile Indians . . . from 1868 to 1882,* 19; Crawford, *Kansas,* 328.

44. *Ibid.;* Moore, "The Nineteenth Kansas Cavalry," 44–47; Hadley, "The Nineteenth Kansas Cavalry," 456.

45. George W. Martin, Secretary, Kansas State Historical Society, to E. C. Manning, Winfield, August 29, 1908, Letter Pressbook, Correspondence, KSHS, vol. LXXVII, 193.

46. Diary entry dated January 16, 1869, Spotts, *Campaigning with Custer,* 104; Moore, "The Nineteenth Kansas Cavalry," 43–44; Crawford, *Kansas,* 330.

47. Spotts, *Campaigning with Custer,* 124–25; Leavenworth *Evening Bulletin,* March 8, 1868; Junction City *Union,* March 13, 1869.

CHAPTER 9

1. The Topeka *Leader,* March 11, 1869, carried the story of Crawford's return on the "City News" page.

2. Crawford, *Kansas,* 345; a review of *Kansas in the Sixties* in an Emporia newspaper sometime in 1911, a clipping from Crawford Scrapbook, III (KSHS); March 3, 1870, entry, Deed Record J, Jefferson County Register of Deeds Office, Oskaloosa, Kansas.

3. Lawrence *Tribune,* July 15, 1869; Wilder, *Annals* (1886 edition), 523; Crawford to editors, *Topeka State Record,* August 17, 1870, clipping in Crawford Scrapbook, I (KSHS).

4. See a poster headed "$200,000 Lost! Lost! (KSHS) and the reprint of an Anti-Clarke cartoon in Gates, *Fifty Million Acres,* 182; Wilder, *Annals* (1886 edition), 523–24.

5. Crawford, Emporia, to James Hanway, October 15, 1870, James Hanway Collection (KSHS).

6. Wilder, *Annals* (1886 edition), 430–38; Crawford to James Hanway, November 15, 1870, James Hanway Collection (KSHS).

7. From the Garnett *Plaindealer* as reprinted in the Emporia *News,* November 25, 1870.

8. Crawford, *Kansas,* 346; Oswego *Register* reprinted in Emporia *News,* January 20, 1871; Emporia *News,* January 13 and 20, 1871.

9. *Ibid.,* January 20, 1871; Junction City *Union,* December 31, 1870; Crawford, *Kansas,* 345–46.

10. Leavenworth *Evening Bulletin,* December 10, 1870, January 14, 18, 20, 1871. Junction City *Union,* December 31, 1870.

11. Emporia *News,* January 20, 1871.

12. Leavenworth *Evening Bulletin,* January 27, 1871.

13. Junction City *Union,* January 28, 1871.

14. This account is based on reports found in the Junction City *Union,* January 28, 1871, and the Lawrence *Tribune,* January 26, 1871

(both supported Clarke); the Emporia *News*, January 27, 1871 (supported Crawford); and the Leavenworth *Evening Bulletin*, January 27, 1871 (a Caldwell supporter). Clarke subsequently admitted that he had agreed to take "expense" money from Caldwell's supporters, a fact which will be documented later in this chapter.

15. This account was taken from the Emporia *News*, February 2, 1871; Junction City *Union*, January 28, 1871; Leavenworth *Evening Bulletin*, January 26 and 27, 1871.

16. Salina *Herald*, as quoted in the Leavenworth *Evening Bulletin*, February 1, 1871; Emporia *News*, February 3, 1871.

17. Lawrence *Democratic Standard*, February 2, 1871, a clipping in Crawford Scrapbook, I (KSHS).

18. Lawrence *Democratic Standard*, January 17, 1872, reprinted in the Council Grove *Democrat*, January 25, 1872; *Report of the Joint Committee of Investigation Appointed by the Kansas Legislature of 1872 to Investigate All Charges of Bribery and Corruption Connected with the Senatorial Elections of 1867 and 1871* (Topeka, 1872), 7–9, 36, 109–10.

19. A copy of the Carney-Caldwell agreement in McDowell's handwriting may be found in the James L. McDowell Collection (KSHS); see also "Report of the Committee on Privileges and Elections," 42 Cong., 3 Sess., *Senate Report No. 451* (Serial 1548), 249, 251.

20. *Ibid.*, i–vi.

21. Emporia *News*, February 3, 1871, and April 27, 1872; Crawford's letter to Thoman is reprinted in *ibid.*, April 12, 1872.

22. Topeka *Commonwealth*, April 11,

1872; Wilder, *Annals*, 576; Norma L. Peterson, *Freedom and Franchise; The Political Career of B. Gratz Brown* (Columbia, Missouri, 1965), 211.

23. Atchison *Daily Champion*, April 12, 1872; White Cloud *Chief*, quoted in Emporia *News*, May 3, 1872.

24. "Another Recruit" appeared in the Emporia *News*, April 12, 1872; Crawford's reply was addressed to the Emporia *Democrat* and is found in Crawford Scrapbook, II (KSHS); Stotler's answer to Crawford is found in the Emporia *News*, April 26, 1872.

25. Details of the Liberal Republican movement and the convention at Cincinnati may be found in Earle Dudley Ross, *The Liberal Republican Movement* (New York, 1919).

26. Crawford to J. F. Warwick, May 20, 1872, Council Grove, printed in Council Grove *Democrat*, May 30, 1872.

27. Topeka *Commonwealth*, September 5 and 11, 1872; Crawford to S. N. Wood, August 12, 1872, Samuel Newitt Wood Collection (KSHS).

28. Topeka *Commonwealth*, September 11 and 12, 1872.

29. Wilder, *Annals*, 586–599.

30. *Ibid.*, 606; for a more complete story of the 1873 election, see Albert R. Kitzhaber, *"Gotterdammerung* in Topeka: The Downfall of Senator Pomeroy," *KHQ*, XVIII (August 1950), 243–78. See also James C. Malin's reinterpretation in "Some Reconsiderations of the Defeat of Senator Pomeroy of Kansas, 1873," *Mid America*, XLVIII (January 1966), 47–57.

31. Crawford, *Kansas*, 350. A letter written by Crawford to E. G.

Ross, November 17, 1873, indicates that he had begun to practice law once again and that he was not giving much attention to politics; see Edmund G. Ross Papers (KSHS).

32. Topeka *Commonwealth*, September 5, 1874; Crawford to S. N. Wood, July 25, 1874, Samuel Newitt Wood Papers (KSHS); Wilder, *Annals* (1886 edition), 651, 654, 662, 663.

33. Crawford to the editor of the Emporia *Globe*, December 4, 1874, Crawford Scrapbook, I (KSHS).

34. Topeka *Commonwealth*, August 17 and 24, 1876; Wilder, *Annals* (1886 edition), 706, 713–15, 717–18.

35. The vote was given as 53 to 37 in the Emporia *Ledger*, August 31, 1876, while the Topeka *Commonwealth*, August 27, 1876, said Crawford was beaten 62 to 22. Reports of the two convention proceedings are found in the Emporia *News*, September 1, 1876; Emporia *Ledger*, August 31, 1876; and Topeka *Commonwealth*, August 25, 26, and 27, 1876.

36. Topeka *Commonwealth*, September 7 and 8, 1876; the letters of Davis were republished in most of the state Republican papers including the *Commonwealth*, October 15, 1876.

37. Davis's withdrawal, dated October 17, was published in the Topeka *Commonwealth*, October 19, 1876; Crawford's new canvass was described in the Emporia *News*, October 27, 1876; Crawford's October

20 speech at Emporia is recorded in the Kansas City *Times*, October 24, 1876.

38. Kansas City *Times*, October 22, 24, 31, 1876; Wilder, *Annals* (1886 edition), 729–32.

39. "Another Correction," an unidentified newspaper clipping in Crawford Scrapbook, III (KSHS); Emporia *Ledger*, January 4, 1877.

40. *Kansas Senate Journal* (1877), 296, 408–09, 510, 518, 727–28, 749, 768, 774; *Kansas House Journal* (1877), 1086; Topeka *Commonwealth*, February 10, 16, 24, and March 6, 1877; Emporia *News*, March 9, 1877.

41. A more detailed account of his tenure as state claims agent will be found in the next chapter. The Paola *Western Spirit*, October 11, 1878, reported that he had secured $300,000 for school lands and $500,000 reimbursement for war claims.

42. Topeka *Commonwealth*, September 24, 1878.

43. *Ibid.;* Emporia *Ledger*, September 26, 1878; Paola *Western Spirit*, October 11, 1878.

44. Atchison *Champion*, October 4, as quoted in the Topeka *Blade*, October 9, 1878; Emporia *Ledger*, October 17, 1878; Topeka *Commonwealth*, October 6, 1878.

45. Wilder, *Annals* (1886 edition), 819–22; Hallowell was appointed U.S. district attorney in 1879, see Lewis Publishing Company, *The United States Biographical Dictionary, Kansas Volume* (Kansas City, Missouri, 1879), 680.

CHAPTER 10

1. *Kansas Senate Journal* (1877), 749, 768; "Official Kansas Ros-

ters," *Kans. Hist. Coll.*, XVI (1923–25), 703; Governor Anthony Pressbook, VII (Archives, KSHS), 151; "Official Bonds and Trade Marks, Secretary of State's Office, State of Kansas," Book 2 (Archives, KSHS); *Kansas Session Laws* (1877), 232–33.

2. *Ibid.;* "Report of Hon. S. J. Crawford to the Governor of Kansas" (November 28, 1884), 11. Most of Crawford's reports, briefs, and arguments may be found in a bound volume called *Briefs and Arguments, S. J. Crawford,* in the KSHS Library.

3. A copy of the contract may be found in Governor George T. Anthony's "Message to the Legislature" (January 13, 1879).

4. Crawford, Washington, D.C., to [George S. Chase], May 30, 1877, an unidentified clipping found in Crawford Scrapbook, I (KSHS), 7.

5. "Application to the Commissioner, General Land Office for the Re-Adjustment of Accounts Between the United States and the State of Kansas for Moneys due Said State from the sale of Public Lands" (Topeka, 1877); "A Statement Relating to the Claims of the State of Kansas, for Money Expended for the United States, for which Reimbursement is Asked" (Topeka, 1877); "Report of Hon. S. J. Crawford, State Agent, to Governor John P. St. John, in Relation to the Claims of the State of Kansas Against the United States, December 2, 1882" (Topeka, 1882); all may be found in *Briefs and Arguments, S. J. Crawford,* Library, KSHS.

6. Charles Hanford Landrum, "A History of the Kansas School Fund," *Kans. Hist. Coll.,* XII (1911–12), 206; "Opinion of At-

torney General Willard Davis," dated February 24, 1879, found in a bound volume *Messages and Documents, Hon. S. J. Crawford, 1880,* Library, KSHS.

7. A copy of the March 6, 1883, act which empowered Crawford to look into the railroad grants is included in "Report of Hon. S. J. Crawford to the Governor of Kansas . . ." (Washington, D.C., 1884). Crawford's brief on behalf of the state is entitled "Before the Hon. Henry M. Teller, Secretary of the Interior, in the Matter Relating to the Excess of Lands Certified to the Atchison, Topeka and Santa Fe Railroad Company within the State of Kansas" (Washington, D.C., 1883). Short titles to some of the individual cases handled by Crawford include: "E. Baxter vs. A.T. & S.F. R.R. Co." (1883); "W. W. Turner vs. A.T. & S.F. R.R. Co." (1883); "Definite Location of A.T. & S.F. R.R. through Rice County, Preemption Rights of Aaron Bobb and Other Settlers" (1883). The Kansas Pacific case was briefed in "Before the Commissioner of the General Land Office in the Matter of Adjustment of Railroad Land Grants with the State of Kansas" (Washington, D.C., 1887); and "To the Commissioner of the General Land Office Relative to the Definite Location of the Kansas Pacific Railroad" (Washington, D.C., 1887).

8. "Kicking Bird" [Milton Reynolds], Topeka *Commonwealth,* March 23, 1882.

9. Kirke Mechem, editor, *The Annals of Kansas,* 2 volumes (Topeka, 1954–56), II, 72–73.

10. Topeka *State Journal,* October 27, 1891; Kansas City *Times,* August

2, 1891; Florence Crawford, "Journal, June 19, 1891, to February 19, 1892" (KSHS); Homer E. Socolofsky, "A Kansas Romance of the Gay Nineties" *The Midwest Quarterly*, III (Autumn 1961), 81–96; Socolofsky, *Arthur Capper Publisher, Politician, and Philanthropist* (Lawrence, 1962), 39–40.

11. Topeka *Commonwealth*, October 6, 1880.

12. Junction City *Union*, March 24, 1883; Topeka *Commonwealth*, August 25, 1883; Kansas City *Times*, September 2, 1883; Chicago *Tribune*, March 15, 1883; Lawrence *Standard*, September 1, 1883; New York *Truth*, September 24, 1883, the last three references are clippings found in Crawford Scrapbook, I (KSHS). Crawford's efforts to return the unearned railroad lands to the public domain are mentioned in Leslie E. Decker, *Railroads, Lands and Politics: The Taxation of the Railroad Land Grants, 1864–1897* (Providence, Rhode Island, 1964), 49, 71, 81.

13. Kansas City *Journal*, reprinted in Topeka *Commonwealth*, September 22, 1883.

14. *Ibid.*, September 30, 1883.

15. Crawford to Glick, October 12, 1883; Glick to Crawford, October 12, 1883, both from *ibid.*, October 13, 1883; Crawford to Glick, October 18, 1883, *ibid.*, October 19, 1883.

16. Crawford's arguments before the House Committee on Public Lands of the 48th Congress were dated February 22 and March 6, 1884; they were entitled: "Adjustment of Land Grants, To Aid in the Construction of Railroads in Kansas," and "Adjustment of Railroad Grants within the State of Kansas, Supplemental Brief for the State." The Wichita *Daily Beacon*, January 23, 1885, suggested Crawford's name as a replacement for Ingalls.

17. Crawford's letter was dated Washington, July 15, 1886, found in unidentified newspaper clipping, Crawford Scrapbook, I (KSHS); election statistics from W. W. Admire, *Admire's Political and Legislative Handbook for Kansas*, (Topeka, 1891), 348.

18. Topeka *Daily Capital*, June 23, 1890.

19. Topeka *Advocate*, July 30, August 27, and September 17 and 24, 1890; Topeka *Weekly Capital*, September 18, 1890; Topeka *Daily Capital*, August 17, 1890.

20. Topeka *Advocate*, August 6, 1890; Kansas City *Times*, August 2, 1891.

21. *Annals of Kansas*, II, 110–11.

22. Governor Humphrey, "Annual Message," *Kansas Senate Journal* (January 14, 1891), 50–51; *Annals of Kansas*, II, 116; Lawrence *Daily Journal*, March 10 and 12, 1891; Kansas City *Star*, March 12, 1891; *Kansas Senate Journal* (1891), 243, 253, 317, 353, 385; *Kansas House Journal* (1891), 1069, 1131, 1141.

23. Landrum, "A History of the Kansas School Fund," *Kans. Hist. Coll.*, XII (1911–12), 206; Kansas City *Star*, March 12, 1891.

24. The appropriations for Crawford's compensation as state agent are recorded in *Kansas Session Laws* (1879), Chapter XXI; (1881), Chapter II; (1883), Chapter XVII; (1885), Chapter LIII; (1887), Chapter XL; (1889), Chapter CCXXXVIII; (1891), Chapter

XVI. "M.B.," the Topeka correspondent of the Kansas City *Times,* in the August 2, 1891, edition, reported that Crawford had netted $200,000 in Indian claims.

25. Boston *Herald,* n.d.; St. Louis *Globe Democrat,* April 15, 1891; Chicago *Times,* April 15, 1891; all clippings found in Crawford Scrapbook, II (KSHS).

26. Topeka *Daily Capital,* August 1, 1891.

27. Topeka *Democrat,* December 23, 1891.

28. Topeka *State Journal,* June 24, 1895.

29. Letter to the Washington *Post* (n.d.) reprinted in the Topeka *Mail,* September 9, 1898, from Crawford Scrapbook, I (KSHS); letter to editor of the Topeka *Daily Capital,* September 21, 1898.

30. "Folder No. 52" may be found in "Campaign Literature, 1900," KSHS Library. Crawford also endorsed Bryan in a letter dated October 21, 1900, printed in the Baxter Springs *News,* November 3, 1900.

31. Washington *Times,* January 11, 1902, a clipping from Crawford Scrapbook, II (KSHS); Topeka *Daily Capital,* July 5, 1909; Topeka *Mail and Breeze,* June 17, 1905.

32. "Washington Topics," Topeka *Daily Capital,* January 22, 1899; Washington *Post,* February 6, 1899, and January 2, 1904, clippings taken from Crawford Scrapbook, I (KSHS); Crawford to George W. Martin, June 1, 1905, Incoming Correspondence at the KSHS; Henry W. Blair, Washington, D.C., to George W. Martin, November 6, 1905, *ibid.;* Martin to Frank H. Hodder, Lawrence, November 9, 1905, Letter Pressbook, KSHS, LXXIII, 138; Martin to Blair, November 11, 1905, *ibid.,* 156.

33. Crawford to Martin, July 8, 1905, Incoming Correspondence at the KSHS; Martin to Crawford, October 13, 1905, Letter Pressbook, KSHS, LXXIII, 28; C. M. Foster to Crawford, October 21, 1905, *ibid.,* 62; Martin to Crawford, October 31, 1905, *ibid.,* 100; Crawford to Martin, November 15, 1905, Incoming Correspondence at the KSHS; Martin to Crawford, April 13, 1910, Pressbook, KSHS, LXXXIV, 21; Martin to Henry W. Blair, Washington, D.C., November 8, 1905, *ibid.,* LXXIII, 136; "Review" in *Dial* sometime in 1912, Crawford Scrapbook, III (KSHS); Kansas City *Journal,* March 18, 1891.

34. Crawford, *Kansas,* 368–70.

35. Topeka *Daily Capital,* October 22, 1913.

BIBLIOGRAPHY

Newspapers

Atchison *Daily Champion*, August 1865 to April 1869.

Atchison *Freedom's Champion*, May 1859 to May 1869.

Baxter Springs *News*, November 3, 1900.

Burlington *Kansas Weekly Patriot*, September 1864 to October 1868.

Chicago *Tribune*, July 17, 1866, and March 15, 1883.

Council Grove *Democrat*, May 30, 1872.

El Dorado *Republican*, February 26, 1886.

Emporia *Ledger*, August 1876 to November 1878.

Emporia *News*, December 1864 to December 1876.

Fort Scott *Weekly Monitor*, June 1867 to December 1869.

Fort Smith (Arkansas) *New Era*, September to November 1864.

Junction City *Smoky Hill and Republican Union*, September 1861 to November 1864.

Junction City *Union*, April 1865 to December 1877.

Kansas City *Star*, March 12, 1891.

Kansas City *Times*, October 1876 to August 1891.

Lawrence *Daily Journal*, March 1891.

Lawrence *Kansas State Journal*, February 1861 to January 1868.

Lawrence *Kansas Tribune*, November 1863 to February 1871.

Leavenworth *Daily Conservative*, September 1864 to September 1868.

Leavenworth *Evening Bulletin*, September 1864 to March 1871.

Leavenworth *Times*, September 1864 to February 1886.

Olathe *Mirror*, May 1861 to December 1875.

Oskaloosa *Independent*, July 1860 to August 1870.

Paola *Western Spirit*, October 1878.

Seneca *Nemaha Courier*, November 1863 to November 1865.

Topeka *Advocate*, July to October 1890.

Topeka *Daily Capital*, April 1879 to November 1913.

Topeka *Daily Commonwealth*, May 1869 to October 1888.

Topeka *Democrat*, December 23, 1891.

Topeka *Kansas State Record*, February 1865 to April 1875.

Topeka *Mail and Breeze*, June 17, 1905.

Topeka *Tribune*, July 1866 to August 1867.

Topeka *Weekly Capital*, September 18, 1890.

Topeka *Weekly Leader*, December 1865 to April 1869.

White Cloud *Kansas Chief*, October 1864 to July 1873.

Wichita *Daily Beacon*, January 23, 1885.

Wichita *Daily Eagle*, February 16, 1886.

Manuscripts and Archives

Governor George T. Anthony Pressbook, vol. VII, Archives, Kansas State Historical Society.

Florence Crawford, "Journal, June 19, 1891 to February 19, 1892," on deposit at Kansas State Historical Society.

Isabel Marshall Chase Crawford, "Family Bible," on deposit at Kansas State Historical Society.

Governor Samuel J. Crawford Copybook, Archives, Kansas State Historical Society.

————, Incoming Correspondence 1865–1868, Archives, Kansas State Historical Society.

————, Telegrams Copied, Archives, Kansas State Historical Society.

Department of the Interior Records, Railroads and Wagon Roads (microfilm copies), Natural Resources Division, National Archives.

Jefferson County Register of Deeds Office, "Record Book J," Oskaloosa, Kansas.

James Hanway Collection, Kansas State Historical Society.

Kansas State Historical Society, Incoming Correspondence, 1905–1911.

————, Letter Pressbook, vol. LXVII.

James H. Lane Papers, University of Kansas Libraries.

James L. McDowell Collection, Kansas State Historical Society.

Muster Roll of the Second Kansas Cavalry from the Files of the Kansas Adjutant General's Office (microfilm copy), Kansas State Historical Society.

Records of the War Department, Office of the Judge Advocate General, Record Group No. 153, "Court Martial of Lt. Col. Owen A. Bassett, 2d Kansas Cavalry," No. 48, Inventory Entry 18 (microfilm copies), National Archives.

Secretary of State, "Commissions, September 7, 1863 to April 15, 1877," Archives, Kansas State Historical Society.

————, "Official Bonds and Trade Marks, Book 2," Archives, Kansas State Historical Society.

Charles and Sara Robinson Collection, Kansas State Historical Society.

Edmund Gibson Ross Collection, Kansas State Historical Society.

Samuel Newitt Wood Collection, Kansas State Historical Society.

Scrapbooks and Pamphlets

Samuel J. Crawford, "Messages and Briefs, 1880" (a collection of printed pamphlets), Kansas State Historical Society.

————, "Briefs and Arguments, 1889" (a collection of printed pamphlets), Kansas State Historical Society.

————, Scrapbook, 3 vols., Kansas State Historical Society.

————, "The State of Kansas: A Home for Immigrants," Topeka, 1865.

————, "A Veteran's Letter Giving Sound Reasons Why Union Soldiers and Everybody Else Should Vote the Democratic Ticket in 1900, Views of Hon. S. J. Crawford, Ex-Governor of Kansas," Folder No. 52, Campaign Literature, Library, Kansas State Historical Society.

Kansas Legislative Scrapbook, 2 vols., Kansas State Historical Society.

Government Publications

A. Federal Government

The Congressional Globe. 39 Cong., 2 Sess. and 40 Cong., 1 Sess.

Journal of the Executive Proceedings of the Senate of the United States of America. Washington D.C., 1877.

U.S. Army, Military Division of Missouri. *Record of Engagements with Hostile Indians within the Military Division of Missouri from 1868 to 1882, Lieutenant General P. H. Sheridan, Commanding.* Chicago, 1882.

U.S. Bureau of the Census. *Eighth Census of the United States, 1860: Population.* Washington, D.C., 1864.

————. *Ninth Census of the United States, 1870: Population and Social Statistics.* Washington, D.C., 1872.

U.S. Congress. Department of the Interior. *Report of the Secretary of the Interior.* House Exec. Doc., 39 Cong., 1 Sess., No. 1. Washington, D.C., 1865.

————. Senate. *Report of the Committee on Privileges and Elections.* 42 Cong., 3 Sess., No. 451. Washington, D.C., 1873.

U.S. Statutes at Large. 1866, vol. XIV.

The War of the Rebellion: A Compilation of the Official Records of the Union and Confederate Armies.

128 vols. Washington, D.C., 1881–1901.

B. State of Kansas

Kansas Session Laws. 1865–1891.

Official Military History of Kansas Regiments During the War for the Suppression of the Great Rebellion, included in a volume entitled *Report of the Adjutant General of the State of Kansas 1861–'65.* Topeka, 1896.

Report of the Joint Committee of Investigation Appointed by the Kansas Legislature of 1872 to Investigate All Charges of Bribery and Corruption Connected with the Senatorial Elections of 1867 and 1871. Topeka, 1872.

Reports of the Adjutant General of the State of Kansas for the Years 1862, 1865, 1866, 1867, and 1868. Topeka, 1902.

Senate and House Journals of the Legislative Assembly of the State of Kansas, 1865–1891.

Books

Admire, W. W. *Admire's Political and Legislative Handbook for Kansas.* Topeka, 1891.

Allison, Nathaniel Thompson, ed. *History of Cherokee County, Kansas and Representative Citizens.* Chicago, 1904.

Athearn, Robert G. *William Tecumseh Sherman and the Settlement of the West.* Norman, Oklahoma, 1956.

Bearss, Edwin C. *Steele's Retreat from Camden and the Battle of Jenkins' Ferry.* Little Rock, 1967.

Berthrong, Donald J. *The Southern Cheyennes.* Norman, Oklahoma, 1963.

Berwanger, Eugene H. *The Frontier Against Slavery: Western Anti-Negro Prejudice and the Slavery Extension Controversy.* Urbana, Illinois, 1967.

Blackmar, Frank W. *Kansas: A Cyclopedia of State History, Embracing Events, Institutions, Industries, Counties, Cities, Towns, Prominent Persons, Etc.* 2 vols. Chicago, 1912.

Brown, Lula Lemmon. *Cherokee Neutral Lands Controversy.* Girard Kansas, 1931.

Bumgardner, Edward. *The Life of Edmund G. Ross.* Kansas City, 1949.

Castel, Albert. *A Frontier State at War: Kansas, 1861–1865.* Ithaca, New York, 1958.

Connelley, William Elsey. *The Life of Preston B. Plumb 1837–1891.* Chicago, 1913.

———. *A Standard History of Kansas and Kansans.* Chicago, 1918.

Cornish, Dudley Taylor. *The Sable Arm: Negro Troops in the Union Army, 1861–1865.* New York, 1956.

Crawford, Samuel J. *Kansas in the Sixties.* Chicago, 1911.

Decker, Leslie E. *Railroads, Lands, and Politics: The Taxation of the Railroad Land Grants, 1864–1897.* Providence, Rhode Island, 1964.

Gaeddert, G. Raymond. *The Birth of Kansas.* Lawrence, Kansas, 1940.

Gates, Paul Wallace. *Fifty Million Acres: Conflicts over Kansas Land Policy 1854–1890.* Ithaca, New York, 1954.

Johnson, Ludwell H. *Red River Campaign: Politics and Cotton in the Civil War.* Baltimore, 1958.

Johnson, Robert Underwood, and Clarence Clough Buel. *Battles and Leaders of the Civil War.* 2 vols. New York, 1887–1888.

Jones, Douglas C. *The Treaty of Medicine Lodge: The Story of the Great Treaty Council As Told by Eyewitnesses.* Norman, Oklahoma, 1966.

Leckie, William H. *The Military Conquest of the Southern Plains.* Norman, Oklahoma, 1963.

Lewis Publishing Company. *The United States Biographical Dictionary, Kansas Volume.* Kansas City, Missouri, 1879.

Mechem, Kirke, ed. *The Annals of Kansas.* 2 vols. Topeka, 1954–56.

Monaghan, Jay. *Civil War on the Western Border: 1854–1865.* Boston, 1955.

Oates, Stephen B. *Confederate Cavalry West of the River.* Austin, Texas, 1961.

Peterson, Norma L. *Freedom and Franchise; The Political Career of B. Gratz Brown.* Columbia, Missouri, 1965.

Richardson, Elmo R., and Alan W. Farley. *John Palmer Usher, Lincoln's Secretary of the Interior.* Lawrence, Kansas, 1960.

Ross, Earle Dudley. *The Liberal Republican Movement.* New York, 1919.

Sheridan, P. H. *Personal Memoirs of P. H. Sheridan, General United States Army.* 2 vols. New York, 1888.

Socolofsky, Homer E. *Arthur Capper, Publisher, Politician, and Philanthropist.* Lawrence, Kansas, 1962.

Speer, John. *Life of Gen. James H. Lane, "The Liberator of Kansas": with Corroborative Incidents of Pioneer History.* Garden City, Kansas, 1897.

Spotts, David L. *Campaigning with Custer and the Nineteenth Kansas Volunteer Cavalry on the Washita Campaign, 1868–'69.* Los Angeles, California, 1928.

Stephenson, Wendell Holmes. *The Political Career of General James H. Lane.* Publications of the Kansas State Historical Society, vol. III. Topeka, 1930.

Tuttle, Charles R. *A New Centennial History of the State of Kansas.* Madison, Wisconsin, 1876.

Wilder, Daniel Webster. *The Annals of Kansas.* Topeka, 1875.

———. *The Annals of Kansas.* 2nd ed. Topeka, 1886.

Articles

Abel, Anna Heloise. "Indian Reservations in Kansas and the Extinguishment of Their Title," *Kansas Historical Collections*, VIII (1903–04), 72–109.

Ballard, David E. "The First State Legislature," *Kansas Historical Collections*, X (1907–08), 232–**279.**

Blunt, James G. "General Blunt's Account of His Civil War Experiences." *Kansas Historical Quarterly*, I (May 1932), 211–265.

Brown, George W. "Life and Adventures of George W. Brown," *Kansas Historical Collections*, XVII (1926–28), 98–134.

Caldwell, Martha B. "When Horace Greeley Visited Kansas," *Kansas Historical Quarterly*, IX (May 1940), 115–140.

Connelley, William E., ed. "Some Ingalls Letters," *Kansas Historical Collections*, XIV (1915–1918), 94–122.

"Extinct Geographical Locations," *Kansas Historical Collections*, XII (1911–12), 471–490.

Farley, Alan W. "Samuel Hallett and the Union Pacific Railway Company in Kansas," *Kansas Historical Quarterly*, XXV (Spring 1959), 1–16.

Garfield, Marvin H. "Defense of the Kansas Frontier," *Kansas Historical Quarterly*, I (November 1931 and August 1932), 50–62, 326–44.

———. "The Indian Question in Congress and in Kansas," *Kansas Historical Quarterly*, II (February 1933), 29–44.

Hadley, James Albert. "The Nineteenth Kansas Cavalry and the Conquest of the Plains Indians,"

Kansas Historical Collections, X (1907–08), 428–456.

Harris, Thomas L. "Crawford, Samuel Johnson," *Dictionary of American Biography*, IV (New York, 1946), 523–24.

Humphrey, James W. "The Administration of George W. Glick," *Kansas Historical Collections*, IX (1905–06), 395–415.

Jenness, George B. "The Battle of Beaver Creek," *Kansas Historical Collections*, IX (1905–06), 443–52.

Kitzhaber, Albert R. "Götterdämerung in Topeka," *Kansas Historical Quarterly*, XVIII (August 1950), 243–278.

Landrum, Charles Hanford. "History of the Kansas School Fund," *Kansas Historical Collections*, XII (1911–12), 195–217.

Learnard, O. E. "Organization of the Republican Party," *Kansas Historical Collections*, VI (1897–1900), 312–316.

Malin, James C. "Some Reconsiderations of the Defeat of Senator Pomeroy of Kansas, 1873," *Mid America*, XLVIII (January 1966), 47–57.

Manning, Edwin C. "A Kansas Soldier," *Kansas Historical Collections*, X (1907–08), 421–28.

———. "The Kansas State Senate of 1865 and 1866," *Kansas Historical Collections*, IX (1905–06), 359–75.

———. "Samuel Johnson Crawford," *Kansas Historical Collections*, XII (1911–12), 271–73.

McBee, John. "Account of the Expedition of the Nineteenth Kansas," *Kansas Historical Collections*, XVII (1926–28), 361–74.

McKenna, Sister Jeanne. "With the Help of God and Lucy Stone," *Kansas Historical Quarterly,* XXXVI (Spring 1970), 13–26.

McNeal, T. A. "The Indians Agree to Abandon Kansas," *Kansas Historical Collections,* VI (1897–1900), 344–46.

Mead, James R. "The Little Arkansas," *Kansas Historical Collections,* X (1907–08), 7–14.

Miner, Craig. "Border Frontier: The Missouri River, Fort Scott & Gulf Railroad in the Cherokee Neutral Lands, 1868–1870," *Kansas Historical Quarterly,* XXXV (Summer 1969), 105–29.

Moore, Horace L. "The Nineteenth Kansas Cavalry," *Kansas Historical Collections,* VI (1897–1900), 35–52.

"Official Kansas Rosters," *Kansas Historical Collections,* XVI (1923–25), 703.

Runyon, A. L. "A. L. Runyon's Letters from the Nineteenth Kansas Regiment," *Kansas Historical Quarterly,* IX (February 1940), 58–75.

Socolofsky, Homer E. "A Kansas Romance of the Gay Nineties," *The Midwest Quarterly,* III (Autumn 1961), 81–96.

Stanley, Henry M. "A British Journalist Reports the Medicine Lodge Peace Councils of 1867," *Kansas Historical Quarterly,* XXXIII (Autumn 1967), 249–320.

Thrasher, Luther A. "Diary, October 15 to December 31, 1868," *Kansas Historical Collections,* X (1907–08), 660–63.

Ware, Eugene F. "The Neutral Lands," *Kansas Historical Collections,* VI (1897–1900), 147–169.

White, Lonnie J. "Warpaths on the Southern Plains: The Battles of Saline River and Prairie Dog Creek," *Journal of the West,* IV (October 1965), 485–503.

———. "Winter Campaigning with Sheridan and Custer: The Expedition of the Nineteenth Kansas Volunteer Cavalry," *Journal of the West,* VI (January 1967), 68–98.

Wilder, Daniel W. "Where Kansans Were Born," *Kansas Historical Collections,* IX (1905–06), 506–08.

Willey, William J. "The Second Federal Invasion of Indian Territory," *The Chronicles of Oklahoma,* XLIV (Winter 1966–1967), 420–430.

INDEX

Adams, Charles W., 14, 31, 66-67
Akin, Judge Andrew, 77
American Emigrant Company of Boston, 86, 88
Anderson, John A., Congressman, 164
Anderson, Thomas J., 21, 31, 46, 52, 106
Anthony, Daniel Read, 26, 28-29, 57, 59, 61, 77-79, 107-8
Anthony, George Tobey, 70-72, 150, 152-53, 159
Atchison, Topeka and Santa Fe Railroad Co., 96, 160, 164
Atchison *Champion,* 57, 75-76, 80, 99, 144, 155

Babcock, Carmi William, 7
Bailey, Lawrence D., 55, 108
Ballard, David E., 27-28, 32, 46, 53
Banks, Gen. Nathaniel P., 23
Barker, Rinaldo A., 111
Bartholow, E. M., 97-98
Bassett, Owen A., 13, 15-16, 18-20
Battles, map of, 12. *See also* Beaver Creek, Kans.; Big Blue, Mo.; Cane Hill, Ark.; Jenkins' Ferry, Ark.; Lexington, Mo.; Little Blue, Mo.; Mine Creek, Kans.; Newtonia, Mo.; Old Ft. Wayne, I.T.; Poison Springs, Ark.; Prairie Grove, Ark.; Washita, I.T.; Westport, Mo.; Wilson's Creek, Mo.
Baxter Springs, Kans., home of Crawford, 172
Beaver Creek, Kans., battle of, 119
Benteen, Col. Frederick, 36
Big Blue River, Mo., battle of, 34
"Black flag" policy of Confederates, 23
Black Kettle, Indian chief, 130, 192n
Blackwell, Lucy Stone, 105
Blair, Charles W., 11, 79, 90
Bloss, William W., 38, 40
Blunt, Gen. James G., 4, 13, 17-18, 21-22, 31, 33-37, 40, 45, 57, 66, 70-71, 179n
Bond, Thomas L., 141
Brown, Gov. B. Gratz, of Mo., 144, 146-47
Browning, Orville H., 86
Bryan, William J., 171
Burlingame, Ward, 58, 60, 76, 78, 106
Burlington *Kansas Patriot,* 70

Cabell, William, Confederate gen., 21-22, 37
Caldwell, Sen. Alexander, 139-43, 148
Camden, Ark., campaign, 1864, 23, 31
Camp Beecher (Wichita), 128-29
Camp Crawford, near Topeka, 127
Camp Supply, I.T., 126-31
Canby, Gen. Edward, 50
Cane Hill, Ark., battle of, 17
Capper, Sen. Arthur, 82, 161
Carney, Gov. Thomas, 20, 25, 33, 36, 39-41, 43, 48, 57-59, 61-62, 68, 77-78, 93, 102-3, 137-39, 142-43
Chase, George S., 153
Chase, Isabel Marshall, 81
Chavez, Major, 72-73
Cherokee Neutral Tract: map of, 84; 85-91, 101, 136, 186n
Chicago *Tribune,* 65-66
Civil War battles. *See* Battles
Civil War regiments. *See* Regiments
Clarke, Sidney, 28-31, 38, 45, 47, 52, 58, 77, 88, 91, 102, 106-7, 109-11, 136-40, 142-43, 145
Cloud, William F., 11, 18-19, 46, 70-71, 81
Coates, Kersey, 87
Construction of state capitol, 51
Cooper, Douglas H., Confederate gen., 14
"Copperheads," 38, 80, 160
Council Grove, raid on, 1868, 122
Cox, John T., 73

Crawford, Florence (daughter of S. J.), 82, 111, 161

Crawford, George, 26-27, 29, 55, 110

Crawford, George Marshall (son of S. J.), 82, 161

Crawford, Samuel Johnson: birth of, Apr. 10, 1835, near Bedford, Ind., 2; law practice in Garnett, Kans., 3; elected to Kans. legislature, 1859, 4-8; recruits soldiers, 1861, 9-10; in battles at: Wilson's Creek, 10-11; Old Ft. Wayne, 15; Cane Hill, 17; Prairie Grove, 18; Indian Territory, 1862, 21-22; Jenkins' Ferry, 23-24; Westport, 35; Mine Creek, 36-37; his Civil War engagements shown on map, 12; physical description of, 13; commands Second Kans. Colored Inf., 22-24; nominated for Kans. gov., 25-32, 178n; disputed 1864 letter of acceptance, 32, 73-77, 179n; role in Great Price Raid, 33-37, 41; as candidate for gov., 37-39, 41-42; takes office Jan. 9, 1865, 43-46; protests draft of Kansans, 47-50; and Price Raid claims, 52-53, 136, 158, 182n; encourages immigration, 53-55; views on reconstruction, 57-63, 79; appointment of Ross to U.S. Senate, 1866, 65-72; 1866 reelection of, 72-81; marriage, Nov. 27, 1866, 81-82; daughter, Florence, born, 82, 111; son, George, born, 82; in Cherokee lands controversy, 85-89; in Osage lands controversy, 89-92; relationship to Union Pacific, Eastern Division, Railroad, 92-97; investigated by legislature, 1868, 97-100; second term of, 101-3; supports impartial suffrage amendment, 104-6; favors impeachment of Pres. Johnson, 107-8; seeks congressional seat, 1868, 109-10; resigns as gov., Nov. 4, 1868, 111-12; attitude toward Indians, 114-17, 121, 134; organizes Eighteenth Kans. Reg., 1867, 117-19; and Medicine Lodge treaties, 119-22; organizes First Frontier Battalion, 1868, 124-25; leads Nineteenth Kans. Cav. on Indian expedition, 126-34; resigns commission, Feb., 1869, 132-34; moves to Emporia, 1870, 135-36; joins "purifiers," 1870, 136; seeks Senate seat, 1871, 136-43; joins Liberal Republicans, 1872, 144-47; affected by Panic of 1873, 148; Greenback candidate for Congress, 1876, 149-52; Greenback views of, 149-52, 154, 170; serves as state agent, 1877-1891, 153, 157-68; Independent candidate for Congress, 1878, 154-55; investments and profits of, 161, 166-68, 198n; returns to Republican party, 1888, 161-62; dispute with Populists, 165-67; opposes Spanish-American War, 170; supports W. J. Bryan, 1900, 171; publishes Kansas in the Sixties, 172; dies Oct. 21, 1913, 173; summary of career, 173-74

Crozier, Sen. Robert, 60, 62

Curtis, Gen. Samuel Ryan, 19, 33-37, 39-40

Cusey, James C., 148

Custer, Brevet Major Gen. George A., 112, 130, 132, 192-93n

Davis, Thomas L., 150, 152

Davis, Atty.-Gen. Willard, 159

Deitzler, George W., 33, 36

Delahay, Mark W., 58, 60, 62

Draft in Kans., 47-50

Dunlavy, Cpl. James, 37

Eighteenth Kans. Cav., 106, 118-19, 126, 132, 134

Elder, Peter Percival, 10, 167
Elections. *See* S. J. Crawford; Republican party; senatorial elections; suffrage
Eleventh Kans. Reg., 108
Emporia *News,* 108, 137-38, 141, 145
Endicott, G. J., 86
Eskridge, Charles V., 151
Ewing, Thomas, Jr., 107-9

Farmers Alliance, 165-67, 169
Fenlon, Thomas P., 139
First Frontier Battalion, 124-26, 134
First Kans. Colored Inf., 23, 47
First Kans. Volunteer Inf., 11
Fisher, Rev. Hugh Dunn, 66, 68-71
Fitzpatrick, William H., 53
Fort Bascom, N.M.T., 126
Fort Cobb, I.T., 131
Fort Hays, Kans., 128
Fort Larned, Kans., 123
Fort Lyon, Colo., 126
Fort Sill, I.T., 132
Fort Wayne. *See* Old Fort Wayne, I.T.
Forts, maps of, 12, 127. *See also* Camps
Fourteenth amendment to U.S. Constitution, 102, 104
Fourteenth Kans. Cav., 21, 22
Fremont, John C., 2, 92
Fry, James B., provost marshal, 47-48
Fuller, Perry, 102-3, 109

Garfield, Pres. James A., 162
Garnett *Plaindealer,* 78, 103, 137
Gillett, Almerin, 153
Glick, Gov. George W., 160, 162, 164
Goodin, John R., Congressman, 149
Graham, George, of Nemaha, 77
Grant, Pres. Ulysses S., 49-50, 107, 116, 146, 148
Greeley, Horace, 3, 146-47, 155
Green, Gov. Nehemiah, 77, 111, 118
Greenback party, 108, 148-52, 155-56, 166-67
Greer, John P., 71, 80, 96

Hadley, James A., 131
Hallett, Samuel, 92
Hallowell, James R., Congressman, 155, 195n
Hancock, Gen. Winfield S., 116, 118, 162
Hanway, James, 136-37
Harlan, James, Secy. of Interior, 85-86, 93, 95
Harney, Gen. William Selby, 120-21
Harvey, Gov. James M., 110-11, 137, 148
Hayes, Pres. Rutherford B., 150
Hazen, Gen. William B., 131
Henderson, Sen. John B., 67, 91
Herron, Gen. Francis, 17
Hindman, Thomas, Confederate gen., 17, 18
Hinton, Richard J., 108
Hodder, Frank H., 172
Hopkins, Henry, 15, 27
Hoyt, George H., 91
Hudson, M. E., 150, 152
Humphrey, Gov. Lyman U., 167, 169

Impeachment of Pres. Johnson, 99, 101, 107-10, 136
Indian lands: map of, 84; 84-91, 102. *See also* Cherokee Neutral Tract; Osage Lands
Indians, government policy toward, 114-17, 119-26
Indian Territory, map of, 127
Ingalls, Sen. John J., 6, 8, 76, 147, 164, 167
Insley, Merritt H., 60, 62, 67
Investigation of U.S. senatorial elections in Kans: of 1867, 103-4, 136; of 1871, 142-43; of 1873, 147
Ives, John N., 168

Jenkins' Ferry, Ark., battle of, 23-24, 31, 35
Jennison, Charles R., 92, 97-98, 187n
Johnson, Pres. Andrew, 56-57, 62, 68, 71-72, 79, 86, 91, 93, 99, 107, 123

Joy, James F., 86-89, 138, 146
Julian, George W., 87, 90-91
Junction City *Union*, 72, 76, 108, 134

Kansas City *Times*, 152, 163
Kansas Farmer, 161, 166
Kansas in the Sixties, 172
Kansas Pacific Railroad Company, 142, 160. *See also* Union Pacific, Eastern Division, Railroad
Kansas regiments. *See* Regiments

Land speculation, 51, 83-89, 97-100
Lane, James Henry, 3, 6, 7-8, 20, 22, 33, 37, 39, 41-42, 44-48, 56-59, 61-63, 65, 68, 70, 73, 78, 93-94, 101, 110, 144-45
Latta, Samuel N., 60, 62
Laughlin, W. R., 147
Lawrence, William W. H., 26-29
Lawrence *Democratic Standard*, 141-42
Lawrence *State Journal*, 54
Lawrence *Tribune*, 42, 61-62, 68, 99, 110, 112
Leavenworth *Conservative*, 40-42, 48-49, 54-55, 58, 61-62, 67, 69, 72, 76, 78-80, 96, 99, 103, 106, 108-9, 120
Leavenworth *Evening Bulletin*, 102, 112, 134, 139
Leavenworth *Times*, 40-41, 48-49, 54, 61-62, 69
Lee, Albert L., 103
Legate, James, 141
Lexington, battle of, 33, 40
Liberal Republican party, 144-46, 166
Lincoln, Pres. Abraham, 5, 13, 41, 50
Lindsey, John G., 9, 132
Little Blue River, Mo., battle of, 34
Lone Wolf, Kiowa chief, 131
Lowe, David P., 136-37
Lowe, Joseph G., 165
Lyon, Gen. Nathaniel, 10-11

McAfee, Josiah B., 27-29, 44, 46, 52-53, 97-98, 106, 108, 126

McDowell, James L., 57-59, 79, 81, 142-43
McEckron, Boyd H., 141
McNeil, Gen. John, 20
McVicar, Peter, 90

Manning, Edwin C., 16, 27-29, 32, 132, 172
Marmaduke, John, Confederate gen., 37
Martin, George W., 72, 76, 132-33, 171-72
Martin, John, of Topeka, 150, 152
Martin, John A., of Atchison, 46, 58, 110
Martin, William Wallace, 168
Mead, James R., 128, 133, 192n
Medicine Lodge treaties, 119-21, 123, 125, 191n
Miller, Solomon, ed. *Kansas Chief*, 37-38, 42, 61-62, 70-71, 80, 109, 144
Mine Creek, Kans., battle of, 36, 41
Mitchell, Robert Byington, 11, 13, 147
Mobley, Richard D., 97-98
Moore, Horace Ladd, 15, 132-33
Murdock, Marshall M., 29-30
Murdock, Thomas B., 29

Negro suffrage, 3-4, 102, 104-5
Negro troops. *See* First Kans. Colored Reg.; Second Kans. Colored Reg.
Newtonia, Mo., battle of, 14
Nineteenth Kans. Cav. Reg., 111, 113, 122, 125-34
Northern plains Indians, 119-20, 125

Olathe *Mirror*, 107
Old Fort Wayne, I.T., battle of, 15-16, 20, 27, 35
Osage Indian land controversy: map of, 84; 89-91, 101, 186n
Osborn, Gov. Thomas A., 26-29, 32, 60, 62, 146-48, 153
Oskaloosa *Independent*, 108-9

Pacific Railroad, 92, 125
Panic of 1873, 148

Panic of 1893, 170
Parrott, Marcus J., 6-8, 110, 144
Pawnee Fork, Kans., attack on, 116
Peace commission, 1867, 119-21, 124-25
Peffer, Sen. William A., 166
Perkins, Sen. Bishop Waldo, 169
Perry, John D., 45, 92-93, 95, 97, 99, 104, 116
Philbrick, John L., 97-98
Pleasonton, Gen. Alfred, 33-36
Pliley, Allison J., 129-30
Plumb, Sen. Preston B., 153, 169
Poison Springs, Ark., battle of, 23-24
Polk, Leonidas L., of N.C., 165
Pomeroy, Sen. Samuel C., 5-8, 33, 49, 57-58, 68, 81, 88, 90, 103, 106-9, 144-45, 147
Populist party, 167-68
Prairie Dog Creek, battle of, 191n. *See also* Beaver Creek
Prairie Grove, Ark., battle of, 17-18, 20, 69
Price, Sterling, Confederate gen., 10-11, 23, 32-37, 39-42
Price raid claims, 136, 158, 182n
"Purifiers," political faction, 1870, 136, 140-41

Railroad lands recovered, 163-65
Railroads in Kans., 51, 83, 85, 96-97, 160, 162. *See also* Union Pacific, Eastern Division; Atchison, Topeka and Santa Fe
Rankin, John K., 46
Reconstruction, 56, 58-59, 72, 79, 102
Red River Campaign, 1864, 23
Regiments. *See* First, Second, Seventh (U.S.), Tenth, Eleventh, Twelfth, Fourteenth, Eighteenth, Nineteenth; *also* First Frontier Battalion
Republican party, 2-4, 26, 73, 76-79, 107, 136, 144-48, 150, 155, 161, 165, 169-70
Reynolds, Milton W., 30, 121, 160

Rice, Gen. Samuel, 23-24
Richardson, Albert D., 77
Riggs, Samuel A., 147
Roberts, J. W., 38
Robinson, Gov. Charles, 4, 6, 8, 10, 13, 18, 20, 25, 31, 37, 39, 41-42
Root, Dr. Joseph P., 77, 79, 82
Rosecrans, Gen. William S., 33
Ross, Sen. Edmund G., 46, 57, 67-69, 71-72, 86-88, 91, 101-3, 106, 108-10, 121, 136, 145, 151
Ryan, Thomas, Congressman, 151-52

Safford, Jacob, State Supreme Court Justice, 43
Sanborn, John S., 120
Santa Fe Railroad. *See* Atchison, Topeka and Santa Fe
Satanta, Kiowa chief, 131
Schofield, Gen. John M., 17-18, 21
School lands, 91
Scott, Harvey D., 93-94
Scott, Dr. J. W., 110
Second Kans. Cav., 12-14, 17-21, 31, 46, 68, 77, 122, 132
Second Kans. Colored Inf., 21-23, 27, 46-47, 105
Second Kans. Inf., 10-11, 13
Sells, Elijah, of Douglas County, 141
Senatorial elections in Kans.: 1861, 8; 1865, 45; 1867, 101-4; 1871, 137-44; 1873, 147-48
Seventh Cav., 119
Sheridan, Gen. Philip, 112, 123-26, 128-31, 133-34
Sherman, Gen. William T., 95, 112, 116-20, 125, 131, 133
Shoemaker, Robert M., 95, 116, 118, 120
Simpson, Apache Bill, guide, 128
Simpson, Benjamin F., 138, 141
Simpson, Jeremiah, 167
Simpson, Samuel N., 98
Smith, Kirby, Confederate gen., 23
Smith, Leonard, 67, 143
Snoddy, James D., 140

Southern plains Indians, 119, 125
Speer, John, 7, 29-30, 41, 45, 59, 61-
    62, 66-73, 75-77, 80, 110
Spotts, David, 133-34
Spriggs, William, 103
Stanbery, Henry, Atty.-Gen., 86
Stanley, Henry M., 191n
Stanton, Edwin M., Secy. of War, 48-
    50, 116
Statehood, Kans., 1861, 6
Steele, Gen. Frederick, 23
Stone, Lucy, 105
Stotler, Jacob, 26, 29-30, 52, 56, 73,
    77, 138, 140, 145
Stover, Elias S., 122
Sturges, William, 89, 92
Suffrage election, 1867, 101, 105-6
Sully, Gen. Alfred, 123

Tappan, Samuel F., 120
Taylor, N. G., Commissioner of In-
    dian affairs, 119-20
Teller, Henry M., Secy. of Interior,
    160
Tenth Kans. Reg., 50
Thacher, Solon O., 37, 39-40, 42, 110
Thayer, Gen. John, 23-24
Thoman, Alois, 144
Tilden, Samuel J., 150
Topeka *Advocate*, 166
Topeka *Commonwealth*, 154, 163

Topeka *Daily Capital*, 161, 165
Topeka *Leader*, 108, 110, 112
Topeka *State Record*, 67, 110
Topeka *Tribune*, 71, 96
Twelfth Kans. Inf., 14

Union Pacific, Eastern Division, Rail-
    road, 45, 55, 82, 92, 94, 96, 102,
    116, 120, 145, 188n
Usher, John P., 93, 96, 98-99, 189n

Vaughan, John C., 60, 62

Walker, Thaddeus H., 147
Ware, Eugene, 88
Washita, battle of, 130
Washita Campaign, 1868-1869: 126;
    map of, 127
Watie, Stand, Cherokee Indian leader,
    14
Westport, battle of, 34-35, 40
White Cloud, Chief, 61, 69, 112
Wichita *Daily Beacon*, 164
Wilder, Abel Carter, 30-31
Wilder, Daniel Webster, 7-8, 31, 39
Wilson's Creek, Mo., battle of, 10-11
Woman suffrage, 105
Wood, Samuel Newitt, 105
Wright, W. W., 82
Wyandotte Constitution, 1859, 4

York, A. M., state Senator, 147